Drought, Water Law, and the Origins of California's Central Valley Project

Drought, Water Law, and the Origins of California's Central Valley Project

TIM STROSHANE

UNIVERSITY OF NEVADA PRESS *Reno & Las Vegas*

University of Nevada Press, Reno, Nevada 89557 USA
www.unpress.nevada.edu
Copyright © 2016 by Tim Stroshane
All rights reserved
Cover design by Martyn Schmoll

LIBRARY OF CONGRESS CATALOGING-IN-PUBLICATION DATA
Names: Stroshane, Tim, 1957– author.
Title: Drought, water law, and the origins of California's Central Valley project / Tim Stroshane.
Description: Reno : University of Nevada Press, [2016] | Includes bibliographical references and index.
Identifiers: LCCN 2016018417 (print) | LCCN 2016029397 (ebook) |
    ISBN 978-1-943859-21-4 (hardback) | ISBN 978-0-87417-001-6 (e-book)
Subjects: LCSH: Central Valley Project (Calif.) | Water resources development—California—History. | Water rights—California—History. | Water-supply—Political aspects—California—History. | BISAC: NATURE / Environmental Conservation & Protection. | POLITICAL SCIENCE / Public Policy / General.
Classification: LCC HD1694.C2 S77 2016 (print) | LCC HD1694.C2 (ebook) |
    DDC 333.91/15097945—dc23
LC record available at https://lccn.loc.gov/2016018417

The paper used in this book meets the requirements of American National Standard for Information Sciences—Permanence of Paper for Printed Library Materials, ANSI/NISO Z39.48-1992 (R2002).

Paperback © 2017 by Tim Stroshane
ISBN 978-1-943859-06-1 (paper : alk. paper)

This book has been reproduced as a digital reprint.

Manufactured in the United States of America

Contents

List of Illustrations and Tables	vii
Acknowledgments	ix
Introduction	3
Chapter 1. Artificial Cascades	11
Chapter 2. Mere Trespassers and Monopolists	26
Chapter 3. Showdown at the Calloway Canal	47
Chapter 4. The Dead Hand of Henry Miller	66
Chapter 5. A Large Permanent Usefulness	76
Chapter 6. District, Rule, Decree	101
Chapter 7. A Lawsuit Is a Poor Match for a Dam	120
Chapter 8. Junior and Senior Partners	143
Chapter 9. Glass Half Full	168
Chapter 10. Parable, Prophecy, Present	183
Appendix A Summaries of Key Miller & Lux–related San Joaquin River California Supreme Court Cases	203
Appendix B Text of Proposition 7 from 1928 California Constitution	209
Appendix C Authorities	210
References	211
Index	223

Illustrations

FIGURES

1.1. Mean annual precipitation in California, 1961–1990 — 12
1.2. Typical high-pressure ridge near west coast, winter 1976–1977 — 14
1.3. How water reaches the Delta and where exported water goes — 19
2.1. The Gate — 34
2.2. Sluice flumes at Timbuctoo, Yuba County — 34
3.1. Calloway Weir, June 2012 — 49
3.2. Calloway Canal, Kern County, California — 49
3.3. Real estate loans from savings banks in San Francisco, Los Angeles, and Sacramento Counties, 1879 — 50
3.4. Real estate loans from savings banks in San Francisco, Los Angeles, and Sacramento Counties, 1899 — 50
3.5. The principality of Henry Miller in three western states — 55
4.1. Miller & Lux and subsidiary California Pastoral & Agricultural Company lands downstream of Mendota Pool along the San Joaquin River — 70
4.2. Miller & Lux and Herminghaus lands riparian to Fresno Slough and the San Joaquin River, western Fresno County — 71
4.3. Henry Miller about the time of the *Lux v. Haggin* case — 74
5.1. Artesian wells, late nineteenth and early twentieth centuries, San Joaquin Valley — 79
5.2. Horse-drawn cart beside artesian well, Kern County, California — 80
5.3. Development of irrigated acreage in San Joaquin Valley, 1886, 1912, and 1922 — 81
5.4. Groundwater areas and developed areas with deficient water supplies, upper San Joaquin Valley, 1931 — 98
7.1. Rights to the Use of Water in California (pamphlet cover), 1927 — 131
8.1. Proposed San Joaquin River pumping system — 156

9.1.	Drought effects on runoff, Tulare Lake Basin	169
9.2.	Drought effects on runoff, Sacramento River Basin	169
9.3.	Drought effects on runoff, San Joaquin River Basin	170
9.4.	Sidney T. Harding	176
10.1.	Critically overdrafted groundwater basins, January 2016	199

TABLES

2.1.	Largest landholdings in California, 1871	41
8.1.	Sacramento River Basin water rights, 1915–1927	147
8.2.	Major state filings, July 30, 1927, pursuant to the Feigenbaum Act	150
8.3.	Central Valley water right claims compared with median river flows as of 1927	154
8.4.	Riparian and pre-1914 appropriative water rights on the San Joaquin River	160

Acknowledgments

I LIVED THROUGH the 1976–77 drought in California. As a young man, I became interested in human cultures, societies, planning, and collective organization. Exploring California on my own road trips, I often stopped at dams and canals, hoping to glimpse the meaning of each silent edifice. By 1980, the subject of water had full hold on me and has not let go since. At the University of California, Santa Cruz, I took courses on hydrology and groundwater. A year later, I completed my senior thesis on the proposal, then current in California, to construct a "Peripheral Canal" around the Sacramento-San Joaquin River Delta. Since then, millions of other Californians and I endured two more droughts: 1987 through 1992 (and 1994), and 2007 through 2009. More recently, between 2012 and 2015, California underwent another drought that called into question the state's infrastructure needs, allocation priorities, and commitment to efficient water use. At this writing, in mid-2016, the drought continues.

In this account of Californians' relationship to their water resources, my method is more or less scholarly but from an activist's point of view: I do not assume that state and federal water agencies make choices that are always in Californians' best interests. It is my wish that others confirm for themselves the value of my lines of reasoning and build on what I assemble here.

My interest in writing about water, coupled with the emergence of the Internet, enabled me to become an activist and contribute to the efforts of scrappy environmental organizations such as the California Water Impact Network, the California Sportfishing Protection Alliance, AquAlliance, and most recently Restore the Delta, as well as the California Environmental Water Caucus.

There are many colleagues and friends to whom I owe debts of gratitude large and small. The first of these are the late independent scholar, salmonid-ophile, and thinker Michael Black, and now-retired water-resources archivist Linda Vida. Michael's support was invaluable at a time when I was just starting to write about California water, and though we took separate paths, his love of salmon (if not his knowledge) rubbed off on me. Linda's generosity of time and interest was an unending source of joy to this independent scholar showing up at the Water Resources Center Archive when it was still housed at University of California, Berkeley. Her patience was abundant. She provided full answers to my questions about sources, research, and cataloging practices in the archive, what was restricted and not restricted. Her answers greased the skids for someone without extended periods of time to really get things done. She also shared my excitement at finding gems such as Henry Holsinger's "Necessity" manuscript (see chapter 10); the remarkable 1931 bank examiner's drought hearing transcript in Sidney Harding's papers; and Samuel Wiel's Tom Paine-like pamphlet from 1928. At the University of California, Riverside, where she helped move the Archive in 2011, her good cheer and professionalism continued until her recent retirement. I worry for the future of the Water Resources Collections and Archives at Riverside but try to remain hopeful that it will eventually become the online resource for all Californians and all water scholars, as promised when the University's division of agriculture and natural resources decided that relocating it from its fifty-year home at Berkeley was a good idea. The jury is still out on that move, but Linda did her part to make the transition work.

I owe a phalanx of teachers and peers a debt of gratitude from my days at the University of California, Santa Cruz: professors Dudley J. Burton, Langdon Winner, Jim Pepper, my thesis adviser Jan Dekema, Ann and Warren Lane, and Randall Wilson. These people were unflagging in their encouragement of my intellectual and professional growth.

I am also grateful to Jim O'Connor, Barbara Laurence, and Eddie Yuen among the folks at *Capitalism Nature Socialism,* where my writings on capitalism, Nature, and California water first appeared over a span of nearly ten years. While my subjects were about nature, their nurture of me demonstrated enthusiasm and support. I learned much from opportunities they provided, despite my busy life raising a family and working a full-time job in the city of Berkeley.

My entry into California water activism would have been impossible without encouragement, beginning about 1998, by people whom I interviewed long before this specific book was conceived: Barbara Vlamis, then of Butte Environmental Council, now of AquAlliance in Chico; Carolee Krieger, Michael B. Jackson, and Tom Stokely of the California Water Impact Network; Bill Jennings of California Sportfishing Protection Alliance; Dante John Nomellini Sr. of the Central Delta Water Agency; the late Alex Hildebrand and John Herrick of the South Delta Water Agency; Randy McFarland, the media man for Friant Water Authority who, along with Steve Ottemoeller, introduced me to the San Joaquin River Exchange Contractors. Mr. McFarland kindly arranged a tour for me of Friant Dam in February 2001. It was during this trip that he and Mr. Ottemoeller provided my "aha!" moment about the Exchange Contractors. Mr. McFarland also pointed me to M. Catherine Miller's landmark history, *Flooding the Courtroom,* from which I learned much about the history of water rights and conflicts in the San Joaquin Valley. Mr. McFarland generously offered many puzzle pieces to this story on that unforgettable day.

I am also grateful to historian Donald Pisani. We met at the Green Versus Gold conference at the University of California, Santa Cruz, in the summer of 1999, and he joined me on the bus tour of Miller & Lux territory around San Luis Dam. His patience with the slow evolution of this book, punctuated with "tough love" for my elephantine book outlines, tedious prose, and book prospectus, has been invaluable. I doubt I have applied the shrewd discipline, systematic research, and well-informed rigor he brings to history and the American West, but I for one have pored through and gained much insight from his own labors, and for that, as well as his professional collegiality, I am eternally grateful.

The observations of irrigation engineer Sidney T. Harding (1883–1969) about climate and water storage (above and below ground) also proved compelling to me. While timid about recommending public policies to his clients that might successfully address contemporary concerns regarding groundwater overdraft and the significance of past droughts in climate records for future reservoirs, he at least wrote his concerns down, published them in *Engineering Record,* and preserved them in his papers, much to my gratitude.

I cannot adequately express my gratitude for the confidence in the manuscript shown by Justin Race, director of the University of Nevada Press. And it goes to press deftly touched by editor Jeff Grathwohl, whose suggestions clarified passages, big and small, that otherwise might have been let through permanently muddy.

The day I fell at age four into the Capri Motel pool in Redwood City in 1962 and my brother Rich fished me out, coughing and crying since I did not swim, my mother Ruth Stroshane calmed me down and comforted me. Was that the genesis of my interest in large structures holding water? Maybe, maybe not. But she has been as interested in my progress on this book as any aspiring author could hope. Ditto, the loving interest shown me by Rich and Siu Wai Stroshane and my in-law parents, Arnold and Sylvia Ambrosini. *Finally!* I am only sorry that my father Richard Carlisle Stroshane did not live to see this book.

Last, but definitely not least, I owe a debt of gratitude to my family for their undying love, good cheer, support, and patience. None of them share my passion for things water, nor would I wish it upon any of them. But daughters Lauren and Kelsey know what this book means to me; thanks for putting up with those occasional side trips to dams and canals and power plants. But no one knows it more than my best friend since 1975, Jan Ambrosini. Beloved wife, through sickness and health, good times and bad, here it finally is.

*Drought, Water Law, and the Origins
of California's Central Valley Project*

Introduction

AT THIS WRITING, California is in the grip of a four-year drought. In fact, eight of the preceding nine years were below normal precipitation— at least. People are conserving water.[1] Some question the state's water right system (Pitzer 2015). Others question whether we should let rivers "waste" their flowing water to the sea. Lack of water in California provokes all manner of thought and thoughtlessness about water and its efficient use.

This book is about efficient use of water. From early statehood almost to the Depression, California's agricultural monopoly players appeared to hoard and waste water for vast expanses of grassland and cropland flood irrigation. For nearly eighty years, the poster child for waste and unreasonable use was monopoly control of the San Joaquin River by Miller & Lux, the historic cattle and meatpacking conglomerate. Yet some people also thought not just in terms of optimal inputs per unit of output but also about how institutions of law, business, and government should change to accomplish greater efficiency of water use. They hoped to limit monopolistic control by turning the Central Valley watershed's economic development and its abundant water resources to more widely distributed public benefit. Hence, the definition of efficiency of water use included social and economic dimensions.

In the following pages, I itemize and detail some of the strategies used to counterbalance monopoly. This includes passage of Prop 7 in 1928, creation and financing of irrigation districts, adjudication of rights, and planning of the Central Valley Project. One way or another, all aimed toward greater water-use efficiency. In an age where Silicon Valley's hyper-technological capitalist ethic of "disrupting" the marketplace dominates, California's water rights law, customs, and contractual arrangements may seem antique. This book is my attempt to retrieve water rights law from the perception that it is ancient, impenetrable, and arcane. It need be none of those things. As Henry Holsinger, one of California government's leading water attorneys during the mid-twentieth century, wrote,

> According to an ancient precept, "He that knoweth the law and knoweth not the reason for the law, knoweth not the law." Theories are more important in the field of California water law than is usually the case with respect to our jurisprudence generally, for the reason that our law of waters resides more in judicial decision than in legislation. (Holsinger 1936)

It is my hope that knowing the reasons for our water laws will help all interested citizens to know the law better, first in California but well beyond.

The dominant type of water right in California is appropriative: one's right to divert and use water is based on the date its holder first put water to use for an economic purpose. Such a right may be handed down from generation to generation, transferred like other, more stationary forms of property. These are family or corporate jewels, precious assets that may have passed through three, four, five generations in some families—some almost to California statehood in 1850.

Buildings rise and decay; great landed estates subdivide into smaller grids; companies split or reacquire stock. But make no mistake: water rights—claiming before all the world a certain rate, volume, place, and season of water use—tend toward gravitational stability. Much like the full outer electron shells of Nature's noble gases, they can seem inert in the absence of direct, energetic, and compelling confrontation. If they weather the slings and arrows of courtroom rules of evidence and cross-examination, such tested water rights can be one of the most stable, reliable forms of property a corporation or individual can own, providing a benefit "stream" commensurate with its seniority: first in time, first in right. Shoring up legal doctrine, as Miller & Lux did, can further buttress property value.

Generations later, such a system can seem quaint. How can an economy like California's—a state whose gross domestic product ranks high among the industrial nations of the world—find its regions engaged at times in bitter conflict over such a basic element of life? "I don't understand," a California water blogger wrote in 2015, "why a farmer should get more water now because his grandfather claimed it a century ago. As between current users of water, having better grandparents doesn't seem like it should make someone more worthy of having water" (On the public record 2015). I will address this perplexity historically.

Water properties assembled by Miller & Lux figure prominently in the design and operation of Central Valley Project water works, affecting not just its form but also its operations. The Central Valley Project, owned and operated today by the U.S. Bureau of Reclamation, is California's preeminent agricultural irrigation water-supply system. Its grasp on water extends from the CVP's reservoirs in rural Trinity River country (Trinity and Lewiston Lakes), rugged regions of the upper Sacramento River near Mount Shasta (Shasta Lake), up the American River catchment near the city of Folsom (Folsom Lake) and the Stanislaus River watershed east of Modesto (New Melones Reservoir), to the rolling hills of the San Joaquin River northeast of Fresno (Millerton Lake). The CVP extended its reach to deliver water to places that were historically and geographically deficient with the hope of turning the driest parts of the Central Valley's vast plains to full bloom. The Corning and Tehama-Colusa Canals serve the west side of the Sacramento Valley; the Delta-Mendota Canal serves the San Joaquin Valley's west side; and the Madera and Friant-Kern Canals serve the San Joaquin's east side from Chowchilla to Bakersfield.

But the origins of the CVP, as distinct from its era of development, lie in the shadow cast by the Miller & Lux cattle empire. The importance of its origins matches the CVP's extended reach and large grasp. It spans development of California water law, historic droughts through which early California suffered, and the state's struggles with land and water monopoly. For the better part of eighty years, Miller & Lux shaped and was shaped by California's law of water rights and the land and water resources of the San Joaquin Valley. I contend that you cannot grasp the Central Valley Project today without understanding Miller & Lux's legal and economic legacy. That legacy extends from statehood to current controversy over groundwater overdraft. It encompasses the efficient allocation of water during drought, whether a river wastes water to the sea, and whether water rights are matters of individual ownership or community interest. The economic and political power for California's water system was born of Miller & Lux's monopoly over water rights. And that power moves among Californians even today: ghostly and forgettable to most in the wet years, vexing and implacable to many in the dry.

Like the gathering of clouds into a storm, or a river's tributaries joining its main stem, this book draws together legal, economic, climatic, and hydrological analysis and events to tell a story of California water rights, and Californians' resistance and accommodations to them as reflected in the origins of its Central Valley Project.

Drought drove public and private actions toward more reasonable use of water, because drought caused shortages and forced Californians to rely on water law to allocate what they still had. Case by expensive case, water law became the language and institutional means by which people perceived and resisted monopolies during drought. Water rights and drought intertwine, since it is through water rights that human social order allocates available supplies when Nature withholds. If we change the water rights system now in place, our new system must solve that problem better than we do now.

This book describes too the origin of a structural conflict of interest in which the state of California came to act as both judge and supplicant in affairs of water. The emergence of this conflict took place during the first half of the twentieth century, when the state began regulating water rights statewide with one hand, and developing and planning to operate the Central Valley Project with the other. Today, the State Water Resources Control Board is supposed to regulate water use, while huge modern bureaucracies of both the state of California and the United States government constantly seek to expand their water supplies with, as one federal judge put it over sixty years ago, "departmental zeal."[2]

One way this conflict of interest has manifested is that far too many water rights claims have been recognized by the state compared to the available water California's climate and geography delivers from year to year. Some of the overappropriation is due to rights claimed by the Bureau of Reclamation and the state of California (Grantham and Viers 2014; Stroshane 2012). The origin of some of these rights in the Feigenbaum Act of 1927 is described in chapter 8. By the time these agencies acquired rights for their two large, coordinated water systems, it was already public knowledge (if not widely known) that claimed water rights far exceeded flow in Central Valley rivers and streams. If Californians intend to restore natural ecosystems and live within their collective financial and ecological means, then something will have to be done about over-promised water rights, while recognizing that the climate becomes drier and warmer. We need to know more about how California got into this hydraulic pickle. Meanwhile, the state's conflict of interest limits available options, at least for now.

This book stands on the shoulders of now-classic works of California and western water history, while adding a new chapter to their stories. The California water canon includes fine histories by Donald Pisani (1984), Norris Hundley (2001), Donald Worster (1985), Marc Reisner (1986), M. Catherine Miller (1993), Carey McWilliams (1949—the chapters on water), and more recently Philip Garone (2011). I have *not* written a history of the Central Valley Project here. Readers looking for histories of the project from its inception to present configuration should consult the works mentioned above. Also, the U.S. Bureau of Reclamation commissioned a series of basic histories of various parts of the Central Valley Project in the 1990s (United States Bureau of Reclamation 1994a–c, 1996).

Given that the title of the present work includes "the origins of California's Central Valley Project," I explore the foundations of the Central Valley Project, not its subsequent history. The lead-up to the CVP was a period full of litigation, engineering concepts, drought, and institutional change in California and in many ways is more important to the current situation. But rather than a history of legislative policymaking, this book lets other forms of human power take center stage—forms that are more economic and legal than overtly political (at least in the governmental sense of politics). My inspiration is Samuel C. Wiel, an early twentieth-century San Francisco water lawyer, who admonished, "much historical store is in law records" (Wiel 1949, 110).

An urban planner by training, I am also interested in how these forms and expressions of power affected the built environment of water facilities and the institutions that build, operate, and maintain them. It took my breath away when I first learned the role monopolists like Henry Miller and Charles Lux played in shaping the San Joaquin River and beyond. They could not have affected CVP design without their economic domination of the river and influence on state water law.

With California water issues, few if any recent writers have focused on the design of the "things themselves"—dams, canals, and hydraulic bureaucracies—and how they impose duties on society and create perceived entitlements to water among private interests. I was pleasantly surprised to find that engineers and lawyers, among others, grappled with the fundamental scientific question of *how water moves* to begin with, because such understanding can help people treat water scientifically and as an *object* of the law and of design. (It also can help you succeed at engineering irrigation systems; see chapter 6.)

Delving into records at the Water Resources Center Archives (housed for fifty years at the University of California, Berkeley, now at the Riverside campus as the Water Resources Collections and Archives), I found that certain engineers and water lawyers thought beyond concrete and steel and earthen artifacts to the public policies, organizations, and bureaucracies needed to design, build, and operate such artifacts.

People such as Sidney T. Harding, Samuel C. Wiel, Henry Holsinger, Edward Treadwell, and numerous other water professionals knew less about the mechanisms of California's climate and its relation to the state's hydrology than perhaps we know now. But despite the state's short history they shared their views with the public, their clients, and their colleagues on how to handle California's water. They also understood that California's agricultural economy was dominated by monopolies such as Miller & Lux, and the politics of monopoly shaped their views on the state's water rights doctrine and water policy.

By keeping their interpretive remarks to the specific context in which they were written, I try to present as fairly as possible what they mean for California water law and policy over the arc of this book. Their views have been largely ignored to date by historians, lawyers, economists, and others, or they were outright defeated, as with Samuel Wiel in the 1928 legal advisory committee to the state legislature. I readily concede they had little lasting or publicized impact on legislative water policy. But defeat or being ignored by history doesn't always equate to being wrong. I recover their ideas for readers of any age interested in California's water, past and present. Hearing these past voices argue in context may stimulate legal and institutional innovations today and tomorrow.

As much as possible, I prefer not to impose today's categories of thought on theirs and try to avoid the temptation to read the present into the past. Here and there I draw parallels with events or realities today but only to show some continuity of conditions or rhetoric with the current era. In foregrounding their ideas on efficiency and reasonable use, groundwater conditions, and other topics, my intent is to give them a voice in historical interpretation emanating from *their* day, not ours.

For example, I first learned the emperor Justinian's Roman-era quote about running water from writings about the public trust doctrine: "The following things by natural law are common to all: the air, running water, the sea, and consequently the seashore."[3] But in the early twentieth century, Justinian's principle had yet to be connected by legal professionals or court precedents to the public trust doctrine, and that doctrine had yet to attach to government legal obligations in California (which is likely another story altogether). I became intrigued when I saw how San Francisco water lawyer Samuel C. Wiel nonetheless used Justinian's insight into the flowing water commons to make a case for preserving river flow because it benefited the progression of all water right holders of whatever stripe along a stream—without resort to the notion of public trust. Wiel thought it in the common interests of proprietary human diverters to maintain flows. But we will see in chapter 8 that he was ultimately unable to persuade others of this truth as the Central Valley Project was coming to life (with desiccating consequences for the San Joaquin River). Still, it strikes me that, ecological sentiments aside, his reasoning provides an important human counterpoint to the idea that rivers should not have their waters "waste to the sea."

This book proceeds only loosely as a chronology, for I am more interested to explain key events (such as surface water shortages, groundwater overdraft, and the frustrating growth of water rights litigation and conflict) in terms of contemporary data, changing legal concepts, institutions, and power dynamics. Some scenes receive detailed analysis while the book skips connecting stretches of time or details of legislative and political history. For that connective historical tissue, see works of the authors I mention above and in my endnote citations.

My method, inspired by Mr. Wiel, involves dislodging technical details in engineering reports, court decisions, contemporary trade and professional magazine articles, and legal journals. In primary documents this includes contracts, agency reports, plans, letters, court transcripts, and data compendia.

Chapter 1 uses California's 1976–77 drought to introduce readers to the state's water system and system of water rights, the Delta's water needs, the state's overall strategy for managing surface and groundwater during drought, and the pivotal role of a "big story" involving San Joaquin Valley water rights, born from land monopoly a century before.

Chapters 2 and 3 summarize monopolized California during the nineteenth century by surveying the insights of other historians and lawyers. Chapter 2 describes the interplay of California's emerging water rights system from the Gold Rush, with subsequent gaming of federal and state land policies in order to encourage settlement and economic development for the benefit of monopolists. Chapter 2 uses backlash against monopolistic development to set the stage in chapter 3 for the legal strategy and arguments of California's preeminent monopolistic water right holders in its precedent-setting water rights case, *Lux v. Haggin*.[4] Chapter 3 studies land- and water-development schemes, including but not limited to those employed by monopolists Miller & Lux and James Ben Ali Haggin to capitalize their businesses. Their competition for land and water in Kern County culminated in landmark litigation provoked by Haggin during the drought of 1877–79.

As early land monopoly and water conflicts played out in Kern County, Miller & Lux also monopolized the main stem of the San Joaquin River from Mendota to the Merced River confluence. Chapter 4 describes how Miller & Lux assembled a concentrated bloc of surface water rights and canal control, then connected this control to its descendants, the San Joaquin River Exchange Contractors. We also see, from key Miller & Lux case law (summarized in Appendix A, with nearly all of it rising to the California Supreme Court) how the Mendota area of western

Fresno County became the physical center of their hold on water rights. The seizure and exercise of this control had much to do with the geography of the company's hydraulic position along the river.

While many rural Californians feared that monopolization of surface water right claims would stunt economic development and land settlement in the Central Valley, these fears lessened by the late nineteenth century when pump technology and hydroelectric energy enabled a boom in Valley groundwater exploitation. Groundwater usage was a vital option, mobilizing more democratic access to land and economic opportunity—an important counter-strategy to the land and surface water monopoly sitting in the San Joaquin Valley. Chapter 5 describes the feverish drilling, economic strategy in groundwater pumping, and the catastrophic legal logic endgame of uncontrolled groundwater usage—partially addressed by the California Supreme Court in the landmark groundwater and reasonable use case, *Katz v. Walkinshaw*.[5] Also in chapter 5, the idea of sustainability is introduced through Sidney T. Harding's work documenting groundwater overdraft and his gracefully apt euphemism, "a large permanent usefulness."

Californians continued to look for ways to break, or at least limit, some of the worst effects of monopoly control of water supplies for economic opportunity, as chapter 6 describes. Such methods included organizing special public municipal corporations called irrigation districts. They hoped that involving the state government in direct regulation of water use would establish a countervailing power. Instead, this period of California's water rights expansion founded the overappropriated system under which the state and its rivers and water systems labor today. Citizens engaged the court system in adjudicating claims, giving a prominent role to the new commission. As part of this role, courts could take advantage of the commission's presumed concentration of expertise to provide factual evidence on which to base court decrees.

California's case law of water threatened to diverge from these countervailing trends by holding to monopoly-dominated legal precedent, however. In the preeminent water law case of the 1920s, *Herminghaus v. Southern California Edison Company*, riparian water rights were upheld as the paramount form of claim in California, unleashing a firestorm of criticism.[6] Chapter 7 highlights Wiel's legal analysis of *Herminghaus* and state water plans, where he derives legal insights about monopoly power from the proposed system of dams and canals, warning ominously, "a lawsuit is a poor match for a dam."

Chapter 8 recounts how practicing attorneys such as Wiel and Edward Treadwell put forward competing viewpoints to address water rights and just compensation issues posed by *Herminghaus*, over-appropriation of water, and state plans for water resource development. The chapter also summarizes the legal and institutional process by which the Miller & Lux water rights bloc became yoked to the equally monopolizing technology of Central Valley Project dams and canals.

In Chapter 9, all the institutional and legal upheaval intersected extended drought and planning for statewide water resource development. The chronic deficit of rainfall and Sierra snowpack that began in 1917 eventually attracted the attention of California's state superintendent of banks in 1931. This dry period lasted through 1934. Coupled with dramatic changes to the lands of California's Central Valley (not least of which included the conversion of over 90 percent of the Valley's natural wetland reservoirs to agricultural use, particularly rice cultivation), the dry times contributed to the urgency for action by state government to develop water resources and to the vehemence of public reaction to the *Herminghaus* decision in late 1926.

Chapter 10, "Parable, Prophecy, Present," is a meditation on California's water rights system and the major legal choices now before the state—even if state leaders keep to their time-honored tradition of delayed reckoning. The chapter documents these choices, centering on the probable need to adjudicate the Sacramento River basin, through legal analyses by Wiel and Holsinger.

In selecting my subjects, I lean toward the founding through case law (and some legislative acts) of legal precedents and their development and occasional overthrow, the spread (or lack thereof) of new ideas and technology, and interpretation of engineered structures in political-legal terms (as offered by Wiel, Holsinger, and Harding, among others). I tasked myself with providing readers compelling and meaningful interpretations of the Central Valley's water heritage, including its riverine properties. For any success I have toward these ends, I will be grateful; errors remain mine alone.

NOTES

1. In 2015, urban Californians surpassed water conservation goals established by Governor Jerry Brown. "For June, July, and August the cumulative statewide savings rate was 28.7 percent," the State Water Resources Control Board said in an October 2015 press release. "That equates to 611,566 acre-feet of water saved—51 percent of the overall goal of saving 1.2 million acre-feet from June 2015 to February 2016," as the governor had sought in his April 1 executive order. Making water conservation a way of life will be increasingly important as drought recurs throughout California under rising greenhouse-gas emissions and climate-change conditions. See SWRCB 2015b.

2. Rank v. Krug, 90 F.Supp. 773 (DCSD Cal. 1950).

3. Institutes of Justinian, A.D. 535, "Thus, the following things are by natural law common to all—the air, running water, the sea, and consequently the seashore." The landmark California decision, National Audubon Society v. Superior Court, 33 Cal.3d 419 (1983), acknowledges Justinian's contribution to the public trust doctrine. See also Hart (1996, 64).

4. Lux v. Haggin, 69 Cal. 255 (1886).

5. Katz v. Walkinshaw, 141 Cal. 116 (1903).

6. Herminghaus v. Southern California Edison, 200 Cal. 81 (1926).

Chapter 1

Artificial Cascades

WATER YEAR 1976 SHAPED UP as one of the driest on record, warned the California Department of Water Resources (DWR) in its first-ever drought report. By February, smaller streams saw decreased flow from the previous fall and early winter; normally they *increased* during the rainy season (generally November through March). California had not had a drought longer than about two years since the extended dry spell that ended in 1934.

Now it appeared dry times might return. On average, California's rainfall varied widely by province of the state's diverse geography, as shown in Figure 1.1. But in 1976, the picture diverged sharply from all geographic averages. In the Bay Area, state data showed that by February 1 precipitation ran 30 to 40 percent of normal.[1] In the mountains of far northern California, rainfall totals ran just 40 to 50 percent of normal; in the Central Valley, 30 to 50 percent of normal; along the coast of California from Mendocino to Los Angeles, 10 to 30 percent of normal. Southern California's populous coast, including Orange and San Diego Counties, reported rainfall of just 10 to 40 percent of normal over this period. Halfway through winter, California's water picture was anything but normal.

Nonetheless, DWR's report struck a reassuring tone.

Less than three years before this report, the state had completed several major new reservoirs, along with the California Aqueduct, which tied the Feather River in the north to the fortunes of large growers to the south in the San Joaquin Valley and the fast-growing cities of the southeastern Bay Area and southern California south of the Tehachapi Range. The "bright part" of the DWR picture was that all of California's large new reservoirs had filled during the abundant spring of 1975, with "normal" quantities still in storage by February 1976.

The agency proudly pointed to the fact that statewide, California had placed in service fifty-nine major reservoirs over the previous thirty years. Of these, thirty-seven were new since 1947, and of these, eighteen more were new since 1963. DWR reassured the public that there was much more publicly owned reservoir storage capacity now than in the 1920s and the last long drought. Californians probably didn't need to worry much, certainly not yet (DWR 1976a). Maybe February and March would be wetter.

They weren't. In fact, DWR officials sensed California was entering uncharted territory for water management and policy.

Two problems loomed if the state had to manage through a drought. For one thing, millions of Californians were new since 1924, when the state endured

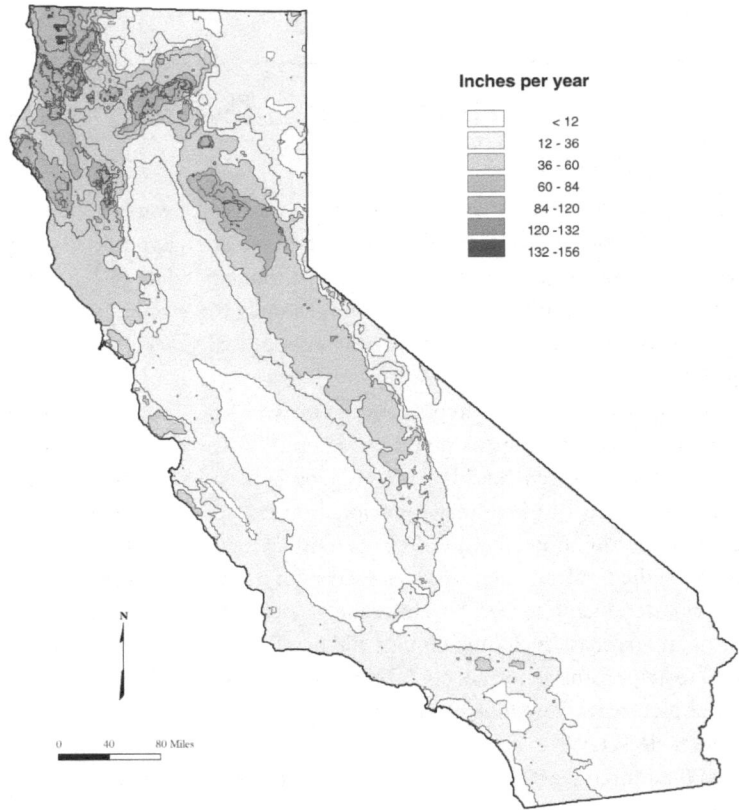

FIGURE 1.1. Mean annual precipitation 1961–1990. Rainfall in California. DWR 2003:22.

its worst recorded drought. In 1920, the U.S. Census reported California's population was 3,426,861 (Thompson 1955, 4, Table I-1; California Department of Finance 2013). By 1976, the state's population reached 21,936,000, an astounding 544 percent increase (California Department of Finance 2000, 10, Table B-1). In 1976, California's economy—its agricultural sector reliant on artificial irrigation systems and urban and suburban development graced with lavish landscaping—was far larger than in the 1920s. So there was little collective memory of the "ancient" drought years. *At least* 18.5 million Californians had no experience or memory of the dry 1920s and 1930s, and the number may have been larger due to normal mortality and outmigration of residents during the intervening decades. How would they react to drought? Could they be convinced to conserve?

Second, you obviously cannot store water if weather fails to deliver it. Reservoir storage in California, especially in the Cascade and Sierra Nevada watersheds, is intended to capture spring snowmelt. But snowpack, the state's natural wintry reservoir, was already low that February. For the State Water Project and the Central Valley Project reservoirs, DWR reported storage levels ranging from 95 to 105 percent of normal on October 1, 1975. But these levels would drop rapidly as sunny day followed sunny day that fall. By the following February, northern Sierra snowpack stood at 27 percent of normal in the Sacramento River basin (including the southern Cascade Range), 14 percent north of Lake Tahoe and 9 percent for the Mokelumne River basin (from which the East Bay Municipal Utilities District imports water to the corridor of East Bay cities from San Leandro and Oakland to Richmond and from Orinda to Walnut Creek). In the San Joaquin Valley, where the Sierra Nevada mountain range reaches its highest elevations (at nearly 15,000 feet above sea level), Kern River snowpack above Bakersfield lagged badly at 1 percent (you read that correctly) to 17 percent of normal for the Stanislaus River basin just south of Lake Tahoe.

Still, DWR offered a comforting perspective: "The dry period 1928–34 had a great impact on the State with 6 dry years in a row, even though any one of the years alone would not have caused serious problems."

But 1924 was the comparison to which DWR returned.

It was one of the few years that was drier on February 1 for most parts than is the case this year [1976]. However, from Bakersfield south, 1975–76 has been even drier . . .

Dry farm crops and rangeland suffered severely in 1923–24, and much irrigated agriculture also experienced substantial water deficiencies. The drought led to formation of the River Problems Committee in the San Joaquin Valley, and the appointment of a water supervisor to closely watch for wasteful practices and to stop waste. Groundwater was the main source of supply at that time since the reservoirs in the Sierras [sic] which we know today were not in existence.

At that time many districts depended on streams with little or no regulatory storage except Nature's snowpack reservoir. Streamflow was very low and many streams and springs that ordinarily flow year-round became dry. (DWR 1976a, 7)

The May 1 report mentioned a cause of continuing dryness: "the persistence, since early November 1975, of a ridge of high atmospheric pressure near the west coast, with above-normal pressures in the surrounding area, including California." Meteorologists, said DWR, "have to conclude that they do not know" how to explain the ridge's persistence. They did know that the ridge's persistence correlated with "floods in Oregon and the Souris River in the Midwest." England, nearly half a world away, was simultaneously experiencing its own worst drought in 200 years. When the ridge persisted through the following winter of 1976–77, DWR produced a map to illustrate it (see Figure 1.2).

The May 1 report said snowpack in California peaked in mid-March 1976 and

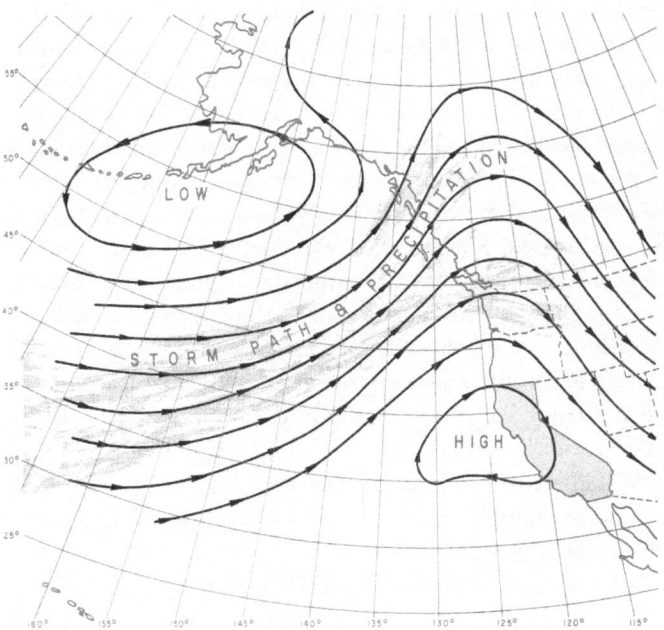

FIGURE 1.2. Typical high-pressure ridge near west coast, winter 1976–77.

full-on snowmelt had begun shortly after. Coastal communities from Jenner on the Sonoma coast to Monterey were hit hard by lack of rain, and many would face rationing or could run out of supplies in their small, sometimes remote watersheds. (DWR 1976b, 38–41, Table 4). In the San Joaquin Valley, however, rainfall and snowpack had improved since February, compared with most other areas of the state. But otherwise, said DWR, dry conditions persisted. In this report, DWR devoted an entire chapter to the question, "What if 1977 is also dry?"

* * *

It is through the institution of water rights that society allocates deficient water supplies (Slater 1999). A water right is a kind of property—a right to take and use water. There are two main types of surface rights in California: riparian and appropriative. Riparian rights to water (which are part and parcel of owning land immediately adjacent to rivers or streams) are the most paramount rights to use water in California. They are followed by appropriative rights claimed before 1914 and then by appropriative rights permitted and licensed by the state of California after 1914. (Further explanation of this pecking order is in chapter 2 and beyond.) Appropriative rights are enforced by the adages, "first in time, first in right" and "use it or lose it." The earlier in time a claim is dated, the more "senior" it is; rights claimed later in time are considered "junior."

Parts of the western Sierra and eastern Central Valley from Redding to Bakersfield owe their senior water rights to the heritage of the Gold Rush and the ensuing agricultural settlement during the late nineteenth century. In the Sacramento Valley, several irrigation and water districts claim large, older blocs of water rights on the Sacramento, Feather, and American Rivers. These water supplies are usually highly reliable due to seniority of their rights: the earlier the date of first diversion, the more likely that even in a dry year right holders can divert, store, and use water even when overall supplies are scarce.

Today, the largest (yet not always the most senior) surface rights typically involve storage and diversions from Sierra rivers just as each leaves the eastern rim of the Central Valley. For each river—Feather, Yuba, American, Stanislaus, Tuolumne, Merced, San Joaquin, Kings, Kaweah, Tule, and Kern—there is a dam—Oroville, New Bullard's Bar, Folsom, New Melones, New Don Pedro, New Exchequer, Friant, Pine Flat, Success, Hidden, and Isabella. These are advantageous sites: topography and geology allow relatively safe and economical dam construction with relative ease of delivery via costless gravity.

From Stockton south to Bakersfield—the San Joaquin Valley—four public and private entities called "exchange contractors" retain paramount riparian and senior appropriative rights to the San Joaquin River that date to the mid-1850s. Their corporate lineage descends from original control by the Miller & Lux cattle corporation of vast acreage along the river and an important canal system inaugurated by other early California movers and shakers.

Some of their rights—the less reliable ones that relied on wet-year flood flows to marshy grasslands in the San Joaquin Valley—were sold permanently through a "purchase contract" to the U.S. Bureau of Reclamation. The exchange contractors' most reliable rights are at the core of the Central Valley Project, and the projects' key rights are still privately held. They are essentially on long-term loan to the Bureau of Reclamation from these contractors. The loan, or exchange, of these rights was executed in a 1939 "exchange contract." Thus, a public-private partnership lies at the heart of California's largest water project, but the private side had the stronger grip in this handshake.

To benefit from *all* the Miller & Lux descendants' rights—those purchased and exchanged—the Bureau built two important reservoirs and two major aqueducts during the 1940s and early 1950s: Shasta Dam on the upper Sacramento River northwest of Redding, Friant Dam northeast of Fresno on the San Joaquin River, and the Delta Mendota Canal linking the south Delta near Tracy with the Mendota Pool on the San Joaquin.

Artificial cascades of exportation followed these purchase and exchange contracts: San Joaquin River snowmelt collected at Friant Dam, so that the river's flood flows once claimed by Miller & Lux could be diverted into the Friant-Kern Canal for irrigation along its 165-mile journey to Bakersfield.

The Friant-Kern Canal cascade from the San Joaquin is the *pro quo* for the *quid* of the Bureau delivering a like amount assured every year from the Sacramento River. This second audacious cascade would be completed through two other engineering feats: the construction and operation of Shasta Dam, and construction of an elaborate pumping system *in* the lower San Joaquin River to deliver the exchange contractors' "replacement water" uphill to Mendota Pool west of Fresno for delivery to the lands of Miller & Lux's corporate descendants. (The 1939 pumping system intended for the San Joaquin morphed into a separate "highline canal," today known as the Delta Mendota Canal.)

The closest analogy I can offer for what the purchase and exchange contracts are to the Central Valley Project might be what the U.S. Constitution is to the union of states. The contracts provide a framework and a point of departure for water project operations every single year. Their effect is nothing if not constitutional and foundational for the Central Valley Project.

Nearly all the San Joaquin River would be permanently diverted toward Bakersfield, and a significant portion of the Sacramento River would be exported, also permanently, to a point 20 miles west of Fresno to irrigate lands held by the exchange contractors. In the process of this accomplishment, Californians endured difficult, politically painful legal, economic, and intellectual challenges accommodating hydraulic technology to the legacy of San Joaquin Valley monopoly water rights.

About one-fifth of Shasta Lake's capacity is apportioned to the exchange contractors each year. Still California's largest reservoir, it was built as a surrogate supply 400 miles north of Fresno in part to accommodate the exchange contractors' senior water rights. Without this design for the Central Valley Project, the exchange contractors could legally insist on their historical supplies from the San Joaquin River. Only in drought years, when Shasta cannot meet its obligations to the exchange contractors, does the exchange contract require release of Friant's waters directly into the San Joaquin River for their use; and in those same drought years, the Friant-Kern Canal loses its source at Friant Dam, leaving to their own devices some twenty-one water agencies and thousands of farmers cultivating a million acres between Fresno and Bakersfield. Such is the power of senior water rights in a drought.

A rung below riparian and appropriative water rights on the ladder of water justice are those jurisdictions and regions that obtained a contract for water service from public or private water systems willing to provide them water. The reliability of a contractor's water service depends on the priority of the system offering the contract. The twenty-one water agencies I just mentioned along the Friant-Kern Canal fit here.

The Bureau of Reclamation went on to add reservoirs at Folsom on the American River in the 1950s and New Melones on the Stanislaus River to the CVP by 1979. In all, the agency would execute water service contracts with over 200 water agencies, corporations, and individuals to deliver water from Redding in the north nearly to Arvin in the south. Still, unique among all CVP contractors, the San Joaquin River Exchange Contractors today have first call on water of the Bureau's storage at Friant (if Shasta fails) because of their vested rights.

* * *

By the mid-1970s, a complex water system operated, with two governmental masters—plus a third, private one, if one accounted for the Exchange Contract. Cities up and down California, the Delta at the center of the state, and the large agribusinesses of the Central Valley depended on the Central Valley Project and the State Water Project to deliver water supplies or protect them through salinity control (in the Delta's case), largely from Shasta Reservoir releases. And the Central Valley Project, especially along the Friant-Kern Canal, released some water in wet years that was simply spread over areas where groundwater supplies were thought to replenish. Drought made it much harder to fulfill each of these tasks for the state's expected and accustomed level of agricultural and urban development.

By the time DWR issued the report (May 1, 1976), agency officials knew they had a very dry year on their hands. Nineteen seventy-six promised the "most severe test of our water management abilities," DWR's director Ronald Robie wrote sternly in the report's cover letter. Robie himself was entering just his second year as director of DWR. Before that, he served from 1960 to 1969 as an expert water consultant to the state Assembly Water Committee. He was appointed the attorney member to the State Water Resources Control Board in 1969, where he served until taking the post at DWR in 1975 under Governor Jerry Brown (during Brown's first administration). His résumé spanned voter approval of the State Water Project in 1960 through initial operation of all its major facilities in 1973.[2] He would oversee operation not only of the statewide water project that had been planned since the late 1940s, but also its coordinated operations with the federal government's Central Valley Project, owned by the U.S. Bureau of Reclamation. As he saw it, his job was to make certain that *all* of California made it through this drought.

The hundreds of local, regional, and statewide public and private utilities and special districts that serve water to agriculture and a largely urban population may be called California's water industry. Robie acknowledged that with the new systems in place, the water industry would have to learn how to manage through drought as it unfolded. He reassured readers of the May 1 report that state and federal reservoirs were planned from the 1920s through the 1960s with enough capacity to get their customers through extended dry periods. But he acknowledged,

Traditionally, projects have been formulated to operate through dry periods, but our experience now is showing vividly the difference between such theories and the realities of operating complex systems in the midst of the myriad of economic, social and environmental counterforces which we see today. These pressures have caused several water agencies to take greater risks in the use of water this dry year than were intended in the design of their projects. (DWR 1976b, i)

Robie did not elaborate on who assumed which risks.

The myriad environmental "counterforces" Robie mentioned came about because by the late 1910s and early 1920s Californians had two unfolding "tragedies of the commons": one in the Delta 80 miles east of San Francisco involving surface water; the other with water underground throughout the San Joaquin Valley, in the Bay Area's Santa Clara Valley, and in southern California.

The northern two-thirds of the Central Valley drains to and through the Delta; the Delta is *the* low place in California's Central Valley (Figure 1.3). In 1959, it was granted a legal definition of its lands in state law. They span a 738,000-acre farming and recreational region between Antioch on the west, Sacramento to the north, Stockton to the east, and Tracy to the south. The Bay and Delta together form an estuary—an often sinuous, dendritic water body where fresh water of the Central Valley meets tidal salt water from San Francisco Bay. From there, the great rivers forming it flow amid huge and rhythmic tidal oscillations to the Golden Gate via Carquinez Strait, the wide river that connects Suisun Bay to San Pablo Bay (CalFED 2000, 10, n. 3). Five counties have pieces of the Delta in their jurisdiction: Contra Costa, Sacramento, San Joaquin, Solano, and Yolo. The latter county, lying to the north, provides abundant floodplain and habitat acreage for the Sacramento River near the city of Davis.

There is *always* water in Delta river channels from Bay tidal flows and from Central Valley and Sierra Nevada rivers, each source varying in proportion. From its river channels, Delta farmers diverted water to irrigate orchards, cornfields, sugar beets, and many other crops. Even today, these lands are among the state's prime agricultural lands.

What matters most in the Delta is whether the water in nearby channels is fresh enough to irrigate crops and for local residents to drink. "Salinity control" used to be one of Nature's services to the Delta, where flows from the Sierra rivers and the Sacramento (which taps the southern Cascade volcanoes) would usually be large enough to keep the tidal salts literally "at bay." Vast, natural wetland reservoirs provided spring and summer valley storage for Sierra snowmelt. But by the early 1920s Sacramento River and San Joaquin River flows were no longer up to the task.

A perfect storm of social and climate factors arrived simultaneously: rice culture emerged as an important Sacramento Valley crop, and an extended dry period

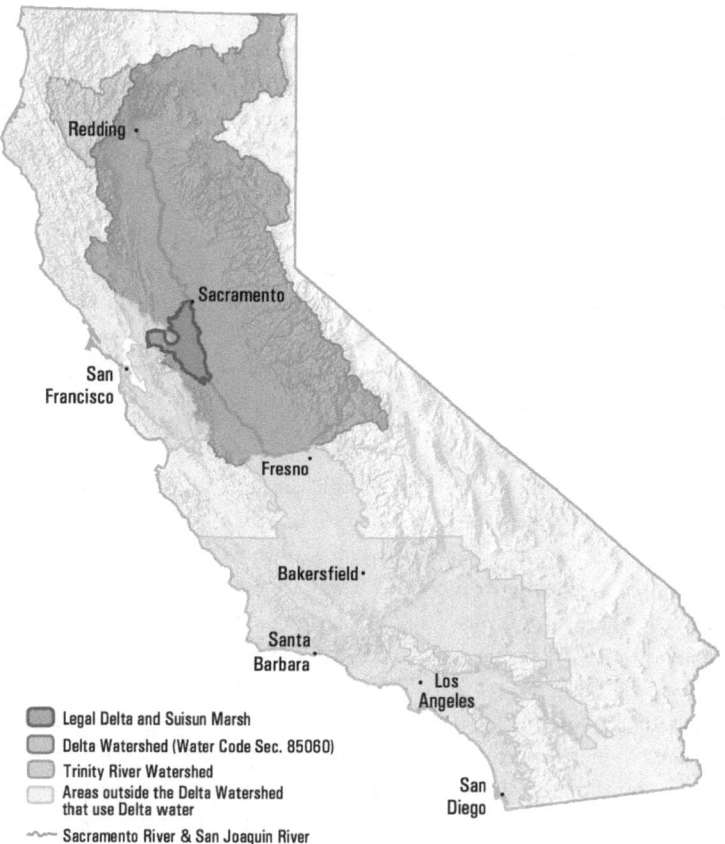

FIGURE 1.3. Delta watershed and modern service area: how water reaches the Delta and where water exported from the Delta goes. Courtesy of Delta Stewardship Council (DSC 2013:6).

withheld rain and snow from the Sierra Nevada and Central Valley. Earlier, crop experiments at the University of California's agricultural extension research station in Biggs (between Chico and Marysville) showed the feasibility of rice culture in California. In 1912, the first commercial rice crop was grown and irrigated in the Sacramento Valley on 1,400 acres. By 1916, irrigated rice acreage grew to 67,000 acres, with nearly 54,000 of them irrigated from the Sacramento and Feather Rivers. By 1920, Valley rice acreage had more than doubled to 154,000 acres. Irrigation and water district formation exploded in the Sacramento Valley so that the region's tax base could be harnessed to develop and control its water for the new export crop, rice (Basye 2011; Davis 1984; State Water Commission 1917, 92). California rice growers joined rice suppliers in Texas, Louisiana, and Mississippi to export the water-intensive grain to global markets, especially Asia.

Why would farmers begin growing rice, one of the most water-intensive crops in the world, in a state where early in the twentieth century water supplies were already known to be at a premium? In 1917, a federal irrigation engineer explained the rationale.

> Rice in the Sacramento Valley has served a two-fold purpose of [first] utilizing land heretofore not used except for scanty pasture or on which grain growing has been declining through decreased production, and [second] of providing a means of utilizing the waters of irrigation systems which had been constructed but which had not been fully developed on account of lack of settlers. (Robertson 1917, 254)

Mr. Robertson described without naming the principle of "due diligence" necessary to retain an appropriative water right under California law. While prior appropriation doctrine set out "first in time, first in right," its corollary was that appropriators must "use it or lose it"—they had to show due diligence to retain their rights. Simply put, growing rice became a way to boost the declining value of Sacramento Valley land, and it was a way to continue use of water by landowners who had obtained water rights that were in danger of loss through disuse.

In the fall of 1917, an extended dry period began even as the rice fields expanded in the Sacramento Valley. Then, a critically dry year came in 1920. As early as September 1919, researchers from the California Water Commission found a much higher concentration of salt in Sacramento River and San Joaquin River waters in the vicinity of Antioch, Port Costa, and Crockett along the Carquinez Strait. Several years before, saltier water enabled a borer mollusk called the "torredo" (or "teredo" in some sources from the period) to migrate up the Strait to the inland port towns of Crockett and Port Costa. Legions of torredos drilled into pilings supporting wharves and ferry berths. "Piles that had been supporting these structures for many years, and which were in first class condition, were suddenly attacked and ruined by these salt water borers," the commission reported at the time. Further upstream, towns such as Antioch had to stop diverting water directly from the Strait because it was too salty for residents and businesses (California Department of Public Works 1926; Sacramento Chamber of Commerce, et al. 1924).

The salt problem in the Strait and in the Delta, where many farmers had also lodged vociferous complaints about salty irrigation water, was a result of both dry weather conditions and upstream diversions for rice culture in the Sacramento Valley. While there was no obvious recourse against Nature for withholding precipitation and runoff, Delta farmers prevailed on the town of Antioch with its diversion from the Sacramento River to sue upstream rice growers to reduce their diversions. But Antioch lost before the California Supreme Court in 1922.[3]

"The salinity problem in the Sacramento and San Joaquin River Delta region has ceased to be a problem of the future," wrote the commission in 1921. "On the contrary, it has become a problem of the present, and one that should be solved at the earliest possible moment" (State Water Commission 1921, 85, Appx. D). Ninety-five years later, those familiar with the Delta's problems know that truer words were never uttered, but lasting solutions have eluded California ever since.

Then came 1923–24, the driest year on record in California at the time and the one that DWR would look to in 1976. Delta farmers again were squeezed by low flows and high salinity. This time, instead of heading to court, farmers from both regions met in Sacramento for a River Problems Conference in early 1924 (Sacramento Chamber of Commerce et al. 1924). The 1920s farm economy had sunk into recession after the boom years of World War I. Few farmers could afford to fight water battles in court. Conferees agreed that upstream diversions would be reduced for the time being, provided that together they would also seek increased supplies in the future for all concerned—especially with help from the state of California. Eventually, the federal government constructed Shasta Dam at the north end of the Sacramento Valley. From 300 miles away, it provided the permanent salinity control that Antioch and Delta farmers sought in the early 1920s (Jackson and Paterson 1977, Ch. 1; Paterson 1978).

By 1976, the water management problem looked very different from 1924 when the Delta water problems conferees met, but it was still an unfolding tragedy of the commons. Both the state of California and the U.S. Bureau of Reclamation were now inextricably immersed in Delta hydraulic affairs. The big state and federal water projects juggled water supply demands of their contractors with requirements imposed by the State Water Resources Control Board, the state's water regulator, to provide salinity control to protect water uses in the Delta. They also knew they had to provide extra water as a hydraulic barrier to tidal salt to deliver supplies across the Delta to their customers. Such "carriage water" was simply a cost, expressed in volumes and flows, of operating the state and federal export systems through the Delta.[4]

In 1967, the state legislature authorized the board to regulate both water quality and water rights. Nowhere is this integrated authority more relevant than in the Delta. By 1976, the Board was in the midst of producing its first water quality control plan for the Delta, as required by the federal Clean Water Act and the state's new water quality control law. When that plan was eventually completed in 1978, the board would reallocate water rights to DWR's State Water Project (which only began full operations in 1973) and the U.S. Bureau of Reclamation's Central Valley Project (which had begun most of its operations by the early 1950s).

DWR icily noted in its May 1976 report that the federal Central Valley Project and the State Water Project must release water to adhere to salinity objectives in the Delta. At the time, the Bureau disputed its obligation to meet Delta salinity rules (a dispute since resolved in favor of it doing so). As owner of the State Water Project, DWR acknowledged that it would probably spend 300,000 acre-feet of its own dwindling water supplies to keep maintaining the Delta salinity targets required by the State Water Resources Control Board without Bureau help.[5] Obviously, those 300,000 acre-feet would be unavailable for other uses during the drought, one of the "myriad environmental counterforces" to which Robie probably alluded.

* * *

DWR also told the public in May 1976 there would be shortages of water to irrigated agribusinesses in the Central Valley that summer. Yolo County's reservoirs (between the Bay Area and Sacramento) had gone dry by the middle of the irrigation season, since its Coast Range reservoirs rely solely on rainfall. After that, farmers would rely solely on groundwater, and in general they would have to rely more heavily on groundwater in that irrigation season. To reduce influx of ocean salt and to harbor upstream reservoir supplies, DWR installed two barriers during 1976 in Delta channels to augment hydraulic protection of Delta water quality. When conditions worsened in 1977, DWR put in *six* barriers, mostly in the south Delta (DWR 1977, 1978).

DWR pledged to do what it could.

> The usual strategy described in discussions with Central Valley surface water project operators who are experiencing a below-normal supply is to serve all the water possible on demand of the users, carrying little or no water over to guard against a dry 1977, except in the Central Valley Project, the State Water Project System, New Don Pedro Reservoir [on the Tuolumne River], and Lake McClure [on the Merced River].

By this reasoning, the water-supply bird in the hand was worth two in the bush:

> This strategy is based on the belief that a good crop this year is desirable, *since next year will probably be a near-normal or better water supply.* In some areas, water was needed and served early in the season to make up for the subnormal precipitation on nuts, fruits, and vineyards. In some instances, where the surface water shortage will be offset by pumping more ground water, the surface water is being held for delivery during the peak months of water demand, July and August. (DWR 1976b, 33, emphasis added)

In the Tulare Lake basin, DWR reported in May 1976 that the Kings, Kaweah, Tule, and Kern Rivers together would have about 35 percent of normal supply. Intensive groundwater pumping by growers would have to make up the irrigation deficiency. By 1976, the San Joaquin Valley already pumped a lot of groundwater for agricultural production. In California, groundwater use was then unregulated. (Recent 2014 legislation qualifies this now.) DWR mentioned in February that groundwater was the main source for irrigation in the 1920s. One reason Valley growers wanted the Central Valley Project in the 1920s and 1930s, and then the State Water Project twenty years later, was that they had been mining once-abundant groundwater supplies since the arrival of pump technology early in the century. As pump technology diffused throughout American agriculture and the Central Valley, irrigation in the Valley expanded by leaps and bounds. Groundwater levels fell, however.

In the 1950s, the state of California acknowledged in its ambitious *California Water Plan* that intensive reliance on groundwater in the San Joaquin Valley had enabled "[e]xtensive areas overlying natural ground water basins" to develop "a high level of productivity." Central and southern California had indeed grown rapidly, in part on the strength of groundwater supplies (as we will see more of in chapter 5). But the cost of this expansive development was overdraft. Like a bank account with insufficient funds to support an owner's spending habits, overdrafted groundwater meant users took more than they allowed Nature to replenish (DWR 1957, 16).

> In many of these areas the overdraft is continuing—in fact increasing—generally with no active measures being taken to correct the serious problem.... If the underground sources of water are allowed to be completely depleted and no other sources of supply are developed in the interim, the economy of the State will not just stand at the current level, but must of necessity regress to one supportable largely by surface developments. Surface water sources are *meager* in the central and southern areas of the State where the water requirements are the greatest. The *calamity* of economic depression attendant on the *excessive depletion* of ground water reservoirs would not be limited to those agricultural areas overlying the reservoirs. *Just as the whole State now enjoys the benefits of an expanding economy, so would the whole state—north as well as south—feel the possible catastrophic effects of the destruction of ground water basins by continued overdraft.* (DWR 1957, 16, emphasis added)

Scary stuff by the standards of 1950s optimism.

The State's water plan disclosed that the most serious overdraft was occurring in the San Joaquin–Tulare Lake basin, (from about Stockton south to Bakersfield) putting the deficit there at 2.5 million acre-feet a year. On the coastal plains of Santa Barbara, Ventura, and Los Angeles Counties, overdraft depleted smaller groundwater supplies there at a rate of about 400,000 acre-feet per year by 1955.

To combat overdraft, state officials in the 1950s and 1960s sought to pour water on the problem, using the Central Valley Project and later the State Water Project. The artificial cascades were already engineered: surface water imports to the Tulare Lake basin via Friant-Kern Canal began in the late 1940s and early 1950s, especially once substitute supplies arrived from Shasta Lake via the Delta-Mendota Canal.

Adding to this, in the 1970s the CVP delivered water from its San Luis Canal (to western Fresno and Kings Counties). State Water Project imports arrived in Fresno, Kings, and Kern Counties through the California Aqueduct also in the early 1970s.

By the 1970s that groundwater overdraft averaged 1.5 million acre-feet a year, reduced by devoting some surface water from the Central Valley Project to groundwater recharge in the Valley. The dry conditions of 1976 would worsen it, DWR predicted. "This extra pumping could exceed normal pumping by about 2,000,000 acre-feet over normal pumpage," said the Department (DWR 1976b, 35). A tragedy of the groundwater commons had festered in the fifty years since the last long drought, and Californians had done little to stem or prevent its recurrence; instead, they had built reservoirs and canals. Growers responded mainly by expanding irrigated crop acreage and kept using water as they always had in the San Joaquin Valley—as though there would always be more, even if it came from somewhere else.

In the San Joaquin Valley, reported DWR by May 1976, "the big story" was the deficiency in Class I water available from the Central Valley Project's Friant Dam. Class I was the Bureau's most reliable water, the exchanged water made available to it by the Exchange Contractors. The Bureau's average annual allocation to the Friant-Kern Canal—a giant concrete flume that transports pristine Sierra Nevada water from the upper San Joaquin River south along the east side of the Valley, delivering water to districts in Fresno, Kings, Tulare, and Kern Counties—was about 1.144 million acre-feet in all. In 1976, however, only about 462,000 acre-feet would be available for delivery to these contractors. As mentioned, the other 682,000 acre-feet they needed, stated DWR solemnly, would have to come from pumped groundwater. Friant Dam also diverts water into the Madera Canal for growers in Madera County northwest of the Fresno area. On average, Madera growers were delivered about 140,000 acre-feet from Friant, but in 1976 Class I supplies would be just 98,000 acre-feet, about 70 percent of average (DWR 1976b, 34). To meet that area's overall irrigation water needs, DWR estimated the growers would need another 215,000 acre-feet from pumped groundwater.

Why was the Friant-Kern Canal deficiency and the need to pump groundwater the "big story"? Eventually during the drought, millions of urban Californians would be enlisted to retrofit bathroom fixtures, drain their washing machines to their gardens (as my father did at our house), and rip out lawns in favor of drought-tolerant landscaping. Eighteen million people were unaware that artificial export cascades of California's water system could be shut off so the San Joaquin River Exchange Contractors might continue to take their legal water, even though they had been receiving Sacramento River water since the early 1950s. It was all because of California's worst drought in over forty years. Even had they known of this exercise of power in the early months of 1976, few Californians could have explained it.

The "big story" behind the Friant water contractors' drought cutbacks lies with the monopolization of land and water rights that began over a century before the 1976 drought, and to which we now turn.

NOTES

1. Hydrologists, civil engineers, and water policy analysts use statistical methods to characterize and compare one water year with another. "Normal" in these drought reports, as well as many other government reports about water, refers to the statistical average (mean) value of all water years that make up the government's historical record of rainfall, snowpack, and runoff (stream flow) in California for a particular time of year. By 1976, there were about fifty-five years of consistent hydrologic data throughout California, providing ready comparisons of the current year with another in the same historical record (e.g., 1924 or 1928–34). Yet by then, California had been a state for 126 years, so this database accounted for just 40 percent of California's recorded climatic history.

2. Today, he is Justice Ronald B. Robie, a member of California's Third District Appellate Court panel.

3. Antioch v. Williams Irrigation District, 188 Cal. 451 (1922).

4. The state of California decided by the early 1930s that it made more economic and environmental sense to use continuous stream flow as a hydraulic barrier, rather than build a physical barrier and convert the Delta and Suisun Bay into stagnant reservoirs (California Department of Public Works 1931a, 44–45; Hyatt 1934, 1935a, 1935b). This is the principle of "through-Delta conveyance" that the DWR and the U.S. Bureau of Reclamation use today to move their upstream reservoir supplies across the Delta for export to the San Joaquin Valley and southern California. Damming of the Bay–Delta estuary with a physical saltwater barrier is no longer under serious consideration for good ecological, economic, transportation, navigation, and water quality reasons. But in the late 1950s and early 1960s, numerous studies of the flow of water into and through the Delta revealed several existing channel pathways or "Trans-Delta" canals (as DWR called them in the 1957 *California Water Plan*) to convey water from the lower Sacramento River at Walnut Grove all the way to the south Delta pumps. As a result, DWR considers various kinds of physical barriers (such as rock barriers, Obermeyer dams, control structures, and fixed radial operable gates associated with boat locks and fish passage) still potentially useful at a local scale within the hydraulic barrier that now exists.

5. An acre-foot is a unit of volume: imagine an acre of land covered to a depth of one foot. It represents 325,828.8 gallons of water (one cubic foot equals 7.48 gallons). An acre-foot is about equal to the amount of water that *two* California households consume annually today. However, in the 1970s, it was often stated that an acre-foot was about the volume of water used by *one* California household in a year.

Chapter 2

Mere Trespassers and Monopolists

CHILDREN GAIN IMMEDIATE INSIGHT into the unbridled, bare-knuckled dynamics of capitalism by playing the board game Monopoly®. Let's recall for a moment what it's like to play.

As the game begins, players take turns rolling dice, advancing to new locations on the board that, at the outset, they can choose to buy as individual properties. Soon the motivation of individual greed takes over, with players accumulating properties around the board for personal gain. Landing on properties owned by others, players must pay rent—a familiar transaction. Once players own all properties on the board, they may strike deals to obtain properties grouped by color, since having all the properties of one color confers investment privileges to their owner—a monopoly over a future stream of revenue from other players.

Having acquired individual monopolies—be they the two- or threesome colored properties, the railroads, utilities, or waterworks that dot the board—players may then develop their properties with houses and hotels, commanding higher rents from nonowners who land on them. Such combinations elevate some players into evermore high-stakes development with even higher rents. Unlucky or unwise players spiral into abject poverty, praying to their dice for a modest cash infusion by passing "GO," avoiding Boardwalk, Park Place, and Pennsylvania Avenue, or collecting the accumulated pot from Free Parking (the latter an informal anticipation of a public lottery not expressly permitted by the board game's written rules) so as to receive an unearned windfall forestalling bankruptcy.[1] The rate at which both poverty and immense wealth accumulate determines how long (or short) the game continues before someone goes bankrupt. The last player standing is the Monopolist. If the game has a lesson, it is this: from equal economic opportunity great wealth and crushing poverty can emerge.

Capitalism's central profit motive is easily grasped as the game proceeds. It does not really matter for educating the young that Monopoly's® invisible hand is found in the roll of dice, rather than through investment in lobbyists or favorable laws. The competitive existential fear and insecurity the game induces is a palpable, virtual analog to life under real capitalism.

Monopoly® the game teaches at least two other lessons of economics: one about the pivotal importance of acquiring and controlling property in economic life; and another about how organizing property into strategic blocs can lead to greater profits by restricting competition from other economic actors.

Playing Monopoly® also demonstrates the real estate truism of "location,

location, location"—the idea that property value derives from the physical placement or position of a property relative to the advantages and disadvantages of others.

As in Monopoly®, so in life. Power of location, design, and priority are claims on the economy, ecology, and political future of watersheds.[2] Design is the exercise of conscious arrangement of human and physical relationships to land and water resources. Priority under water law determined who got first claim to California's rivers and streams prior to those arriving later. Water politics is therefore not just about elections, policy, and legislation. Monopolized water politics must describe the workings of the ownership and control of key locations in a watershed; it must pay attention to design of engineered systems that intervene in the natural workings of the watershed; and it must itemize the pecking order established by a priority system of water allocation dominated by monopoly interests. What came of monopoly power playing out in California's Central Valley was most certainly unexpected by California Indians, who generally allocated land and water resources in common, and by subsequent pioneer settlers.

In the monopoly board of early California, Gold Rush miners trespassed onto federal, public-domain lands where they asserted possessory control of Sierra mining regions. Not long after, organized corporate interests assumed dominance first of the mines, and soon after, the fertile and most easily irrigated lands of the Central Valley. Thus, the emergence of the law of California water rights is situated in the florescence of U.S. industrialization and civil rights for corporations and individuals, and government's creation of commission forms of authority in response.

* * *

In the decades before James Marshall found gold at Sutter's Mill in January 1848, California had little appeal. Three thousand miles east, Congress was preoccupied by conflict over Missouri's admission to the Union, dealing with the fugitive slave problem, and the question of whether the South's institution of plantation slavery would be allowed to spread west. Between 1846 and 1849 the United States had prosecuted a war with Mexico over the Republic of Texas. Through the Treaty of Guadalupe Hidalgo, which concluded the war, the United States pressed beyond its conquest of Texas to acquire Alta California from Mexico. Ratification of the Treaty gave the U.S. government contiguous territory from Atlantic to Pacific. It was the largest land acquisition since the Louisiana Purchase in 1803. Mexico ceded to Washington some 336 million acres.[3] About one-third of that acreage contained what became modern California. Most of California's public domain was located in its desert and mountain regions. The Treaty would ignite a century and a half of uninterrupted east-to-west migration by Americans, transforming their economy and collective self-understanding in the process.

By federal law, acquisition of territory by the U.S. government meant that property not already privately owned by individuals or companies (and which could be documented as legitimate) came into its possession. Starting with lands beyond the Appalachians, the Louisiana Purchase, and the Northwest Ordinance, the government aggressively used its real estate acquisitions as sources of revenue for the federal budget, selling off lands (patent) to private speculators and settlers (Rohrbaugh 1968; Wiel 1949, 5–16).

But California would get more awkward and ambiguous treatment. The chaotic early years of California's statehood and the lead-up to the American Civil War exposed a power vacuum.[4] Into that vacuum flocked new immigrants to mine gold, to serve the miners with food, to manufacture mining and agricultural tools, and to finance the new western economy. This "growing population of urbanized American civilians was demanding self-government and such traditional rights as trial by jury," writes historian Kevin Starr (Starr 2005, 91). In March 1849, San Francisco convened its own fifteen-member assembly to draft a code of laws for the city.

That June, U.S. military governor of California Brigadier General Bennett Riley took notice, deciding that, in Starr's words, "Neither military law nor the *alcalde* system currently in use . . . could cope with the complexity of California." He called for a constitutional convention. By October, "California stood redesigned as an American state," with a new constitution informed by examples from New York and Iowa. Women could own property in their own name, hardly a universal policy in the day. But only white males could vote, denying the same right to Native Californians and longtime Californios, as well as the more recent African Americans and Chinese. Individuals from these groups could not testify against whites in a court of law. And the framers came "dangerously close" to prohibiting African Americans—whether slave or free—from entering California at all. The constitution did ban slavery after much debate and "despite the knowledge that the admission of California as a free state would destabilize even further a shaky and fragile Union," writes Starr. The lands of Mexican California were trimmed to exclude from the new state of California the territories of what later became Arizona, Nevada, Utah, and southern Colorado in hopes of making California more acceptable to an agitated and fractious Congress (Starr 2005, 92–93).

* * *

The idea of priority is central to California and western American water law. Prior appropriation is today California's distinctly capitalist water right in perhaps its purest form, its most legible statement of a tangible property right to use water, especially when compared with unquantified riparian rights. Prior appropriation also relies on usufruct—a right to *use, season, and method of diversion* (but not possession) of actual water. It provides legibility to owner and government alike, since the right is *quantified,* limited to diversion from a specific point, and to use at a specific place. It is only as good a right as it is diligently used; appropriative rights can be lost or revoked through disuse.[5]

Because appropriative water rights today are a key institutional basis for California's modern water system, some recent observers of water law have viewed the doctrine's history as an inevitable result of state historical development. California's water system, particularly the State Water Project and the federal Central Valley Project, is today controversial, but it was certainly not inevitable. Water lawyers defending the appropriative doctrine undergirding these systems either represent the state's interests in owning and operating (or even regulating) the system, or they represent the interests of customers who depend on continuity of those appropriative water rights. William Attwater and James Markle, for instance, gloss over historical difficulty with the emergence and elaboration of appropriative doctrine (Attwater and Markle 1988).[6] Discussing early California Supreme Court cases in *Eddy v. Simpson* (1853) and *Irwin v. Phillips* (1855), they write that the doctrine of prior appropriation was developed "as the courts worked out the characteristics of the appropriative right."[7] Such a statement assumes what it concludes: that state justices in the 1850s knew a priori that California would adopt the doctrine of prior appropriation. At that time, as we shall see, prior appropriation's modern role was hardly a foregone conclusion.

Attorneys Clifford Schulz and Gregory Weber begin from a different but equally faulty premise, that California's doctrinal evolution went "from prior appropriation to riparian rights" (Schulz and Weber 1988). They recognize that miners' appropriative rights were merely possessory and did not run with the land as do riparian rights. They also acknowledge that the California Supreme Court's early appropriative rights cases expressed uncertainty over the status of such rights. They also cite *Kidd v. Laird* (1860) as showing the early court's view of property in water as a usufruct (a right to use), deserving constitutional protection. But *Kidd* did not specify this property right as *private*.[8] Schulz and Weber inflate the significance of an 1863 case describing appropriative rights as "vested" with a private veneer (Schulz and Weber 1988, 1051). They then jump ahead to a 1912 case claiming appropriative rights as private, though by then public entities had been appropriating water since enactment of the Wright Act of 1887 enabled irrigation districts to appropriate water under the California Civil Code in effect at the time. In this instance, a lack of attention to connecting periods of doctrinal development from real-life conflicts and court cases suggests that brevity does not always yield clarity.

Priority in law conferred advantage to owners of lands immediately bordering rivers. Such locations, as the state found, benefited the design of California's legal framework in the run-up to statehood. Having adopted its constitution in 1849 prior to statehood, the California legislature passed legislation on April 13, 1850, adopting the Common Law of England, "so far as it is not repugnant to or inconsistent with the Constitution of the United States, or the constitution or laws of the state of California" to apply in California courts of law.[9] Under English Common Law, a water right is a *usufruct*, "a right for a certain period to use and enjoy the fruits of another's property without damaging or diminishing it, but allowing for any natural deterioration in the property over time."[10] California was in essence applying riparian water rights to all real property within its borders adjacent to streams and lakes. These rights run with the land, meaning they inhere in the definition of a given parcel of land in perpetuity (Shaw 1922, 447). Riparian right holders possess a pro rata right to a proportion of the flow in relation to the riparian rights of other owners of land along the same stream from headwaters to or straddling its mouth at the sea. Lawyers call this proportional relationship "correlative," since your rights must correlate with the rights of others. Absolute quantities go unspecified in this commons. By holding riparian rights through your ownership of land next to a stream, you do not lose them, even if you don't use your fair share from the stream (Hutchins 1956, 285, 291; Littleworth and Garner 2007, 44).[11] Only if you sell your riparian water rights to someone else, or separate them from riparian access, say by subdivision, would a riparian parcel no longer enjoy use of the adjacent water (Hutchins 1956, 182). And, by virtue of its early adoption, the legislature provided riparian water rights paramount priority in most cases over water right doctrines that emerged later.

Common law riparian rights establish a clear connection between waters flowing in a stream and the adjacent land where the riparian owner may use the water. These rights implicitly respect an ecological basis to the economic relationship between human use of water on the adjacent land, the vagaries of Nature, and the hydrologic cycle. In litigation involving riparian rights, it is not uncommon for a riparian's defense to invoke the "fertility" of the lands that floodwaters provide (Pisani 1996, 15; and the *Herminghaus* case examined in chapter 7).

Despite its justifiable claims to aridity, California is laced, bisected, and ringed with rivers and streams. And along every river and stream are riparian landowners, the vast majority of whom enjoy the use of waters adjacent to their lands while participating in a legally enforceable commons. But if one acquired enough lands along its banks, a monopolist could potentially control the use of water along a river.

Those seeking or holding appropriative water rights—whether private investors or government agencies—have long distrusted riparians as monopolists. Riparians lack accountability to public, social, and economic interests outside their own common property regime. Their water must be available when desired, without having to quantify its use. Paradoxically, quantification of their rights has never been legislated.[12]

* * *

By examining the record of state supreme court water law cases, and the writings of Samuel C. Wiel and more recent historians, a more complete, if complex, picture emerges of prior appropriation's doctrinal trajectory. Gold Rush miners are often credited by historians with inventing appropriative water rights for California and the American West after staking claims for mining operations on public lands where they could claim no riparian rights (as the U.S. government owned the land they mined; Wiel 1909, 482, n. 4). The credit given by some historians for miners' innovation is a bit undeserved (McCurdy 1976). In the East, prior appropriation emerged to support industrialization of eastern rivers (Horwitz 1977; Steinberg 1991). In California, priority of use also has roots in the state's reliance on English common law.

In April, 1851, the state legislature passed a bill stating:

> In actions respecting "Mining Claims," proof shall be admitted of the customs, usages, or regulations established and in force at the bar, or diggings, embracing such claim; and such customs, usages, or regulations, when not in conflict with the Constitution and Laws of this State, shall govern the decision of the action. (Harding 1960, 32, 34; Young 1960)

While the bill said nothing directly about water, "customs, usages, and regulations" bundled appropriative water rights into any mining district dispute that went to court. Mining claims were earned on the basis of priority—first come, first served—and on the basis of sustained and diligent use for some useful purpose (the requirement of "due diligence"). That purpose was mining, but water at hand was critical to the value and returns of a claim. Without diligent use, an appropriator could lose his mining claim and his water, essentially "use it or lose it," and others could step in, an action known as "claim jumping."

But in the open-access situation of early California's public lands, the legislature and the courts provided miners only possessory claims *relative to each other;* most had no title to lands they worked as mining claims and therefore had no *absolute* property rights to their claims.

Early on, some judges thought the new state of California owned the gold fields and the rivers running through them, but "the Eastern part of the country then as well as now held it all to be federal property and part of the public domain of the United States," Samuel Wiel wrote in 1909. Easterners argued that the miners had no rights at all and that they should be evicted so that the federal government could regain control of the public domain in California. It could then lease the mines in a more orderly fashion "to those who would pay the Government for them, and so increase the Government's revenue" (Wiel 1909, 487).

This activist, regulative stance toward public lands and the public domain extended back at least to the Northwest Ordinance of 1787, passed by the Continental Congress, and was included in the U.S. Constitution.[13] The federal government opened branches of the U.S. General Land Office (GLO) throughout the western territories beginning in 1812. Established as part of the Treasury Department, the GLO was shifted to the Department of the Interior in 1849. It surveyed, platted (mapped), and sold public lands in the western U.S.

As the government's realtor, the GLO controlled the process of selling off the public domain to private individuals or companies, a process called "patenting." A land patent is evidence of land ownership granted by the government to an individual or private company. A claimant had to fill out "entry" papers to select the parcel, and the land agent at the office would check local records for availability. The entry application was then sent to the GLO central office in Washington D.C. for further review. If everything checked out, the central office issued the land patent to the claimant. Patent claims could take months or years to process, but once obtained they were as good as gold to the patent holder.

Given this time-consuming process, however, California's pre-statehood military officials viewed the miners in the public domain of the Sierra foothills as trespassers. Military deserters from around California rushed to the gold fields without heed of the established process for acquiring government-owned land.[14] Because miners had to work their claims diligently to avoid having them jumped, they could not and often did not care to initiate the patenting process. It wasn't until 1861 that the California Supreme Court ruled "emphatically" that the federal government held title to the land (Wiel 1909, 486, citing *Moore v. Smaw*).[15]

Historian Leonard L. Richards shows that the miners, despite their questionable legal status on the public domain, strove not only to protect their claims from jumping, they headed off entry of Southern-owned slave labor to work the mines. Miners fashioned mining and water law not just to address on-the-ground concerns in the Sierra foothills but also to buttress local opposition to slavery, the most pressing political issue at that time in the United States.

On the Yuba River, miners decided in April 1849 that they needed laws to resolve claim disputes. "Meeting at [Jonas] Spect's store at Rose's Bar, they had drafted a legal code. Among other provisions," wrote Richards, "it limited the size of the mining claim to what one man could work by himself. They also elected a committee of the oldest miners to enforce it." From Richards' information, we can infer that due diligence applied to a mining claim could limit an attached water right claim, effectively forcing the presence of a water claimant to work the mining claim; by definition, slaves were not claim owners. Therefore, slave owners could not just leave their slaves to work the claim in their absence. This became an early reason for applying the "use it or lose it" requirement of prior appropriation doctrine in antebellum California. (Miners sometimes even used extra-legal means to resist slaveholder entry to the mines. [16])In addition, miners feared that allowing slave labor in the mines could concentrate wealth in the hands of a few slaveholders and unfairly increase competition for the limited number of working claims in the mining districts (Richards 2007, chap. 3). The mining districts sent representatives to the first

California constitutional convention in early 1849 to advocate for their newly won codes, and the state's new constitution banned slavery in California (Starr 2005, 93, 96–99).

California judges charged with deciding cases under California laws could rely on few local or regional precedents. Often, judicial activism was necessary under the framework of common law. Early mining cases assumed that miners could dig gold on the public domain based on a franchise from the government. As they constructed it, California judges inflated miners' possessory rights to their mining claims into a "species of property" defensible "as against all the world but the [United States] government" (McCurdy 1976, 240). But in several cases state supreme court justices acknowledged the challenges posed by possessory claims on federal land.[17]

With time, the interests of established Gold Rush miners and later arrivals to the mines diverged. Charles McCurdy wrote,

> Those who arrived late and found the best tracts already occupied frequently called public meetings to "persuade" prior claimants "to diminish the prescribed size of claims so as to give all an equal chance. . . ." By the mid-1850s, population pressures on the available supply of mineral land had transformed many of the miners' assemblies into powerful legislative bodies of "fraternal cooperation". (McCurdy 1976, 240–41)

Such changes posed classic constitutional issues of police power versus vested property rights, writes McCurdy. But where legislative exercise of police power might attempt to pare back vested rights of established miners, there was potential for an unconstitutional taking of property and denial of due process (McCurdy 1976). In addressing these claims, California judges, led by State Supreme Court Justice Stephen J. Field (soon to join the U.S. Supreme Court), stressed that resolving claim jumps and other attempts to reduce prior vested mining claims had to depend upon facts specific to the case.

Eventually, to work gold deposits located long distances from watercourses, it became necessary, says McCurdy, to establish permanent rights to use certain amounts of water to operate a mining claim. Water was essential to the mining claim, given the level of capital investment needed to divert that water for gold extraction from its placer resting place (McCurdy 1976, 254).

New water companies were formed to appropriate and supply water to mining claims by legally separating claims to water from the mining claim. It took lots of capital to supply mines with water under hydraulic pressure through ditches, flumes, gates, dams, and monitor nozzles (Figures 2.1 and 2.2). Once capitalized by private investors, water companies proceeded to construct hundreds of miles of flumes throughout the Sierra mining regions to transport water over great

FIGURE 2.1. The Gate, illustrating an appropriative mining district diversion. With permission of the Society of California Pioneers.

FIGURE 2.2. The sluice flumes at Timbuctoo, Yuba County. With permission of the Society of California Pioneers.

distances—and with the vital drop in elevation needed to generate the intense pressures used in hydraulic mining operations.

Yet on the public domain, the federal government owned not only the land beneath the mining claim but the flowing water on or across it too. Prior appropriation by miners mobilized water from the public lands. As a system of water law, it "was built up for the encouragement of the pioneers, who, though they refused to admit it, were all mere trespassers; a system for the encouragement of trespass" for development of a region, wrote Wiel (1909, 509).

Two California Supreme Court decisions found that the miners trespassed against the federal government's public lands in the Sierra foothills. In *Conger v. Weaver* (1856), Justice Heydenfeldt wrote for the majority that permission for the disputants to be on the federal government's lands could only be presumed under common law, since no evidence of government approval could be produced for their trial.[18] Heydenfeldt and the other justices relied upon the doctrine of presumption for the basis of their decision—the idea that "for the purpose of settling men's differences, a presumption is often indulged, where the fact presumed cannot have existed."

An earlier case, *Irwin v. Phillips* (establishing prior appropriation amongst those with possessory interests on public lands), likened an appropriative right to a "franchise"—a right conferred by government to engage in a specific business. The "attending circumstances" indicated to the *Irwin* majority that the government granted this franchise privilege, provided the prior rights of others "are not interrupted." The franchise consisted of "construction of ditches, flumes and canals, for the purpose of conducting waters from their natural channels to supply the wants of gold miners." Among trespassers, the party diverting the water—in case of *Weaver*—won the right from the California Supreme Court to divert water for miners elsewhere from the nearby stream that Conger hoped to use in his gristmill. But it was a very specific situation: the conflict between Conger and Weaver occurred entirely on public land in Sierra County.

In *Moore v. Smaw* a few years later (1861), the California Supreme Court clarified that when the federal government issues a patent on public land to a private individual it transfers everything: water, land, minerals, and soils.[19] From *Moore* came the finding that riparian water rights were embedded in federal title to land, and that if the land was patented, the water rights would of necessity transfer to the new patentee—even if the claims of a (trespassing) miner were established before the patent was issued.

The patentee's rights obtained from the government were complete and total, when compared with those of the miner-as-possessor-but-trespasser. Since the parties in *Conger* and *Moore* were "trespassers" they all could have been evicted from the public lands had the government cared to act. Also, a private person receiving a government patent to land riparian to the stream could extinguish the trespasser's rights claimed under prior appropriation, since California law recognized riparian rights as paramount to any obtained under prior appropriation on the public domain. (*Conger* and *Moore* were key cases that Schulz and Weber ignore in their abridged reconstruction of prior appropriation doctrine.)

Wiel characterizes the trespasser legal narrative as "a dangerous theory in the pioneer days," paraphrasing the theory this way:

> [T]he Government had, by silently permitting free exploitation, bound itself to the pioneers as completely as though it had actually *granted* them a fee in the mines and waters; the theory that appropriation is actually a grant from the United States of waters on the public domain, equal in force to a patent. (Wiel 1909, 489)

This theory implied that silence from the U.S. government represented consent to the miners' exploitation of the Sierra Nevada mineral resources. The federal government had tacitly granted its lands to the miners, wrote the *Conger* court, since

> [it failed to] attempt any rights of ownership to any of the large body of lands within the mineral region of the United States.... Now, can it be said, with any propriety of reason or common sense, that the parties to these acts *acquired no rights*? If they acquired rights, they rested upon the doctrine of presumption of a grant of right, arising either from the tacit assent of the sovereign, or from expressions of her will in the course of her general legislation, and, indeed, from both. (Wiel 1909, 489)

In upholding prior appropriation, says Wiel, "the Court was announcing a political theory rather than one of law," one that "probably had no foundation; it was political rather than judicial, and can be understood today only when the history of the times and the free exploitation of the public domain is recalled to mind, and the absolute political necessity of such a policy and such an announcement is seen" (Wiel 1909, 496, 497).

President Abraham Lincoln's flirtation in 1863 with confiscating the New Almaden quicksilver mine illustrates this political necessity. Judges and other officials feared that enforcing evictions against the miners would lead to violent backlash against the judiciary and the government, since so much potential wealth and emotional investment was at stake.

Lincoln's initial impulse to evict miners indicates their contingent status on the public domain continued in the eyes of the U.S. government fifteen years after gold was discovered at Sutter's Mill. That Lincoln backed down from confrontation suggests the sudden dawning in the minds of federal officials to tacitly except California from past U.S. policy on earning revenue from the public domain—a crucially expedient exception at that.

President Lincoln faced this situation in the spring and summer of 1863 even as he prosecuted the Civil War. He chose New Almaden, a mercury mine south of San Jose, rather than a gold mine, against which to flex Union muscle under the 1807 Ordinance. The owners of New Almaden had problematic title to the land from Mexico, predating the 1848 cession of California. Between May and August 1863, Secretary of the Interior John Usher and Attorney General Edward Bates telegraphed California-based military officials regarding confiscation of the New Almaden mine to demonstrate Union ability to enforce control of the public domain.

At a moment when Lincoln was distracted by the Union's stunning defeat at Chancellorsville, Usher and Bates argued to the president that New Almaden would serve as an example to miners elsewhere in California. In the days following Chancellorsville (over which Wiel suggests Lincoln was "depressed"), Lincoln signed an order to seize the New Almaden mine. Troops ferried from Benicia to San Jose in July 1863 to start their march south to New Almaden but were soon recalled. Lincoln learned through channels separate from his Cabinet advisers that the order whipped up intense fear and resistance throughout northern California, especially in San Francisco, the West's trade center and headquarters for mining and financial corporations. The possibility of provoking a California rebellion forced Lincoln to recall the Benicia troops, "simply to keep the peace," as he put it in a statement to Californians in August 1863.

Other reasons were available to Lincoln. The "trespassers" produced Union gold. It was certainly in Union interest to keep California out of Confederate hands at all costs and to maintain an undistracted military presence in the Bay Area, given active Confederate sympathizers in California. In addition, Lincoln was already repulsed by the horrors of war. His order to seize New Almaden "never had any direct or indirect reference to any mine, place, or person, except the New Almaden Mine and the persons connected with it," Wiel later maintained.[20]

The transoceanic and transcontinental rush for gold overwhelmed federal control of California, even had the government, as the new state's preeminent landed proprietor during the Civil War, wanted somehow to control it, guide it, and derive revenue from it. Infusion of California and western gold helped finance the war, and apparently the government settled for a more steady source of income.[21]

Had adoption of prior appropriation in the mining states not occurred, says Wiel, "the history of the West would have been entirely different." As private owners patented riparian lands obtained from the federal government, the rights of appropriators would "long since have perished." After the Civil War, Congress adopted its Act of July 26, 1866, expressly stating that the miners were never trespassers and that "they were on the lands *of right* from the beginning, as the California Court had declared when it announced the theory that they were federal grantees."[22] This Act may be where the seeming "inevitability" of prior appropriation doctrine originates—Congress itself rewrote doctrinal history in 1866. (Schulz and Weber, and

Attwater and Markle, ignore Congress's role in providing political cover to prior appropriation.) The 1866 law recognizing the future of appropriative doctrine probably represents reasonable appreciation from a grateful Union, acknowledging California's rapid economic development, as well as its vital contribution to the "manifest destiny" of the victorious North.

In 1872, the State Legislature passed Civil Code Sections 1410 through 1422 to formalize the process of appropriating water. This law permitted a diverter to post a notice on a stream stating intent to divert; in the mining districts, diligent use of the appropriative right of the "trespasser" could be defended against late-coming appropriators and possibly even patented riparians.[23] They also had to record the same notice with the county where the streamside notice was posted. Section 1422 continued to protect riparian rights, however. California was moving ahead postbellum with two distinct water rights doctrines that added frustration and confusion atop the myriad economic changes America faced in the late nineteenth century.

Some Californians began to assume erroneously that Congress had legalized appropriation of water for private lands; but the 1866 legislation covered only appropriative claims moving forward from 1866, and only on federal lands (the public domain). It did not grandfather appropriative claims before 1866. Out in California, however, riparian doctrine continued its winning streak on private lands. In *Creighton v. Evans*, April 1878, the California Supreme Court affirmed the right of a riparian owner to have water from Elk Bayou run through his land as a vested right.[24] A little over a year later, the California Supreme Court agreed in *Pope v. Kinman* that the plaintiff, Pope, had "an interest in the living stream of water flowing over the land: their interest is called the riparian right. . . . Under settled principles, both of the civil and common law, the riparian proprietor has a usufruct in the stream as it passes over his land."[25]

* * *

By the 1880s, America was well into its industrialization and the growth of corporate control of economic development. Within a few more decades, corporations amassed the largest concentrations of capital ever seen. Invention and diffusion of new technologies knitted the United States of America as a single, unified market and polity with roads, railroads, and telegraph communications. Movement of people, goods, and information accelerated, as did the pace of social, economic, and political change.[26]

What did it mean to be an individual in such a rapidly industrializing economy?

The controversy over monopoly was partly about how industrialization was to proceed and whether it could be harmonized with American principles of freedom and equality of opportunity. It was not about whether industrialization was a good or bad thing (Lustig 1982, 44). The friends and owners of corporations fought to construct new liberties for corporations out of the political rhetoric, institutions, and culture of America's Lockean individualism. Their enemies saw a frightening encroachment by huge, unaccountable, and well-lawyered organizations on the opportunities available to small farmers, urban merchants, and other ordinary, flesh-and-blood Americans. But in retrospect, as corporate influence expanded, the field of traditional American freedoms shrank. Ultimately, the presence and activity of monopolies would dramatically restructure the relationship of individuals to all levels of government and to the economy. Critics of monopoly such as Henry George, various populist leaders, the Grange, and others saw in this "liberty" the carving out of privilege, of literal "private law." Monopoly, in their assessment, was a label used to identify "corporations gone wrong, of private companies possessing significant power over the commons (which for traditional liberals meant the market), yet spurning responsibilities to it" that individuals had otherwise to bear, wrote the late California political scientist R. Jeffrey Lustig.

For supporters of corporate development, the major legal fights of this period, including the conflict decided in *Lux v. Haggin* (discussed in chapter 3), were about protecting vested property rights in order for owners to use their assets as they wished, as well as enjoy the right to acquire more. Railroads, land and canal companies, and hydroelectric utilities all sought to vest property rights so that risky investments in steam engines, refrigerator cars, irrigation colonies, dam building, and the like would enjoy sufficient security and longevity to return a healthy profit.

But what did "monopoly" mean, *politically,* beyond the liberty of capital accumulation promised by vested property rights?

Earlier in American history, corporations were highly distrusted institutions. They were usually only chartered by the government or state legislatures to undertake specific public purposes, such as operating a ferry or constructing and operating commercial canals and bridges (Wood 1991, 318–322). A charter carved out a very specific public purpose, assigned the task to the corporation, and usually severely limited the corporation's actions and operations to that purpose alone. If the purpose ended, or the corporation failed in its service, its charter could be readily revoked, extinguishing the chartered corporation. Later, states passed laws to facilitate corporate chartering at the option of private persons, making it easier to create limited liability corporations and raise capital to conduct business.[27]

Few legal issues were as contentious in late nineteenth-century America as the definition of a person or an individual and what rights individuals possessed, especially compared with the rights of nonpersonal collectivities chartered as corporations. The fear spread by such disparity had a profound emotional impact on American and California politics of this period (Goodwyn 1976, 1978).

In the wake of the 1857 Dred Scott decision by the U.S. Supreme Court and abolition of slavery in 1865 with the Thirteenth Amendment, the U.S. Constitution lacked clear, positive definition of personhood. Before then, it addressed personhood largely as a matter of counting male heads for purposes of apportioning political representation: white males would be counted as one indivisible vote; slaves of African descent were regarded as three-fifths of a person. Count the heads of slaves, and multiply by 0.6 and that's your three-fifths addition. The Thirteenth Amendment had simply abolished the latter category of personhood by banishing slavery and involuntary servitude from the United States.[28] It said nothing specific about what being a person in America *meant*. But among other things, it implied that a free person possessed certain rights.

Shortly before Congress passed the Act of July 26, 1866, recognizing appropriative water rights on the federal public domain, it passed in June 1866 (and the states subsequently ratified) the Fourteenth Amendment to the constitution whose first section squarely addressed personhood.[29]

In order to define the rights of *all* Americans, the Fourteenth Amendment takes up the *person as citizen* ("all persons born or naturalized . . . are citizens of the United States and the State where they reside"). A citizen may not be stripped of rights to "life, liberty, and property" that originate with citizenship without due process of law. Moreover, the amendment states that all persons are entitled to equal protection of the law.

The rest of the nineteenth century saw corporations seek out these same protections for collective organizations. Beginning in the late 1860s and continuing through the early 1890s, a series of cases reached the U.S. Supreme Court to test and clarify the meaning of personhood. We will not go through them here, but in the main, corporations sought and won the right to have due process, equal protection, and free speech apply to them. Achieving legal personhood would enable them to hold the same collective rights to "life, liberty, and property" as a citizen.[30]

* * *

The legal trend of this period helped remake the place of law in American society. The emerging water rights framework helped structure the monopolization of California's economy.

Riparian rights would become associated with land monopoly in California (Igler 2001; M. Miller 1993). One of the largest early-California land-and-water monopolies was Miller & Lux, a major cattle and beef corporation of the late nineteenth and early twentieth centuries. Its empire reached from southern Oregon and northern Nevada to San Francisco and the northern San Joaquin Valley.[31] As a riparian landowner along the San Joaquin River and Kern regions, Miller & Lux did its utmost to install and buttress California's riparian doctrine through numerous court case precedents and diligent and vigilant willingness to subject its riparian rights to trial—including establishment of riparian priorities over those of appropriators. The corporation also thoroughly remade much of central California's land and waterscapes to benefit its beef production and water sales from the San Joaquin and Santa Clara Valleys to the upper San Francisco Peninsula.[32]

TABLE 2.1. Largest Landholdings in California, 1871

OWNER	1871 ACREAGE (APPROXIMATE)	DESCRIPTION
Charles McLaughlin	300,000	Western Pacific Railroad land grantee
William Chapman	350,000	"pioneer scrip speculator"
Edward Beale	300,000	Ex-U.S. Surveyor-General. "Across his estate it is said one can ride for seventy-five miles."
Miller & Lux	450,000	San Joaquin Valley cattle ranching integrated with abattoirs in San Francisco. "Around one of their patches of ground there are 160 miles of fence."
J.F. Houghton	300,000	Ex-state surveyor for the State Land Office
Bixby, Flint & Co.	150,000	San Francisco–based
George W. Roberts & Co.	120,000	Comprised of swampland, may refer to lands in the Delta, including today's upper and lower Roberts Islands
Isaac Friedlander	100,000	San Francisco grain merchant
S.R. Throckmorton	146,000	Mendocino-based
John Foster	120,000	Los Angeles–based
Thomas Fowler	200,000	Acreages in Fresno, Tulare, and Kern Counties
Murphy Family	150,000	Santa Clara–based
Philadelphia Petroleum Co.	200,000	Acreage marketed for sale by a Santa Barbara–based company

Source: George 1902, 71–72.

In 1871, populist economist and journalist Henry George published a list of the largest land monopolists in California (Table 2.1) and thundered, "It is not only the land and the timber, but even the water of California that is threatened with monopoly." He noted that because of the appropriative water rights doctrine emerging from "the construction of mining and irrigation ditches, [and] the mountain streams and natural reservoirs . . . being made private property, . . . already we are told that all the water of a large section of the State is the property of a corporation of San Francisco capitalists," possibly an oblique reference to Miller & Lux, which, as we shall see in chapter 4, acquired appropriative rights as well (George 1902, 67).

To Californians enduring the prerogatives and privileges enjoyed by James Ben Ali Haggin in Kern County and the Miller & Lux cattle, land, and water monopoly in the greater San Joaquin Valley, the trend was a reversal of the table for American individualism and small proprietorships, orchestrated by legal precedent and the emergence of new regulatory, bureaucratic tools of government. "Administrative law, rather than contractual law, becomes the paradigmatic form of law in the modern state" under monopoly conditions, observed Lustig (1982, 25).

With rising control of the economy held by corporations such as Miller & Lux, Californians feared that the "monopoly board" of early California was rigged in favor of the big players willing to press their advantages. Historian M. Catherine Miller observed,

> As Miller & Lux knew, the command of resources is not simply a matter of physical control, but one of law, particularly the laws defining property. As settlement increased and the practice of irrigation agriculture spread, water became an object of physical, ideological, and legal contention. These struggles were a complex array of forces tied not only to the local environmental problem of aridity but also to broader concerns of American law and political economy at the turn of the century. (Miller 1993, 5)

Where American individualism is often referred to as "liberalism" (in the sense of free individuals pursuing life, liberty, and property), the new economic and political reality in which modern industrial corporations operated during the late nineteenth and early twentieth centuries was one of "corporate liberalism." Government, to paraphrase Lincoln, was becoming more of the *corporations*, by the *corporations*, and for the *corporations*—attributing public status, purpose, and consequence to the growth of corporate privileges, franchises, geographic markets, and financial reach (Lustig 1982; Sklar 1988).

Lincoln himself is reputed to have been deeply concerned about the potential for corporations to dominate American economic and industrial development after the Civil War ended. "We may congratulate ourselves that this cruel war is nearing its end. It has cost a vast amount of treasure and blood," he wrote in the fall of 1864. But he told army colonel William F. Elkins that, "As a result of the war, corporations have been enthroned and an era of corruption in high places will follow, and the money power of the country will endeavor to prolong its reign by working upon the prejudices of the people until all wealth is aggregated in a few hands and the Republic is destroyed." It was a somber assessment from Lincoln as chief executive, in which he prayed, "God grant that my suspicions may prove groundless" (Lincoln 1864).

In the six decades after the Civil War's conclusion, America invented regulatory commissions to mediate the relationship among individuals, corporations, and the law. California's own state government actively participated in this evolution. In 1887, the legislature passed the Wright Act to enable citizens to authorize "irrigation districts," a locally controlled form of public corporate organization to promote irrigated agriculture as a countervailing power to private monopoly. The legislature in 1911 established a Railroad Commission, for example, to set rates of rail companies operating within California. This same commission was also assigned authority to regulate private water utilities, such as irrigation and canal companies, as well as firms generating hydroelectric energy from new dams and powerhouses nestled into steep Sierra canyons. In 1913, the legislature established the California Water

Commission to regulate the acquisition and protection of water rights in California (more about this in chapter 6).

Commissions and boards are familiar parts of our experience of government today. They are government's tools for intervention into a complex marketplace and society shaped by and for large corporations (public and private), whether the arena is consumer products, local planning and land use, coastal zone protection, Delta stewardship, interstate commerce, food and drugs, rent regulation, telecommunications, nuclear facility regulation, water quality and rights, or countless other regulatory purposes established by Congress, legislatures, and local governments. Individuals may appeal to them for redress against some other regulated party (such as a chartered corporation or water district). Yet the specialized nature of their jurisdiction, their reliance on professional legal, economic, and engineering expertise to carry out their work effectively, and their quasi-executive, quasi-legislative, even quasi-judicial powers (in some California instances), often reinforce and extend the political and emotional distance of government from average citizens.

Commissions are American government's primary ongoing response to the rise of powerful corporations. They attempt to preserve at least a façade of due process and equal protection for all "persons." Yet they also represent a gathering of power and freedom away from individuals *and* their elected representatives in order to protect vested rights, as well as due process and equal protection. Courts defer to their expertise so long as they do not abuse their discretion.

This competition for economic opportunity and political influence in California lay at the heart of the heated rhetoric unleashed by the parties during the court proceedings of *Lux v. Haggin,* to which we turn in the next chapter. The case set lasting precedent in California water law for all subsequent generations, affecting flesh-and-blood people, as well as public and private corporate entities. In 1886, James Ben Ali Haggin's attorneys labeled Miller & Lux a monopolist before the court system and wrapped their own land-baron client in the mantle of an enterprising pioneer "dedicated to freedom and liberty," a community builder turning an irrigation colony into a "garden spot" that would attract thousands of families to farming and community life. By so doing, they tapped into a general public animus toward corporations. But by the 1880s, Miller & Lux had long since remade their early San Francisco partnership into a sprawling, vertically integrated modern business corporation. The charge of "monopolist" would dog the corporation in its business and political dealings until the 1930s (Miller 1993). And in the 1930s, the question emerged: what if government itself became a monopolist?

NOTES

1. Columnist Jon Carroll (2008) quotes *San Francisco Chronicle* opera critic Joshua Kosman: "The single biggest cause of Monopoly games going on too long is the spurious Free Parking rule, which people play by tradition despite the fact that it's not mentioned (and indeed is

more or less explicitly countermanded) in the rules. The basic capitalist dynamic of the game is unchanged (the rich get richer, the poor lose their shirts), but the constant infusions of cash from Free Parking draw out the process to interminable lengths. It's like a really, really generous state lottery that gives the underclass constant hope to ensure that they never rise up and throw off their chains." This diagnosis of Monopoly® resonates with the push and pull of societal tensions between capitalist industry and government policy.

2. This claim to power underlies momentous dialog in the movie *Chinatown* between gumshoe detective Jake Gittes (played by Jack Nicholson) and power broker Noah Cross (played by John Huston). Courtesy of Internet Movie Database, accessed 26 December 2015 at http://www.imsdb.com/scripts/Chinatown.html.

3. In return for $15 million, Mexico ceded about 525,000 square miles of land in what is today southern Wyoming, New Mexico, Colorado, Utah, Nevada, and Arizona. This is equivalent to about $29 per square mile or about 4.5 cents per acre (Treaty of Guadalupe Hidalgo, Encyclopedia Britannica Online 2015).

4. California Supreme Court Justice Lucien Shaw summed up the situation this way, while overstating the existence of "unoccupied" lands in Gold Rush California and ignoring California Indians: "The conditions were novel to these [immigrant] people. There seemed to be no owner of the land. It belonged to the United States, but the national government had not surveyed it and had no persons in actual control of it. It was all unoccupied. There was no known law to govern the rights of the persons desiring to extract the gold from the land and use the water for that purpose. There was no government, no law and no authority. In these circumstances the early adventurers had to form their own government and frame and enforce their own laws in such rude fashions as conditions permitted" (Shaw 1922, 445).

5. McCurdy (1976, 254) writes, "Water in the streams and lakes on the public domain was, like the mines, owned by the federal government. There were no other riparian owners or occupants with legitimate claims to the water, and miners therefore perceived no legal impediments to their appropriating a natural stream so as to conduct it to their claims through artificial ditches or flumes. Consequently, the right to divert water arose as a necessary incident to their right to mine; it universally became one of the mining customs that the right to divert and use a specified quantity of water could be acquired by prior appropriation."

6. Attwater was for many years a high-ranking legal counsel with the California State Water Resources Control Board, and Markle was senior staff attorney in the board's water rights program.

7. Eddy v. Simpson, 3 Cal. 249 (1853); Irwin v. Phillips, 5 Cal. 140 (1855); see Attwater and Markle 1988.

8. Kidd v. Laird, 15 Cal. 161, 179–180 (1860). Schulz and Weber (1988) at the time of this article were, respectively, partner and associate at the prestigious Sacramento law firm of Kronick, Moskovitz, Tiedemann & Girard. Stanley Kronick and Adolph Moskovitz, firm founders, met originally as staff attorneys with the Bureau of Reclamation.

9. Cal. Stat. 1850, ch. 95 (April 13, 1850); see Harding (1960, 32).

10. Black's Law Dictionary, s.v. "usufruct," 9th ed., 2010.

11. "Riparian rights are typically acquired by ownership of riparian land. Because riparian rights run with the land and are not lost through nonuse, title to the rights is acquired as part of the property purchase" (citing Lux v. Haggin, 69 Cal. 255 (1886) at 391). The riparian water right may be severed from the land through subdivision, condemnation, sale, or prescription. See also Walker v. Lillingston, 137 Cal. 401, 403–404 (1902).

12. Some U.S. western states, such as Colorado and Wyoming, abolished riparian rights in the nineteenth century. See Holsinger (1936).

13. U.S. Const. art. IV, § 3, cl. 2. Wiel (1949, 13–16) wrote that President Thomas Jefferson proposed in early 1807 that Congress consider enacting a law to "prevent unauthorized entries or settlements of lands ceded to the United States . . ." and to enforce its interests by use of the military. The Senate passed the bill on February 11th, but it subsequently faced heated debate in the House when members of Congress realized the bill called for U.S. military action to enforce its own real estate interests—even against American citizens. Despite objections to the bill that it would see the "rights to property tried at the point of the bayonet," the bill passed the House in March 1807 as worded in the Senate version, and, in Wiel's words, "laying all the western regions liable to the treatment which the colonies had fought when employed by the Mother Country" (Wiel 1949, 13–16). Wiel (1949, 15) reproduces the 1807 Act, cited as U.S. Stats., Ninth Cong., Sess. 2, ch. 46, p. 445.

14. Wiel (1949) quotes legal historian Curtis H. Lindley (1914): "Of course these pioneer miners were all trespassers. They had no warrant or license from the paramount proprietor"— the United States of America.

15. Moore v. Smaw, 17 Cal. 199 (1861).

16. Early miners were serious about self-governance. Richards (2007, 68) reports that when a Texas slaveholder named Thomas Jefferson Green arrived with some friends and fifteen of his own slaves and took control of a stretch of the Yuba River, the miners acted, using such means as hanging and bodily mutilation. Such could be the nature of law enforcement in the early days of the mines—the "Wild West" supposedly—crossing into vigilante justice.

17. Associate Justice Peter Burnett (who served earlier as California's first governor), writing a pollution case decision between successive appropriators on a stream, with the upper appropriator the polluter: "It may be said, with truth, that the judiciary of this state, has had thrown upon it, responsibilities thrown upon it, responsibilities not incurred by the courts of any other state in the Union. . . . Left without any direct precedent, as well as without specific legislation, we have been compelled to apply to this anomalous state of things the analogies of the common law, and the more expanded principles of equitable justice. There being no known system existing at the beginning, parties were left without any certain guide, and for that reason, have placed themselves in such conflicting positions that it is impossible to render any decision that will not produce great injury, not only to the parties immediately connected with the suit, but to large bodies of men, who, though no formal parties to the record, must be deeply affected by the decision. . . . Yet we are compelled to decide these cases, because they must be settled in some way, whether we can say after it is done, that we have given a just decision or not." Burnett quoted from Bear River Co. v. York Mining Co., 8 Cal. 332 (1857), in Shaw 1922, 449–450.

18. Conger v. Weaver, 6 Cal. 556 (1856).

19. Moore v. Smaw, 17 Cal. 199 (1861).

20. Wiel (1949, 69) recovered this history from Lincoln family archives released only in the mid-twentieth century to the Library of Congress. But earlier, Wiel (1909, 500) concluded of the New Almaden affair that "the escape from entire confiscation [of the mines] was much more narrow than the good people of California ever supposed."

21. Richards (2007, 230, and n. 18, 275) relates that during the Civil War, steamships left San Francisco a few times a month during the Civil War to deliver gold back east and that Union General Ulysses S. Grant believed California gold was critical to winning the war.

22. Act of July 26, 1866, ch. 262, § 9, 14 Stat. 253 (Rev. Stat. § 2339 (1875)); cited in Wiel 1909, 498.

23. Diligent working of the mining claim and diligent use of the water appropriation protected holders of prior rights. If a prior right holder failed to use claimed water diligently, then

another could claim the water for use (McCurdy 1976, 256–257). One possible scenario for an early appropriator to sustain his water right against riparian claims of a patentee was if diligent use occurred for at least five years prior to the riparian's challenge to the appropriator. In that instance, the appropriative right would ripen through the doctrine of prescription.

24. Creighton v. Evans, 53 Cal. 55 (1878).

25. Pope v. Kinman, 54 Cal 3 (1879).

26. These complex and interwoven changes to the U.S. economy and polity are well considered in the works of many geographers and historians. On land ownership concentration in California, see Liebman (1983). On global markets, see Appleby (2010); and for California's nineteenth-century place in them see Jelinek (1982). On economic and financial instability see Kindleberger (1989); and for California's experience with banking instability see Lister (1993). On California's economic and agricultural development, see Henderson (1999); Isenberg (2005); Stoll (1998); and Walker (2004). On irrigation's role in California economic and legal evolution, see Pisani (1984). And on the ideological, legal, and corporate restructuring of American life, see Lustig (1982); and Sklar (1988).

27. Lustig (1982, 44) refers to such privileges as large-scale ownership of land and capital, and railroad rate-setting in the years before public-utility rate regulation was enacted.

28. U.S. Const. art. XIII, § 1, proposed February 1, 1865, ratified December 18, 1865.

29. U.S. Const. amend. XIV, § 1, proposed June 16, 1866, ratified July 28, 1868, stated: "All persons born or naturalized in the United States, and subject to the jurisdiction thereof, are citizens of the United States and of the State where they reside. No State shall make or enforce any law which shall abridge the privileges or immunities of citizens of the United States; nor shall any State deprive any person of life, liberty, or property, without due process of law, nor deny to any person within its jurisdiction the equal protection of the law."

30. Lustig (1982) cites the Slaughterhouse Cases, 83 U.S. 36 (1873) from New Orleans; the Granger cases involving granaries (including Munn v. Illinois, 94 U.S. 113 (1877)); Santa Clara County v. Southern Pacific Railroad, 118 U.S. 394 (1886); and Chicago, Milwaukee & St. Paul Railroad v. Minnesota, 134 U.S. 48 (1890), as key cases among many that helped establish corporations as "persons" with rights to equal protection, due process under the law, and free speech. Ironically, during the period in which corporations achieved personhood, the same court issued its decision in Plessy v. Ferguson, 163 U.S. 537 (1896), announcing that "separate but equal" treatment of African Americans was not prevented by the laws of the United States, making the evil of Jim Crow the de facto civil rights framework in southern states. This policy would not be overturned until the U.S. Supreme Court's 1954 decision in Brown v. Board of Education, 347 U.S. 483 (1954) under Chief Justice Earl Warren, former California governor. See also Barkan (2010); Barley (2007); Gerencser (2005); Handlin and Handlin (1945); Kitch and Bowler (1978).

31. According to Igler (2001), Miller & Lux ranches encompassed over half a million acres in four major areas of California: the Kern River delta northwest of Bakersfield (near rival Haggin's cattle ranches), lands along the San Joaquin River from Mendota almost to the Stanislaus County line, major holdings around Gilroy, and Lux's Buri Buri ranch at the north end of the peninsula south of San Francisco. See also California Department of Public Works (1952, 57–60).

32. Miller & Lux achieved this status through its vast fencing enclosures (contributing greatly to populist sentiment in early California), industrialization of cattle raising, racial segmentation of industrial labor markets, and marshaling of capital to finance construction of a latticework of canals that diverted waters of the San Joaquin and Kern Rivers onto its extensive wetland and grassland acreage. See Igler (2001) and M.C. Miller (1993).

Chapter 3

Showdown at the Calloway Canal

DEPARTING VISALIA on the eastern side of the San Joaquin Valley in mid-April 1864, members of the California Geological Survey, newly flush with funds from a prickly state legislature, trekked south past Coyote Springs and White River. Survey geologist William Brewer logged the stretch in his journal as "a desolate waste—I should call a *desert*." They encountered just two houses. The next day, they made 35 miles to the Kern River only to detour about 10 more miles downstream to ford it. They found the soils and terrain persistently bleak. Despite the river's formidable presence, the area was "a sandy plain, without grass, in places very alkaline—a few desert or saline shrubs growing in spots, elsewhere the soil bare—no water, no feed," wrote Brewer.

William Brewer knew something about desolation. Born in 1828, Pennsylvania-raised, he earned a degree from Yale and spent two years in natural science study in Europe. Back in the U.S. during the 1850s, Brewer enjoyed a number of eastern teaching posts. But in 1860, his young wife and infant died of illness. Not long after, an offer came from noted geologist Josiah Whitney (for whom California's tallest mountain peak is named) to become the California Geological Survey's first member. Brewer decided a trek throughout California would distract him from crushing grief in Pennsylvania (Brewer 1966, xiii–xiv). His journal, covering four years with the Survey, would become a historical classic and go-to primary source for its eyewitness descriptions of early California Nature, landscape, and society.

Eighteen sixty-four found southern Kern County in the second year of a brutal drought. Brewer recorded that they "struck a cabin" near a Kern River ford where they encountered "a man, wife, and several children, all ragged, dirty, ignorant—not one could read or write," adding with not a little Yankee prejudice, "and Secessionists, of course." But in mid-April, the river itself was "a wide swift stream, here about twenty or twenty-five rods wide, with a treacherous sandy bottom."[1]

One man's desert can be another's opportunity. By the early 1870s, civil engineer and land speculator O. P. Calloway was early to the effort of converting undeveloped lands or vast grain fields to farms for pioneering opportunities in California. Developers like Calloway created pioneer farms to facilitate the settlement process—much the way we today think of urban developers as entrepreneurs who organize and build a new town, a subdivision, a mall, or an industrial park.

Where present-day Riverview Park in Oildale and the Bakersfield Metro Recreation Center converge on the Kern River, O. P. Calloway planned the Calloway Weir to provide water via his planned Calloway Canal to an agricultural colony of small 80-acre farms on 35,000 acres north of the Kern River (Figures 3.1–2). Calloway envisioned that over 4,000 new farms would bring some 16,000 new settlers to Kern County once colony lots sold and filled. With the Southern Pacific railroad arriving from the north and hoping for an expanding ridership through settlement, the *Kern County Gazette* enthused, "A populous and prosperous community is certain to spring up along the line of such a canal, especially as the railway is within such easy reach" (Zonlight 1979, 114, quoting *Kern County Gazette*, October 7, 1876).

Developers, newspaper publishers, and merchants counted and traded on Americans' belief in the uncorrupted yeoman farmer, the Jeffersonian ideal, whose fields would be productive (provided adequate amounts of water were delivered), income beneficent, and proprietary livelihood independent. Newcomers immigrating to California brought a belief that this American dream would translate from the eastern and midwestern United States to California, despite its highly capitalized economy and Mediterranean climate—where for six to eight months in most years little or no rain fell from Redding south.

Beliefs and dreams notwithstanding, "It is deeply ingrained that America's agricultural regions are places that 'settlers' made and less appreciated that at times money got there first," writes geographer George L. Henderson (Henderson 1999, xi). California was such a place. Even so, the plans of settlement developers in California too often lacked sufficient liquid assets: capital and water. New homesteaders, accustomed to humid, rainy summers back east, had to plant seeds in the late winter or spring when the last storms visited a few inches of moisture to the San Joaquin Valley, then endure a summer-long drought of both water and income until an uncertain autumn harvest. As George Henderson shows, the solutions for California agriculture centered on the state's young banks extending agricultural credit to develop irrigation systems that would bridge the gap between planting and harvesting (Figures 3.3–4; Henderson 1999, 18–27). For farming to mature, developers like O. P. Calloway learned the hard way that their settlers needed both credit and water.

During 1875 and 1876, Calloway worked to acquire lands from the Southern Pacific Railroad, which was selling off parcels granted to it by Congress that were surplus to its San Joaquin Valley alignment. He also sought to perfect lands claimed directly from the federal government under the Swamp Lands and Desert Lands acts. But he lacked sufficient funds to construct the 35-mile canal himself. He urged prospective colonists to "join in the completion of the canal" by purchasing stock and infusing their own capital for its construction—a risky investment given such arid circumstances. The idea was to give colonists-as-investors not only a share of ownership in their homestead and Calloway's Kern River Island & Canal Company but also to guarantee water for their lands—*if* the project could be built (Zonlight 1979, 114–15). Praising Calloway's project, the *Kern County Courier*, another local paper competing to build readership, argued that land and water should be valued

FIGURE 3.1. Calloway Weir, June 2012. Photo by author.

FIGURE 3.2. Calloway Canal, Kern County, California. Photo by Carleton Watkins, with permission of Kern County Historical Society.

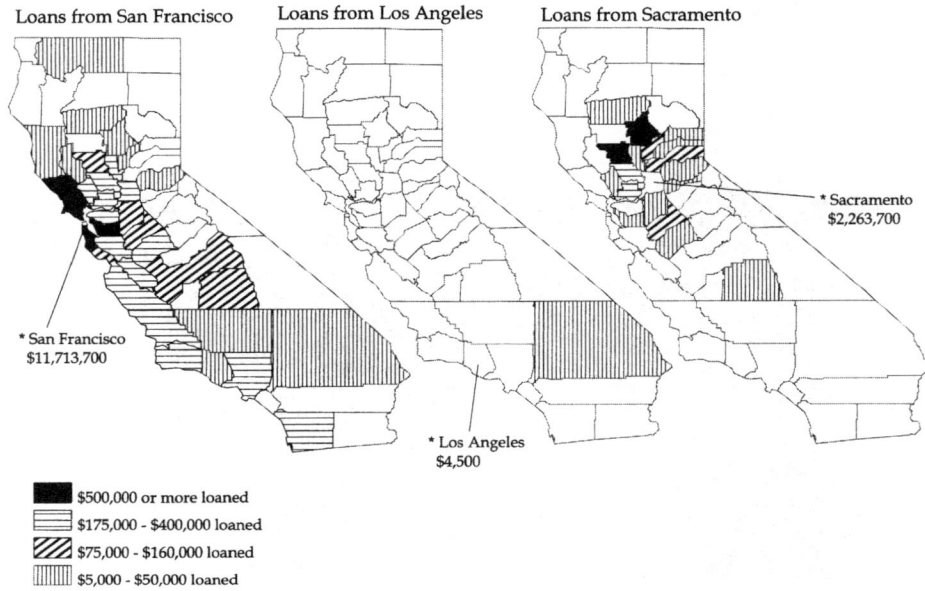

FIGURE 3.3. Real estate loans from savings banks in San Francisco, Los Angeles, and Sacramento Counties, 1879. By permission of Oxford University Press (Henderson 1999:22); original data from California Board of Bank Commissioners, *Annual Reports*.

together and that ownership of one should entail ownership of the other. The *Courier*'s editors endorsed Calloway's project for holding to this principle (Zonlight 1979, 115–16).

Yet Calloway attempted to sell land to settlers that he wound up neither owning nor controlling. In 1876, Calloway's title to colony assets crumbled to dust when the army scrip applications used for acquisition under the federal Desert Land Act were exposed as forgeries (though not of Calloway's doing). Much Calloway project acreage reverted to the Southern Pacific, and to the federal government (Zonlight 1979, 118–21). Of course, in the ensuing confusion, "few of the small farmers that had invested in Calloway lands and canal stock were able to maintain possession of their lands" (Zonlight 1979, 124). The canal's engineer, Walter James, later testified, "At this time there are but few of such persons holding on to these locations, and they are working as laborers on the canal, which for want of encouragement was abandoned by Calloway. . . ." (Zonlight 1979, 124–25). Despite the ills besetting the Calloway project, James believed it would eventually succeed. It did, but not as planned, and not without tumultuous water rights litigation.

* * *

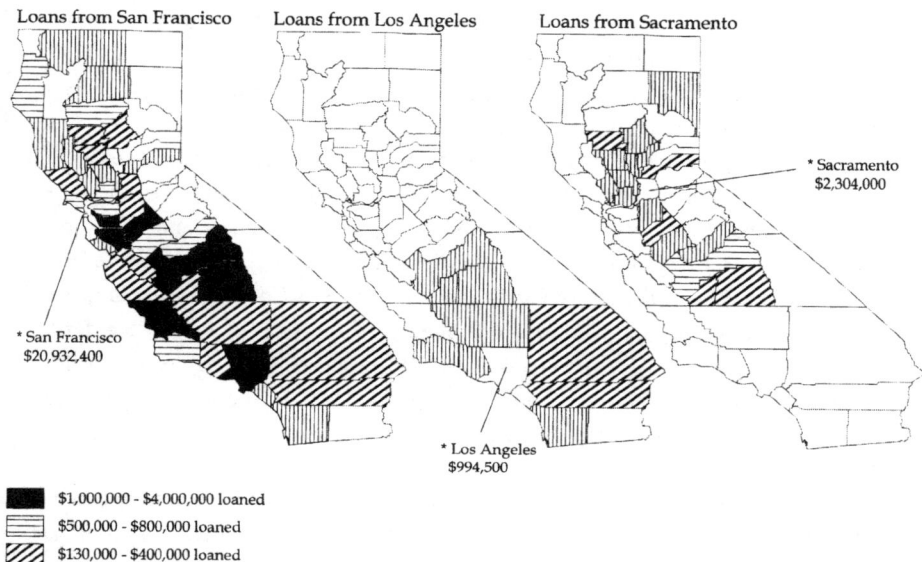

FIGURE 3.4. Real estate loans from savings banks in San Francisco, Los Angeles, and Sacramento Counties, 1899. By permission of Oxford University Press (Henderson 1999:23); original data from California Board of Bank Commissioners, *Annual Reports*.

Just like that, one man's calamity became another's opportunity. At the urging of Southern Pacific political broker William (Billy) Carr, Kern County land and cattle baron James Ben Ali Haggin and his partner Lloyd Tevis swooped in to pay Calloway's debts and take the irrigation colony project off his hands. They also financed the Calloway canal. The headgate on the Calloway Weir in Bakersfield under Haggin's control would become the focal point of the most important water rights lawsuit in nineteenth century California.

In the pantheon of early California capitalism, Haggin and Tevis are among its founding fathers (Zonlight 1979, 62–65). Born in 1822, Haggin was the son of a prominent Kentucky family. He knew Tevis (b. 1824) as a boy, and they reconnected in Sacramento in 1850 where they formed a law partnership. But the investment opportunities in Gold Rush California eventually proved more interesting than the law. As the 1850s gave way to the 1860s, Haggin and Tevis became major figures in the emergence not only of California's real estate industry (they would soon found the Kern County Land and Water Company, today known as the Kern County Land Company) but also in early natural gas, private water, mining, and transportation.

Tevis also ascended to an executive position at Southern Pacific Railroad, complementing Billy Carr's political role there.

Haggin and Tevis excelled at creating competitor companies in these industries that another company would later acquire, allowing them to reap the gains from these mergers. Western Union bought one, and Wells Fargo later absorbed a transportation company they started. They were key initial investors in Homestake Mining Company, still one of America's foremost producers of gold and other precious metals. Each kept homes in the Nob Hill district of San Francisco (the "citadel of the wealthy of the entire Pacific Coast," as a Kern County Land Company historian describes it) where they hobnobbed with the likes of Leland Stanford, Collis P. Huntington, Mark Hopkins, Senator George Hearst (who gained his wealth through industrialized hard-rock gold mining from Homestake with Haggin and Tevis), Darius O. Mills (of Mills College fame), and major financiers of the Comstock Lode silver rush (Zonlight 1979, 61).

Haggin and Tevis professed intent to acquire vast tracts of Kern land to subdivide, develop for agriculture, and then sell to small farmers in order to encourage settlement. They had spent much of 1873 through 1877 creating experimental demonstration farms on their already extensive holdings in the area (largely for cattle, sheep, horses, and forage). The productivity impressed Haggin and Tevis so much that, instead of subdividing land for sale to small farmers as originally planned, they opted to hold and acquire still more.[2] By 1877, Haggin and Tevis, joined by Southern Pacific's former political operative Billy Carr, had acquired some 100,000 acres of land in Kern County alone, land with water rights and accessible to Southern Pacific rail lines.[3]

Haggin and his colleagues used various means to acquire nearly 60,000 acres of land along Southern Pacific right-of-way in Kern County to fill in gaps in his Calloway tract acquisition. He also aggressively litigated (often over water rights) to drain his competitors' finances and force them to sell, even though he apparently seldom if ever won these suits. Extending their entrepreneurial skills to politics, Haggin, Tevis, and Carr also engineered passage by Congress of the Desert Land Act. Within days of its signing by President Rutherford B. Hayes in late March 1877, they took advantage and used dummy entry men from San Francisco-based U.S. Mint employees to file on more than 100,000 acres at $1.25 per acre. After Calloway surrendered his canal and colony project to them, Haggin, Tevis, and Carr completed their landed empire along the Calloway Canal (Pisani 1984, 195–96).

* * *

Haggin had competition in Kern County: Henry Miller, one of his neighbors from Nob Hill in San Francisco.

Miller was a stoic German immigrant who came to California in 1850 to ply his trade as a butcher. He realized that water law in California smiled upon those with riparian land, for they could always expect to have flow in the river. In the spring, Sierra snowmelt coursing through the Central Valley's rivers would mean green and lush pastures on which Miller's cattle could graze, and fat cattle would bring large profits from hungry miners in the gold fields and the discerning, carnivorous urbanites in San Francisco and other growing cities of northern and central California.

Miller proceeded to acquire ranches along the San Joaquin and the Kern Rivers. In 1857, thirty-year-old Henry Miller turned over a cowhide at his San Francisco butcher shop to find a brand: "HH." Actually, it was two "H" letters sharing the middle vertical bar, an image he had dreamt as a younger man. It was the brand of the Hildreth brothers, owners of a large cattle ranch along the San Joaquin River—the two Hs likely stemming from the Hs beginning and ending Hildreth. Miners visiting Miller's San Francisco butcher shop told of cattle driven to the mines from this part of the valley. Seeing the brand, Miller resolved to see the ranch for himself.

Upon arriving at the Hildreth ranch, as his biographer Edward Treadwell tells it, Miller met one of the Hildreth brothers—a "coarse cattle man, booted and spurred and riding a fine horse"—and they struck up a relationship on the spot. Learning Miller was from San Francisco, the financial center of the West at the time, "his hospitable heart was opened," reports Treadwell, and Mr. Hildreth showed Miller his herds and ranch for a few days. "Finally he said he wished he could sell the place," wrote Treadwell, and before Miller left for San Francisco, he had an option to buy 8,835 acres of land and 7,500 head of cattle for a total of $47,660.[4] Along his return route, Treadwell claims that the budding cattle baron stopped at each major rancho along the route from Los Banos (where Hildreth was) through Pacheco Pass to the Santa Clara Valley and up the San Francisco Peninsula. As he traveled, Miller thought through ways in which cattle could be driven from the Hildreth Ranch to other ranches along the route to San Francisco, envisioning geographic and corporate integration controlling beef production in the west. Treadwell reports that Miller visited Charles Lux, a leading beef competitor, at his home along Baden Creek in San Mateo County. They formed a partnership that would last for decades.

Back in San Francisco, Miller visited William C. Ralston at the Bank of California, who endorsed Miller's cattle production and business plan and financed dramatic expansion of this cattle and butchering business almost overnight. "Then began a veritable orgy of land and cattle buying," writes Treadwell, "which continued without abatement for thirty years" (Treadwell 1931, 36). The Panic of 1857 deflated land values, providing an opportunity for Miller's buying spree. As the spree progressed, Miller acquired for Miller & Lux the largest single bloc of riparian water rights to the San Joaquin River—indeed the largest single bloc of rights on any river or stream in California—by using his water rights and his land monopoly along the San Joaquin River to leverage additional rights in a canal utility originated by a separate syndicate in the 1870s. He would ultimately control—without owning—the hydraulic operations of most of the earliest hydropower systems on the upper San Joaquin River. These properties and relationships helped extend his empire from Kern County to the San Joaquin River basin, into northwestern Nevada and southeastern Oregon, and included urban industrial and ranch lands in San Francisco, Gilroy, Fresno, and Bakersfield (as well as other small towns; see Figure 3.5). Historian Catherine Miller estimated that Henry Miller's land acquisition amounted to nearly 100 miles of riparian frontage along the San Joaquin River and nearly 1 million acres and that by 1916, the year Henry Miller died at age 89, Miller & Lux was among the top 200 industrial corporations in the United States with $35 million in net assets.

Miller obtained land by a variety of means. In 1855, California established a land grant commission to evaluate claims and resolve legal conflicts associated with Spanish and Mexican land grants made before California's statehood. He paid close attention to its workings, often approaching heirs of Spanish ranchos beset by legal fees and mounting debts to buy out one or more of them. In so doing, he would acquire a tenant-in-common right to graze cattle there. Gradually, Miller would then buy out the remaining heirs or subdivide the land to avoid conflict with other owners. Maps of Miller & Lux's accumulated San Joaquin Valley properties show Rancho Sanjon de Santa Rita and Orestimba Rancho along the west side of the San Joaquin River where Miller operated.

With enactment of the Desert Land Act in 1877 (spearheaded by Tevis, Carr, and Haggin) and other legislation by Congress to dispose of public lands, Miller and his agents acquired additional lands through the U.S. General Land Office. Miller (as well as Haggin) was known to use dummy entry men to "enter" their names for consideration with the GLO for acquisition of specific parcels. "The method for making a dummy entry," wrote historian M. Catherine Miller, "was well known—hire a man with no ambition and require that he sign a property transfer before actually filing his claim to land." Miller also employed them to buy tracts outright or challenge homesteaders obstructing his designs on "small plots that controlled springs or the headwaters of small streams along mountain valleys of his breeding ranches." Miller allied with a land dealer, F. A. Hyde, to handle land scrip with the GLO, essentially laundering the chain of title through successive property transfers until Miller or his company acquired it. Though Hyde eventually served time in prison, such arms-length chains of title using dummy entry men kept Miller's hands clean of fraud charges (M.C. Miller 1993, 2).

Henry Miller combined his willingness to exploit government land programs with his long-term strategy of holding it for productivity and speculative gain: "Land in California is cheap now, it will be valuable," Treadwell quotes Henry Miller. "Wise men buy land, fools sell."

FIGURE 3.5. The principality of Henry Miller in three western states. Treadwell 1931 [2005].

He preferred to acquire lands he knew would be economically productive by virtue of their natural fertility. When irrigated with water brought naturally via the slough and force of gravity, the grasses would rise, and the cattle would eat and grow. Treadwell labeled this method "wild irrigation."

The basic principle was that water-loving grasses were desired. These were best produced by water reasonably deep on the surface, but kept fresh. This was best done by allowing the water to fill the land behind one levee and then flow over and into the next check. By using almost unlimited amounts of water, which was plentiful, this was accomplished with a minimum of labor. One *zanjero* could cover thousands of acres of land. (Treadwell 1931, 40).

Miller & Lux's corporate monopoly of the lower Kern River and Buena Vista Slough achieved a flourishing agricultural and economic integration. Miller repeated and expanded this model on the San Joaquin River to the north, where the agricultural productivity enabled Miller & Lux to amass land. Treadwell describes the Miller & Lux San Joaquin Valley production-to-profit business model as a continuous flow of inputs to output, with cattle as vessels of productivity: they fattened on the lush grasses of the San Joaquin's floodplain, were transported to San Francisco's abattoirs for slaughter, and the meat was sold in local and regional markets. By vigilantly managing and protecting its riparian water rights, Miller & Lux believed it could keep its production costs low. Apart from the land, the water rights were Miller & Lux's most precious asset (Treadwell 1931, 41; M.C. Miller 1993).

Miller & Lux's vertical integration (in which all the units in the chain of resource extraction, production, distribution, and sales are combined under one or few corporate entities) also enabled the cattle company to use water and beef pricing as economic weapons. Treadwell acknowledges that Henry Miller would refuse to sell water to a cattle competitor in the San Joaquin River basin and instead sell it to others with whom he had more favorable relationships. And during drought, he was known to withhold supplies from competitors he wished to discipline in order to purchase their assets "for a song" (Hope and Sheehan 1985, 36, citing Treadwell 1931). Among the San Francisco butchers, the cattle baron's price fixing at the beef counter was benevolent but effective.

> [T]here was not only no prosecution for violation of the Sherman Anti-Trust Law, but there was never any question raised as to the subject. This was not due to the fact that there was no combination or no restraint of trade, but it was due to the fact that by forty years he anticipated the decision of the Supreme Court of the United States that the test was not whether there was combination, or whether there was a restraint of trade, but whether the combination and restraint were reasonable. (Hope and Sheehan 1985, 42; also Sklar 1988, 86–175, on reasonable combination and restraint of trade)

Where Haggin's lands north of Bakersfield were to be irrigated via the Calloway Canal and other ditches with water diverted from the Kern River, Miller & Lux lands were located downstream of Bakersfield. The rest of Miller & Lux Kern lands hugged both banks of Buena Vista Slough where it turns north toward Tulare Lake. Its flows from the high Sierra finally sank into the ground, exhausted before reaching the Lake. By 1879, Miller acquired some 78,900 acres in Kern County along the lower Kern River and Buena Vista lake and slough, most of it in western and southwestern Kern County. Historian David Igler (2001, 97, 101) found that within the next ten years Miller doubled his company's acreage along Buena Vista.

Miller & Lux built ditches from Buena Vista Slough and the river to water their pastures and ran thousands of head of cattle most years. Drought struck in 1877, however (and was also afflicting India, China, and Brazil; Davis 2001). Rain gauges in San Francisco showed precipitation in California that year at 10 inches, about 46 percent of the average to that date (since 1849).[5]

* * *

When the irrigation season got under way in April 1877, Haggin's field engineer diverted water from the upper Kern into the Calloway Canal, even though flows were lower than usual. Haggin's diversions at Calloway Weir reduced downstream flows to Miller & Lux's system of Buena Vista Lake, Buena Vista Slough, and lower Kern River canals. Miller & Lux's pastures turned brown and forced the early slaughter of thousands of head of cattle before losing them to starvation and dehydration. In retaliation, Miller & Lux sought to perfect riparian water rights to Buena Vista Slough in large part by forming a Riparian Suits Association with other riparian landholders in 1877. The association proceeded to file seventy-eight individual lawsuits against Haggin's diversions to the Calloway Canal and other smaller upstream diversions built by farmers in eastern Kern County.[6]

As the largest landowners in Kern County, Haggin and Miller & Lux were poised for the most important legal showdown over water rights in California's short history. Their battle in *Lux v. Haggin* posed the ultimate water-law question of the day: which legal doctrine would prevail in California, riparianism or prior appropriation?

Direct as this legal question was, it got bound up politically and publicly with another: what effect might choosing one doctrine over the other have on California's economic development? Haggin painted himself as a noble developer of agricultural plots, serving the democratic sentiments of his supporters, a seeker of irrigation water for all. Recall the timing of his test plots; he had not yet determined that he would *not* sell off the colony plots he acquired from Calloway in 1876. So it was expedient for him to hold his long-term plans close to his vest for the sake of winning his case against Miller & Lux on the Kern River.

Miller & Lux and their allies countered that the attack on riparian rights was an attack on vested property rights. If the courts would not protect even the property rights of riparian water right holders, then no property rights were safe from expedience of outcome that a majority of the public might want.

The two water-law doctrines shared roots in American jurisprudence, and arguably, the American psyche. The riparian doctrine in English common law provides a right to divert water for use on one's property commensurate with the length of riparian frontage. The right is part and parcel of owning such land. Riparian owners could be distinguished on a stream not only by their position geographically, but by their acquisition of a riparian right in time. For example, a long-tenured owner subdivides land and ensures a riparian right for the newly created parcel with riparian frontage. The new owner of that parcel may receive a riparian right subject to the older owner taking his portion of flow prior to that of the more recently tenured owner (whether up- or downstream of the long-tenured owner). The idea of prior appropriation in such situations was born from common law practice.

But the two doctrines parted company when the productivity of water usage on a stream became the object of neighborly competition. Legal historian Morton Horwitz, studying late-eighteenth- and early nineteenth-century American jurisprudence in water cases involving New England lumber and textile mills wrote, "If priority is measured not from a common denominator of natural use but from the time a new technology appears, the theory of natural use continues to enforce its antidevelopment premises, but a rule of priority now confers an exclusive right on the first developer" (Horwitz 1973, 250). Riparian owners faced encroachments from flooding and other harms to their property. But early-nineteenth-century courts found increasingly in favor of mill owners who dammed their rivers to create hydraulic heads (that is, the gravitational force translated to water flow) needed to turn water wheels powering their mill machinery. The shift in doctrinal treatment of injuries to water property supported the industrial factory system and capitalist economic development over more pastoral water uses (Steinberg 1991).

Two ideas were key to this shift: risk and efficiency. "In a capital scarce economy, . . ." writes Horwitz, "the first entrant takes the greatest risks; without the recognition of a property right in the first development—and a concomitant power to exclude subsequent entrants—there cannot exist the legal and economic certainty necessary to induce investors into a high-risk enterprise" (Horwitz 1973).

The second idea—efficiency—emerged in appropriative doctrine as capitalist industrial development in America expanded, creating economies of scale through the application of capital, labor, and resources such as water. Dependable access to such inputs was crucial to factory production. Vesting of property in such resources secured that reliance. In turn, this vesting status decreased risk to help ensure profits. "As property rights came to be justified by their efficacy in promoting economic growth," says Horwitz, "they also became increasingly vulnerable to the efficiency claims of new competing forms of property." Efficiency of use, however, raised questions about absolute versus relative efficiency in water use. What criteria should apply? Could there be a fixed standard for efficient water use? Or was it a matter of degree or situation (be it geographic, economic, or climatic)? These and related questions about efficiency led to the introduction into legal proceedings of a "reasonable use" standard for water cases (McCurdy 1976). Newer industrial forms of water use often showed greater efficiency of water use per unit of productive or economic output. While in eastern U.S. courts prior appropriation increasingly preempted or limited riparian uses due to risk and efficiency claims, such claims by appropriators for even newer industries could undermine earlier appropriators on efficiency grounds through a showing that the newer use was more "reasonable" than the prior. Thus,

> [T]he rule of priority, wearing the mantle of economic development, at first triumphed over natural use. In turn, those property rights acquired on the basis of priority were soon challenged under a balancing test or "reasonable use" doctrine that sought to define the extent to which new forms of property might injure the old with impunity. Priority then claimed the status of natural right, but only rarely did it check the march of efficiency. Nor could a doctrine of reasonable use long protect those who advanced under its banner since its function was to clear the path for the new and the efficient. (Horwitz 1973, 251)

But reasonable use as a statewide doctrine would wait a little longer in California—well after the litigation in *Lux v. Haggin* concluded. At the 1881 trial in Kern County, Superior Court Judge Brundage upheld appropriative rights as the law of water in California in 1881. Miller & Lux appealed to the California Supreme Court, and the titanic argument over California water law moved to San Francisco. In San Francisco, the case's theater about California's future political economy reached full rhetorical flower on the statewide stage.

One ground for appeal was that Miller & Lux produced certificates of purchase from 1872 demonstrating they had purchased their property along the Kern far earlier than Haggin had acquired water rights in the Calloway Canal, earlier even than when Calloway himself had acquired the rights to appropriate the Kern into his eponymous canal. Judge Brundage had, however, excluded from evidence Miller & Lux's certificates of purchase in order to make his ruling.

The California Supreme Court reversed the trial court in 1884 in a narrow 4–3 vote, finding simply that state law adopted the common law riparian doctrine first. Moreover, the justices found the trial judge erred by excluding Miller & Lux's certificates of purchase from trial evidence when in fact they represented reasonable evidence that the cattle corporation had owned its riparian land and diverted water from the Kern River before Calloway or Haggin had done so at the Calloway Canal. Miller & Lux's rights to use water from the Kern River were therefore paramount to those of Haggin, both as a matter of time and as vested real property with riparian rights.

The Court issued its 1884 decision to full-throated hue and cry.[7] Haggin turned to Carr, funding and organizing an anti-riparian movement that built a rising drumbeat of public revulsion to the 1884 *Lux v. Haggin* decision. Their movement soon reached a crescendo, convincing the California Supreme Court to rehear the case and allow any and all parties to brief the court about its merits.

Two years later, though, the justices again split their vote 4–3, but this time Justice Elisha W. McKinstry wrote the decision. Justice McKinstry served on the court from 1873 to 1888. Descended of "Revolutionary and Puritan Stock," according to his official court eulogy, he was born in Detroit, Michigan, in 1825 and educated in Ohio and New York. He began practicing law in 1847 in New York. But like thousands of others, in 1849 he departed promptly for California where, according to his eulogy, his "talents and character . . . attracted the notice of his fellow-citizens immediately after his arrival here." He served a stint as a judge in Napa and then relocated to Nevada in 1862, returning to California in 1867 to win election as a judge in San Francisco. The court's eulogy cites his decision in *Lux v. Haggin* as "the most important of Judge McKinstry's decisions, and one by which his fame as a jurist will be transmitted to posterity. . . . [It is] an imperishable monument to the learning and ability of its author."[8]

Lux v. Haggin from 1886 is Justice McKinstry's comprehensive, methodical dissection of the Haggin legal team's wide-ranging arguments. He painstakingly explained why riparian doctrine is the preeminent water-law doctrine in California, reminding the Haggin team of specific facts and why the court came down on Miller & Lux's side.

Haggin's team threw every legal theory they could think of at the California Supreme Court in order to find a fatal flaw to end the reign of riparian water rights. With Miller & Lux having waited two years after Haggin's diversion at Calloway Weir before litigating, Haggin's attorneys argued that Miller & Lux's silence represented consent to Haggin's Calloway diversions. Riparian doctrine should be overthrown, they contended, because it is good public policy to allocate water rights equitably across society, something riparian doctrine fails to do. Riparian doctrine, they argued, is bad water policy in an arid region such as the southern San Joaquin Valley. Thus, the court should honor the principle of the "greatest good for the greatest number of people." Mexican law, Haggin's attorneys argued further, should apply here because it set the precedent, contrary to riparian doctrine, that *aqua profluens* (flowing water) was dedicated in Roman jurisprudence to the common use of the inhabitants of an adjacent community. Upon California's admission to the Union in 1850, its law became vested with all the rights, sovereignty, and jurisdiction in and over the navigable waters on an equal footing with the other states in the Union. And so on.

Haggin's counselors argued that a grant of public land from the United States carries with it common law rights to surface water unless the waters are expressly or implicitly reserved by terms of the federal patent or some other authority. (Recall that Haggin and Tevis had acquired much of their lands through chicanery associated with the Desert Land Act, an act of Congress.)

If those theories wouldn't work, maybe these would help overthrow riparianism: California, Haggin's attorneys surmised, had become owner in September

1850 of the swamp lands described in the complaint, so Miller & Lux couldn't be the owner, despite their certificates of purchase and subsequent grant deeds. Or this: Congress's Act of July 26, 1866, authorizing prior appropriation as a method of acquiring water on the public domain took precedence over riparian rights acquired through the patenting process of the General Land Office, thus California Supreme Court decisions themselves gave prior appropriation dominance over riparian rights.

And they flung still more theories in hopes that one might stick to courtroom walls: certain laws passed by the legislature after statehood "abrogated" the riparian doctrine applicable to Kern County, including township control by water commissions (these were legislated in support of some colony developments that were more successful than Calloway's). They claimed the California Civil Code amendments of 1872, which laid out a more formal process by which appropriative water rights could be acquired, also abrogated riparian doctrine. Passage of the common law would mean that the appropriative doctrine should apply here in California, not the riparian doctrine, since prior appropriation could be traced to the common law.

In his 1886 decision, Justice McKinstry disposed of each and every theory from Haggin's attorneys. He showed that when it came to protecting vested property rights he was a justice for the times. McKinstry furrowed his brow toward the "public policy" arguments that riparian doctrine is poorly suited to California's climate and fails the maxim of allocating water to the greatest number of people. "There is no 'public policy' which can empower the courts to disregard the law," McKinstry wrote. Nor may "an asserted benefit to many persons (in itself doubtful) . . . overthrow the settled law. This court has no power to legislate," he continued, adding, "especially none to legislate in such manner as to deprive citizens of their vested rights."[9] Miller & Lux's point about vested riparian rights evidently resonated with McKinstry and the court majority.

It is not simply the number of people that determines whether a use is public, McKinstry reasoned. To abrogate privately vested rights for a supposed public use by settlers would likely be an unlawful "taking" under the Fifth Amendment of the U.S. Constitution, unless just compensation to the riparian proprietor is paid. Early in the *Lux v. Haggin* decision, McKinstry hinted that riparian doctrine is paramount for rights to use water in California because it was enacted through the adoption of the English common law in 1850. It was "settled law."

> If the law is settled, we cannot override the established rule to secure some conjectural advantage to a greater number. If, however, we were permitted to do this, the inquiry would still remain whether the recognition of a doctrine of appropriation . . . would secure the greatest good to the greater number. Observe, if that be the true rule, the appropriator does not necessarily act as the agent of the state employing the power of eminent domain

for the benefit of the public, but by his appropriation makes the running water his own, subject only to the trust he shall employ it to some useful purpose...[10]

Having scanned the parties sitting opposite him in the San Francisco courtroom during the same case for at least several years, McKinstry could surely see that the pot of Haggin was calling the kettle of Miller & Lux black. The appropriator, Haggin, was a speculator in land, holding at the time nearly one-half million acres of land in Kern County. The riparian, Miller & Lux, was a cattle baron whose landed empire extended to three western states. Clearly, either form of property right in water could be monopolized (Pisani 1984, 245–246). California's courts would not address the policy issue of monopoly underlying *Lux v. Haggin*—that of the impact of combinations and restraint of trade (represented by concentrated land and water rights ownership)—since that issue had not been brought before them.

But the most telling doctrinal reasoning in *Lux v. Haggin* emerged as Judge McKinstry took up the California Civil Code theory. The Civil Code adopted in 1872 provided Californians with a procedure by which private diverters could appropriate and maintain a property right in water.[11] Its language included Section 1422, which simply stated, "the rights of riparian proprietors are not affected by the provisions of this title." This meant that any water appropriated could be subject under Civil Code Section 1422 to challenge from riparian right holders to the extent their vested rights might be injured. "Section 1422 of the Civil Code," wrote McKinstry, was "declaratory of existing law."[12] In essence, the 1872 legislature built in vesting protection for riparian property rights in water.

Haggin's attorneys had attacked the legislature's adoption of English common law, only to be thoroughly repulsed by Justice McKinstry. Under the common law of California, Haggin "has no right to divert the waters from the lands of the plaintiff unless that right *exists* under and by virtue of the common law, as the same was adopted in and by" the state legislature in 1850.[13] While perhaps originating in common-law practice back east, "The doctrine of 'appropriation,' so called," wrote McKinstry, "is not the doctrine of the common law. In examining the numerous cases which establish that the doctrine of 'appropriation' is *not* the common law," he concluded, with apparent judicial relish, "we meet an embarrassment of abundance."[14]

Turning to factual evidence issues arising from trial procedures, the supreme court majority again ruled that Judge Brundage in Kern County erred in omitting from evidence Miller & Lux's certificates of purchase of their Kern County lands. Though at the time they hadn't acquired the land outright, the certificates showed clearly that Miller & Lux had sufficient interest in the property as owner and therefore was entitled to all the benefits of the land, including diverting water from Buena Vista Slough and the lower Kern River. The company had done so years before the Calloway Weir headgates were installed in Bakersfield, and Haggin's field engineer had opened them in 1877.[15]

McKinstry's decision also found that the trial court excluded testimony by a Miller & Lux employee indicating, without contradicting testimony from Haggin's side, that Buena Vista Slough had clearly definable banks and channels, thus meeting the definition in law of a riverbank rather than an undifferentiated swamp region as Haggin's team claimed. The California Supreme Court then found that Miller & Lux's rights came prior to Haggin's appropriative rights, and that therefore the trial court had to take the case back to determine an appropriate remedy.

Back in Kern County after the decision, however, Henry Miller and James Ben Ali Haggin instead opted in 1888 for a commodious settlement between monopolistic titans that allocated between them the privatized waters of the Kern River: one-third of the water each year would be reserved by converting Buena Vista Lake to a reservoir for Miller & Lux's lands along Buena Vista Slough, while Haggin's Kern County Land and Water Company would receive two-thirds of the river's flow.[16] In addition, Haggin would pay to build a reservoir storing Miller & Lux's share of the water for release during the irrigation season. The southern San Joaquin Valley developed quickly into one of the most productive irrigated agricultural regions in the nation during the twentieth century—and not from the monopolized control of surface water alone, as we shall see in chapter 5.

Elisha McKinstry resigned from the California Supreme Court in 1888 to teach at Hastings Law College and conduct private practice. And in 1891, Miller & Lux hired him to represent them in a constitutional challenge to the Wright Act—early enabling legislation for irrigation districts—litigation that failed on appeal (M. C. Miller 1993, 96–97).

* * *

Even in defeat, during the remainder of 1886 and into 1887, Haggin continued to fund what we today might call an "astroturf" movement (organized and funded from the top down to pay activists to simulate a "grassroots" insurgency) against riparian water rights in California. Anti-riparian activists and legislators convinced Governor George Stoneman to convene a special session of the legislature in the summer of 1886 after release of the final *Lux v. Haggin* decision. With much alcohol consumed and lucre exchanged between legislators and interested constituents, riparian defenders (funded in large part by Henry Miller) were able to prevent any legislation to undo or abolish riparian rights, except for repeal of the vexing but redundant Civil Code Section 1422. The English common law and its riparian doctrine, abetted by *Lux v. Haggin*, still reigned in California water law, and the special session adjourned, having accomplished little (Malone 1966; Pisani 1984, 191–249).

As *Lux v. Haggin* was litigated, the area of irrigated land "increased four or five times during the 1880s," despite the supposed antidevelopment and monopolistic tendency attributed to holders of riparian water rights (Pisani 1984, 245).

NOTES

1. A rod is about 5.5 yards. Brewer (1966, 382) was estimating the river channel's width at close to 140 feet, nearly half the length of a modern football field.

2. Historians have not resolved whether this is actually the course of events, and they may never. The experiments could have been simply for Haggin, Tevis, and Carr to evaluate the productivity of the soils in an unknown climate and an untried technology (irrigation). Zonlight (1979) cites on one hand "official and unofficial statements made by or about the Kern County Land Company" professing that Haggin, Tevis, and Carr's original purpose "was to acquire land on which to establish a vast cattle ranch." Downey (1947), in his anti-communist/anti-Bureau of Reclamation book, makes a similar case, cited by Zonlight (1979, 67–68). Zonlight (1979, 68), however, also quotes Haggin, 1877: "I also purchased various water-rights [*sic*] which had been located under the laws of California, and located canals for the purpose of irrigating my lands, with a view that when I had sufficiently demonstrated the subject and rendered my land subject to irrigation, of dividing them up into small tracts and selling them out to farmers, with the water-rights necessary for irrigating the same." Beyond this quote, Haggin and Tevis left scant documentation for historians to dissect and resolve whether Haggin's professed interest in subdivision was company policy or expedient testimony for public consumption. Pisani (1984, 201–202) excerpts this quote as well and questions whether Haggin was serious about subdividing when, in the 1880s, a number of orchard colonies in and around Fresno met with success. See Zonlight (1979, 69–72), Liebman (1983, 70–72), and Pisani (1984, 202–03). Pisani (1984, 203) describes how the Kern County Land Company holdings were but a fraction of Haggin's "vast 'grasslands empire'" comprising 1.4 million acres of land in Arizona, New Mexico, and Kern County. Haggin's comments, writes Pisani, "have the ring of truth when the Haggin-Carr efforts in Kern County are viewed in isolation. . . . Irrigation was valued not as a way to raise high-value crops like those cultivated around Fresno, but to produce alfalfa for stock." Subdividing, concludes Pisani, would have destroyed their expanding livestock business "by driving up taxes and creating a potentially 'intractable' community of small farmers. As it was, Haggin and Carr had a hard time controlling Kern County politics."

3. Zonlight (1979, 79–80) cites news sources stating that Haggin paid $200,000 for this acreage at $3.50 an acre and concludes that having Tevis and Carr as associates "considerably lessened" Haggin's land monopoly ambitions and efforts, since Carr had been a lobbyist and Tevis vice-president of the Southern Pacific Railroad Company. Historian Richard Orsi (2005, 197–98) summarizes Southern Pacific's relationships with irrigation and development companies in Kern County.

4. An option is a contract specifying terms of a sale or other agreement that provides the owner of the option a time-limited chance to line up financing to complete the sale. Dollar value estimated from acreage and cattle head prices. See Treadwell (1931, 34–35).

5. According to San Francisco's oldest continuous rain gage, 047772, rainfall in 1877 was just 10.11 inches, while the historical average from 1850 through 1877 was 23.23 inches. (Precipitation data accessed from Desert Research Institute, August 26 2013.)

6. The members of the Association sold out to Miller & Lux by 1888, according to legal transcripts (Igler 2001, 101; M.C. Miller 1993, 5 and n. 5, 189).

7. Lux v. Haggin, 4 Pac. 919 (1884).

8. McKinstry's eulogy is found at 141 Cal. 745 (1906).
9. Lux v. Haggin, 69 Cal 255, 299 (1886).
10. *Id.* at 308–309.
11. This legal process would assume great importance once the state of California was assigned by its legislature in 1914 to control and regulate new water rights. Appropriations asserted prior to 1914 were grandfathered in as vested.
12. *Lux,* 69 Cal. at 368.
13. *Id.* at 380.
14. *Id.* at 390.
15. *Id.* at 421–439.
16. Treadwell (1931, 60–61) claims that Miller said of the deal with Haggin, "'There is more water than we can use, and it does not come at the right time of year. It comes in a great flood early in the spring, and in the hot months of the summer, the river is dry. . . . You builds [*sic*] me a reservoir, and I gives you two-thirds of the water,' and the difficulty was solved." See Contract and agreement between Henry Miller and James B. Haggin, July 28, 1888.

Chapter 4

The Dead Hand of Henry Miller

IN 1866, BUSINESSMAN ROBERT BENSLEY came to Fresno County with a dream to build a huge irrigation canal using private investment to serve lands on the west side of the San Joaquin Valley. The canal would take water from the San Joaquin River at modern-day Mendota where the river turns northward. By routing the canal at an elevation higher than the river along the western side of the San Joaquin Valley, the waters could be turned downhill in ditch laterals to irrigate the arid west side as far north as Stanislaus County. Bensley's first canal company ran out of money by 1868. But the idea survived as the Southern Pacific Railroad and a drought that lasted from 1868 to 1873 both took hold in the Valley. With help from William Ralston, head of the Bank of California, Bensley reorganized the project into the San Joaquin and Kings River Canal and Irrigation Company. Ralston was its lead investor. They attracted a syndicate of other prominent San Francisco capitalists, including Isaac Friedlander and William Sharon, both noted land speculators of the period. Friedlander owned vast holdings of Sacramento Valley wheat baronages (Table 2.1.). Lloyd Tevis, then president of Wells Fargo Company (before his days with Kern County land baron James Haggin) also joined.

Bensley soon left the picture. Ralston hired British civil engineer Robert Brereton to oversee canal design in 1871. Brereton quickly completed a comprehensive survey of the San Joaquin Valley that offered alternative canal routes in the same year. From there, Ralston, Brereton, and the syndicate soon envisioned irrigating the entire Central Valley, starting with construction of an ambitious 230-mile aqueduct skirting the east side of the Coast Range from Buena Vista Lake in Kern County (at the north end of Miller & Lux's lands there) to Antioch on the western edge of the Bay–Delta estuary in eastern Contra Costa County. They also planned eight east-west lateral canals to serve as a transportation network for the Valley connecting the main canal with the San Joaquin River and its tributaries (Pisani 1984, 107).

Later, Brereton recommended the syndicate reduce the canal's length from 230 to 160 miles by starting it further north at Tulare Lake, probably due to lower runoff and drier climate in the Valley's southern portion. Shortening the canal was probably also a step taken to husband the syndicate's resources for its largest financial challenges.

Brereton and the syndicate addressed what they anticipated would be the project's biggest obstacle: obtaining a right of way from Miller & Lux to build a 40-mile reach of their aqueduct from Firebaugh's Ferry to Los Banos.[1] In exchange for the syndicate gaining a right of way across his land, Miller received clear recognition of the cattle company's paramount riparian rights to the San Joaquin River. Brereton and Henry Miller agreed to terms in which Miller & Lux provided the canal company rights of way across Miller & Lux lands, a cash subsidy, and access to water at low rates. (According to Miller's biographer Edward Treadwell, it was half the rate that Miller charged others.) Miller also received free stock water and rights to "overflow his grass land when the water was not needed by other persons" (Treadwell 1931, 43).

Henry Miller's "subsidy" to the project came in the form of $20,000 toward construction costs, as well as use of Miller & Lux workers, equipment, and horses. Ralston and the syndicate agreed to provide company stock to Miller & Lux in addition to the rights of way and favorable water charges. Hampered at first by the economic depression of the early 1870s, the canal syndicate grew desperate for additional capital as the decade proceeded. By early 1875, their financial picture improved with infusions of capital from British investors, plus the addition of 100,000 acres of Miller & Lux land to the canal's service area in exchange for another 100,000 shares of canal company stock to Miller.

But suddenly that year, two key investors, W. S. Chapman and Isaac Friedlander, went bankrupt, as did the Bank of California. The bank's president William Ralston, who had been deeply involved in the Comstock Lode, died in August 1875, an apparent suicide. Historian Catherine Miller found that a variety of other landowners along the canal's right of way were approached to join the irrigation and canal company with an offer of 100,000 shares of canal company stock (the same general strategy O. P. Calloway employed at about the same time in Kern County to the south). The company possessed no land of its own, only a water right. Brereton believed that the company would be unprofitable just relying on water sales for irrigation. When Brereton approached British bankers later in 1875, they shied away from further investment in the scheme when other such projects failed because of "shoddiness." Nor was Brereton able to win congressional support for the project.

Relations between Brereton's canal company and Miller & Lux became "tempestuous" in these years. One of the original terms by which Miller & Lux granted the canal its right of way was that the canal company furnish water to the cattle corporation either free or with minimal charges. The cattle company then declined to take all its entitled water deliveries from the canal over several years in this period, starving Brereton's canal company of revenue. After failure of the Bank of California in 1875, Miller & Lux asserted its corporate influence over the canal company for which Henry Miller had negotiated years earlier, mooting the bad blood with Brereton. In late 1877, Miller himself became majority owner of the canal company and its system by purchasing canal stock at less than one-third its original value. The canal system would be a friendly and supportive subsidiary within the expanding Miller & Lux corporation for the foreseeable future. By 1908, Henry Miller would control 80 percent of canal company stock. "By that time," wrote Catherine Miller, "the two companies had virtually become one." For example, Miller & Lux routinely used interlocking directorates to control canal company affairs (Miller 1993, 43–44). Catherine Miller also notes that the two companies' offices shared the same building in Los Banos (Miller 1993, 44).

Well positioned by its deals with the canal syndicate, Miller & Lux reaped opportunity from Brereton's failure, acquiring much of Chapman's and Friedlander's best lands in the western San Joaquin Valley, plus the unfinished canal and Brereton's stake in the canal company. Though historian Donald Pisani concludes that Brereton's project "was far too ambitious for a frontier society," it nevertheless delivered into Miller & Lux's control essential building blocks for the growing cattle and water empire in the San Joaquin Valley: additional grazing land served by an extensive water distribution and lateral system into which Miller & Lux could divert its own and the canal company's water from the San Joaquin River, beginning at Mendota Pool (Pisani 1984, 119).

* * *

Because of its location and ephemeral linkage, Mendota Pool eventually became the switchyard of San Joaquin Valley hydrologic activity.[2] The Valley is actually two distinguishable drainage basins. The Pool gathers near the topographic nexus of the San Joaquin River basin with the Tulare Lake basin. The San Joaquin drains north to the Pacific Ocean while the Tulare Lake basin usually has no such outlet. The basins were separated by massive deposits of alluvium brought to the valley floor by the San Joaquin River and its hydrologic neighbor, the Kings River to the south. The Kings River drains Kings Canyon high in the Sierra, and reaches the San Joaquin Valley floor a few miles due east of Fresno. It flows southwest from the Sierra, like its neighbor the San Joaquin River, to the north. But the Kings approaches Tulare Lake where the land flattens and the river splits off Fresno Slough. Although the Kings deposited most of its flow to the lakebed in the nineteenth century, the slough curves around the lake's north shore near Riverdale, siphoning flood flows from the Kings River to reach the sea via the San Joaquin River. The slough and the San Joaquin River meet at Mendota Pool.

The San Joaquin leaves the Sierra Nevada just above the Fresno County hamlet of Friant at about elevation 340 feet above sea level. Here the river's centerline serves as the boundary between Madera and Fresno Counties. Upon reaching the Valley, it meanders the alluvial plains on its way to Mendota, 20 miles west at 170 feet of elevation. As it reaches Mendota, the San Joaquin also reaches the flattest part of the Valley and meanders widely and often, fed from the east by five other Sierra rivers on its way to the Delta and San Francisco Bay.

Where the San Joaquin River turns from its southwesterly journey to a northwesterly course, the land and the river drop another 19 feet in the 10 miles between Mendota and Firebaugh, another 31 feet in elevation from Firebaugh to Los Banos;

and by Gustine it loses another 24 feet. At its confluence with the Merced River, the San Joaquin has lost nearly 244 feet of elevation. Mendota Pool appears to be a perfect place to divert the San Joaquin River.[3] A canal dug at that point from the river could follow the Valley's gently sloping western hillsides at a flatter gradient so that water could be easily and safely brought to thousands of acres of west-side farm and ranch lands using gravity flow, while still enabling those lands to drain. Once available, the arriving waters would have increased their value overnight. Several of Miller & Lux's legal precedents were set among the confluences, diversions, and fluctuating flows at or near Mendota Pool.

Figures 4.1 and 4.2 illustrate the lay of land, river, and slough from early Fresno County cadastral maps. They show Miller & Lux's control of land ownership (including through the California Pastoral & Agricultural Company) on both banks of the San Joaquin River downstream of Mendota Pool, as well as the immediately surrounding area. In one California Supreme Court decision, Miller & Lux's diversion on the west side of the pool was upheld as a riparian claim against a challenge that the diversion interfered with the river's navigability.[4] The challenger, Jefferson G. James and the Enterprise Canal & Land Company, which owned land along Fresno Slough, sought to divert water a few miles upstream along the San Joaquin of Miller & Lux's Mendota Pool diversion, claiming it was exercising a riparian right from Fresno Slough (recall that San Joaquin River waters sometimes back up into Fresno Slough). In 1905, the California Supreme Court found for Miller & Lux that James did not have a riparian right to divert on the San Joaquin.[5] And then in 1915, only when the slough was "hydrologically connected" could James make "reasonable use of flows for diversion from Fresno Slough."[6] In practical terms, "hydrologically connected" meant those times when one of two conditions held: either the San Joaquin River flowed high enough for Mendota Pool to fill and back up behind Miller & Lux's weir into Fresno Slough where James could divert from the slough when it flowed "upstream"; *or* Kings River flows were so high that Fresno Slough flowed past Tulare Lake sufficiently for James to divert as the slough flowed northward (downstream).

The customer base of the San Joaquin & Kings River Canal & Irrigation Company grew as it extended its Main Canal north to western Stanislaus County to the vicinity of Newman. By the start of the twentieth century, public challenges to its water rate-setting and direct control of San Joaquin River supplies forced Miller & Lux to litigate frequently, using its position as premier owner of land and water rights along the river to develop legal doctrine to protect Miller & Lux's water rights.[7] The riparian doctrine became the legal and institutional cornerstone of the cattle corporation's asset value.

But it wasn't all about riparian doctrine. In taking over the San Joaquin & Kings River Canal & Irrigation Company canal, Miller & Lux corporate attorneys creatively protected the canal's appropriative water rights as well. While their riparian

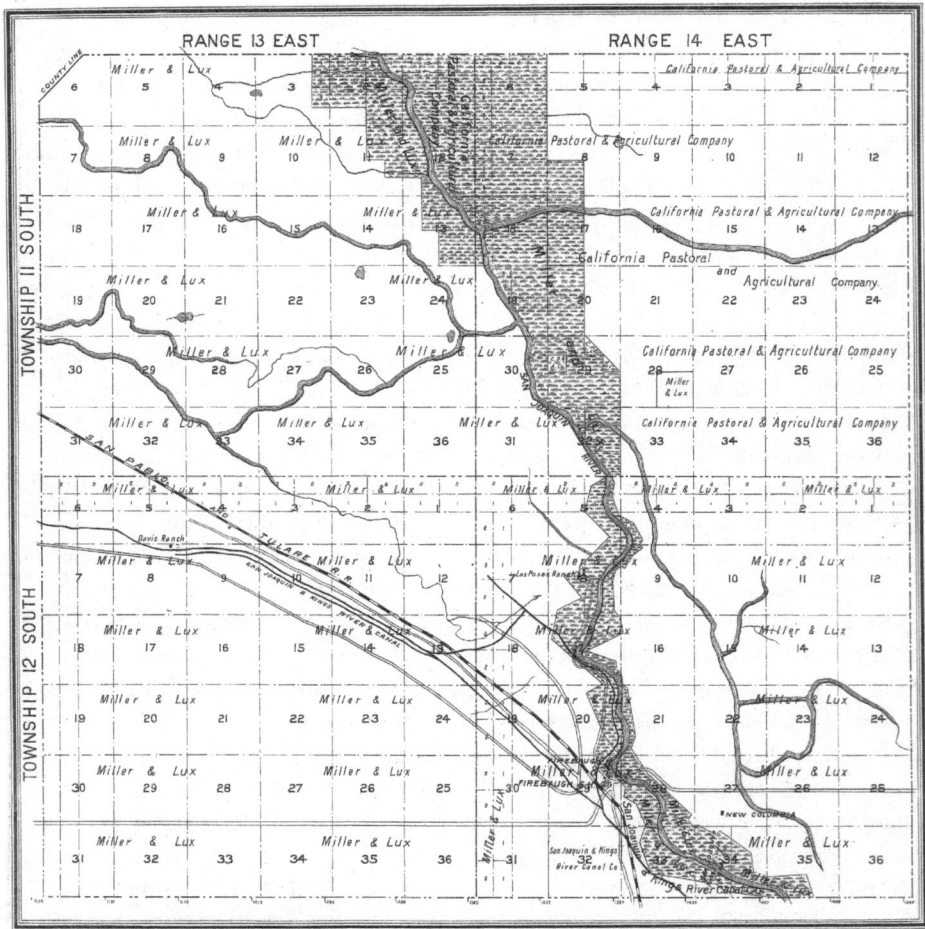

FIGURE 4.1. Miller & Lux and subsidiary California Pastoral & Agricultural Company lands downstream of Mendota Pool along the San Joaquin River. Courtesy of David Rumsey Map Collections and Cartography Associates, http://www.drumsey.com/home.

rights proved vital to production of beef cattle through their use of "wild irrigation" (described in chapter 3), the canal company's appropriative rights proved critical to protecting the sweetheart arrangements they provided to Miller & Lux, delivering both its riparian water and supplying canal customers.

Most of us never get before a state supreme court, let alone the United States Supreme Court. But between 1899 and 1919, Miller & Lux and its closely allied business interests figured prominently in a remarkable *thirteen* California Supreme Court water rights cases. The corporation was a direct party as either Miller & Lux

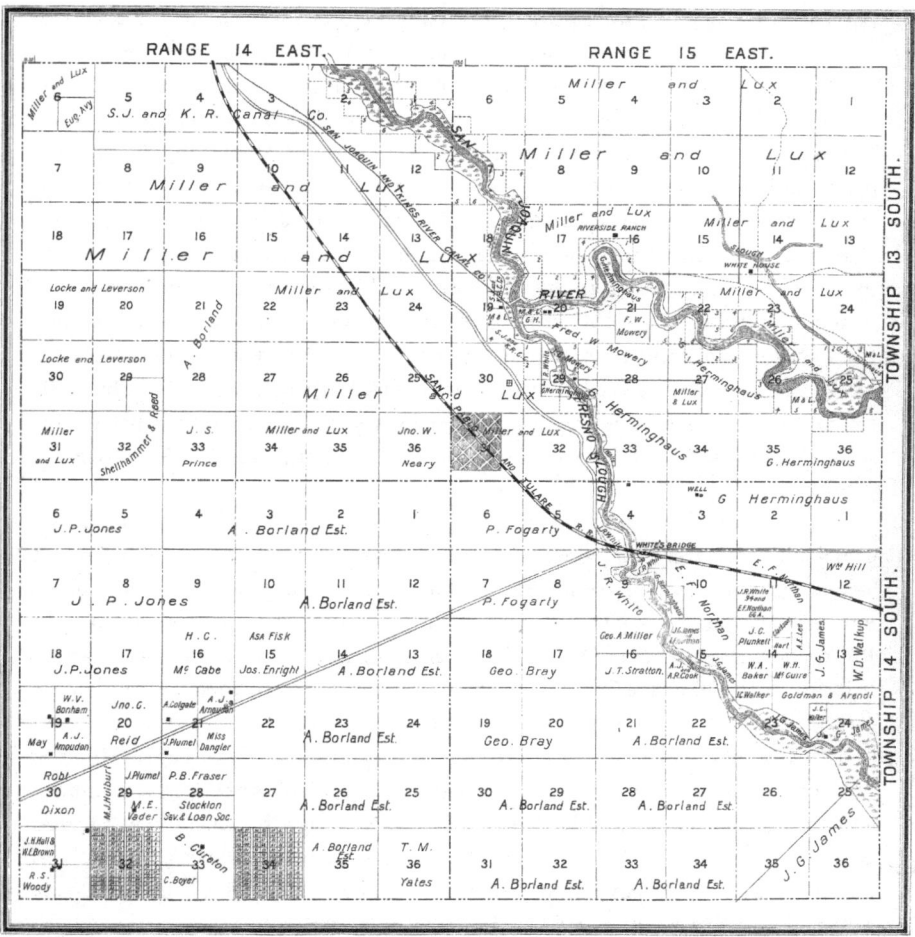

FIGURE 4.2. Miller & Lux and Herminghaus lands riparian to Fresno Slough and the San Joaquin River, western Fresno County. Courtesy of David Rumsey Map Collections and Cartography Associates, http://www.drumsey.com/home.

(the cattle corporation) or as the San Joaquin & Kings River Canal & Irrigation Company (the public canal utility). These entities were also parties at interest as leasing tenants of another landowner (Elizabeth Turner), a direct party in some of the cases and supported by her tenants, Miller & Lux and its affiliates. (Appendix A summarizes these cases.)

With time, Miller & Lux added new canals to irrigate more of its lands east of the San Joaquin River. To reach those lands, its canal company won prescriptive and appropriative rights to divert water from the San Joaquin through its Aliso and

Lone Willow Canals. (Prescriptive rights may vest after five years of "adverse use" diversions when neighboring water users do not stop them from occurring.) Other neighboring competitors downstream built canals of their own, including Chowchilla Canal (by Chowchilla Farms) and the East Side Canal (to a 25,000-acre irrigation colony planned by a downstream riparian owner J.J. Stevinson). These competing canals diverted San Joaquin River water to the east side of the Valley along the 40-plus-mile run that Miller & Lux and its canal company controlled. Whatever water they diverted would be water unavailable to the canal company's right, which diverted San Joaquin River to the west side. Any loss to the canal company's rights would limit the amount of Miller & Lux's riparian rights it could deliver to its lands through the canal company's systems. After a difficult period of litigation, Miller & Lux's canal company succeeded, first, in getting itself legally declared a "public utility," and second, in limiting Stevinson's diversion rights to a fraction of what Stevinson originally sought to develop for its irrigation colony near the Merced River confluence.[8]

Also during this period, Miller & Lux successfully blocked plans by the Madera Canal and Irrigation Company to construct a reservoir on the Chowchilla River, a smaller east side tributary of the San Joaquin. This was on grounds it would interfere with the cattle company's enjoyment of the natural flows in the San Joaquin River, injuring Miller & Lux's riparian water rights in the San Joaquin—again with help from the California Supreme Court.[9] This case soon provided legal precedent for the politically charged *Herminghaus* case of the 1920s.

In still other cases, Miller & Lux was willing to settle out of court. Miller & Lux concluded deals to avoid litigation with Southern California Edison Company and San Joaquin Power and Light Company in exchange for timely flow releases. Between 1895 and 1928, these power companies constructed dams, reservoirs, and powerhouses in the upper San Joaquin River watershed in the Sierra above Fresno. Miller & Lux agreements established schedules by which the two power companies would abstain from storing river flows above 3,000 cfs from snowmelt for the spring and summer irrigation months, as well as absolute limits on how much reservoir capacity might be used in the winter months when storage recharged from snowmelt (California Water Project Authority 1936a, 2–7).

As the largest riparian landowner along the San Joaquin River, Miller & Lux pressed its advantages relentlessly. The company based its cattle production scheme, firstly on "wild irrigation"—the right to free or inexpensive water—and secondly through shrewd dealing with the San Joaquin & Kings River Canal & Irrigation Company syndicate for a canal right of way across Miller land. Thus Miller & Lux came to own over 100 miles of canals. The canals it obtained, and those the corporation subsequently built itself, delivered water cheaply and reliably, though less so to their public customers.

In successfully defending its water rights in the many California Supreme

Court cases, Miller & Lux arguably exerted undue influence over the development of California water law commensurate, at least for a time, with its monopoly power in the western beef market and the world of San Joaquin and Kern River hydrology. Through its quest for cheap and reliable water, the cattle company consolidated its control of San Joaquin River water as the basis for its many hydraulic privileges. "Ironically, the commitment of the courts . . . , to private property also rendered inoperative efficiency models of pricing and economic growth in capitalist society," observes historian Catherine Miller. "Instead, riparian property rights made ownership of a public utility (the San Joaquin & Kings River Canal & Irrigation Company) an effective technique for ensuring a cheap supply of private water and Miller & Lux's repeated litigation helped maintain a system that restricted access to water by skewing the pricing mechanism."[10] The technique was monopoly. It was neither the first time nor the last that California water actors would defy the theories and models of economists and historians alike.

Miller & Lux's economic power and political influence were eventually eclipsed by consolidation in the cattle industry, led by Chicago cattle and beef producers and their increasing control of the national beef market in the early twentieth century. While World War I dramatically increased demand for Miller & Lux beef, the postwar economic depression beginning in 1919 put the whole Miller & Lux empire into permanent decline. Yet despite the company's blunted edge, its water rights remained its most important tangible asset, even as the value of land and other assets (such as its San Francisco abattoirs) plummeted from loss of market share, slack demand, and the larger economic depression of the 1930s. During the 1920s and 1930s, Miller & Lux gradually bequeathed its San Joaquin River lands and water rights to four mutual companies named for the local canals: San Luis Canal Company, Firebaugh Canal Company, Columbia Canal Company, and Gravelly Ford Canal Company. Their rights became the geographical and legal foundation on which the Central Valley Project would be built. (See chapter 8.)

Even as its economic power deteriorated, its water rights were still important to the state of California's plan for coordinated statewide water development into the 1940s. One large portion of this bloc of water rights (their "purchased" water rights) became the basis by which today the U.S. Bureau of Reclamation infuses Kern County and the rest of Tulare Lake basin (including Kings and Tulare Counties) with irrigation supplies exported south from the San Joaquin River.

The other bloc of former Miller & Lux rights is "exchanged" (or borrowed) to augment the "purchased" exports from the San Joaquin to Kern County. But these exchanged rights must be immediately replaced because they are senior to nearly everyone else's. As though the dead hand of Henry Miller (Figure 4.3) reached from the grave, his monopoly of San Joaquin River water rights compelled construction of what today is still California's largest reservoir (Shasta Lake, north of Redding) for direct benefit of Miller & Lux's corporate descendants, the San Joaquin River

FIGURE 4.3. Henry Miller at age sixty, about the time of the *Lux v. Haggin* case. Courtesy of California Department of Parks and Recreation.

Exchange Contractors. From the U.S. Bureau of Reclamation, they receive annually a guaranteed substitute supply of water to replace about 840,000 acre-feet they "exchange" to the Tulare Lake basin counties from water stored at Friant—delivered through the Friant-Kern Canal. And every drought year, the four Exchange Contractors between Gustine and Mendota are still guaranteed no less than 75 percent of their usual water rights, courtesy of the federal government, whether its source is Shasta or Friant or portions from both.

Miller & Lux's attorneys succeeded in recasting the riparian doctrine from one reliant on "natural use" for the mere enjoyment and use of the riparian owner to one representing vested property rights to water integral to the corporation's apparatus of grassland, canals, and beef production.

Not only did Miller & Lux monopolize the riparian lands along Buena Vista Slough in western Kern County, but it also came to control vast acreage on both sides of over 100 miles of the San Joaquin River in the late nineteenth century—from Gravelly Ford to the Merced River confluence. In those days, despite their control, the river still flowed there. That control continued in the twentieth and twenty-first centuries. "Some think Friant Dam is the center of the California water world. Actually, the San Joaquin River Exchange Contractors are the center of that world," said Ron Jacobsma, general manager of the Friant Water Authority, to the State Water Resources Control Board in November 2010.[11] The Exchange Contractors are the corporate offspring of Miller & Lux's water and real estate holdings along the San Joaquin River. But as we shall see, the coming of the Central Valley Project dried up most of that reach of the river.

NOTES

1. The canal's diversion works would be built back to Mendota a few years later. Los Banos was located at the end of a wagon road connecting to Gilroy in the southern Santa Clara Valley near one of Miller & Lux's ranches on the route to San Francisco. Southern Pacific Railroad had completed a connector from Gilroy to San Francisco as well, which would "facilitate construction by carrying workers, heavy equipment, and supplies, as well as potential settlers" to the western San Joaquin Valley" (Pisani 1984, 109).

2. Gudde (1998, 234, s.v. "Mendota") found that the name Mendota derives from "a Siouan language, perhaps referring to the confluence of two rivers," in this case, the meeting of Fresno Slough with the San Joaquin River. Other Internet sources suggest Mendota is merely an Indian term for a confluence of two trails. Like many California place names, Mendota may also echo other town or rail station names back east.

3. Approximate elevations obtained from Benchmark Maps, 1998. Friant, elevation 340 feet; Mendota, elevation 170 feet; Firebaugh, elevation 151 feet; Los Banos, elevation 120 feet; Gustine, elevation 96 feet.

4. Miller & Lux v. Enterprise Canal, 142 Cal. 208 (1904).

5. Miller & Lux v. Enterprise Canal, 145 Cal. 652 (1905).

6. Miller & Lux v. Enterprise Canal, 169 Cal. 415 (1915).

7. See Appendix A for a summary of thirteen cases setting and buttressing water law precedents.

8. J.J. Stevinson v. San Joaquin & Kings River, 162 Cal. 141 (1912); San Joaquin & Kings River v. James J. Stevinson, 164 Cal. 221 (1912); and Elizabeth Turner v. East Side Canal & Irrigation Company, 168 Cal. 103 (1914) and 169 Cal. 652 (1915). See also M. C. Miller (1993, 67–94).

9. Miller & Lux v. Madera Canal, 155 Cal. 59 (1909).

10. Miller (1993, 66) describes what agricultural economist Daniel Bromley means as a "private property regime." Bromley (1991) hints at a larger implication regarding water rights, of whatever stripe, in a market society such as California: that monopoly control of water rights obstructs the free functioning of a market for water. Economists are less than successful persuading a California public that regards a market for water with great suspicion, once they understand what is at stake. We will revisit this issue in a sequel to this book.

11. Quote by Jacobsma (2010) from the author's notes in attendance that day.

Chapter 5

A Large Permanent Usefulness

REFLECTING ON HER FORMER HOME in 2004, writer and journalist Joan Didion wrote, "A good deal about California does not, on its own preferred terms, add up." A Sacramento native, she observed that California "tended to attract drifters of loosely entrepreneurial inclination . . . and to reward most fully those who perceived most quickly that the richest claim of all lay not in the minefields but in Washington." Her example: the "robber barons" of the Southern Pacific "built the railroad that linked California with the world markets and opened the state to extensive settlement, but it was the citizens of the rest of the country who paid for it. . . ."

Paradoxically, though California is a place where "distrust of centralized governmental authority has historically passed for an ethic," its people and history are awash with railroad, flood control, drainage, water subsidies, and land gifts from the federal government. Many such perquisites encouraged first mining, then agricultural and urban development. (Subsidies cover the difference between society's willingness to pay for something and its total cost.) Subsidies continue today, she added, famously so in commodity agriculture. The result of such subsidies is a government-facilitated "vast agricultural mechanism, quite remote from the normal necessity for measuring supply against demand and cost against return" (Didion 2003, 19–26).

She could have easily cited James Ben Ali Haggin and Henry Miller, the largest landowners in Kern County and the San Joaquin Valley in nineteenth-century California, as poster children of monopoly beneficiaries of public wealth. Yet, while they relied heavily on gaming various government land-settlement programs to expand their empires, they did not own all the land. Other people came to own land and found alternative means to settle the valley and its Sierra foothills. Dreamers and schemers arrived in California to establish social experiments by which agricultural and community development might manifest the word of their utopian dreams (Hine 1953). Their dreams often foundered from lack of water, lack of capital, lack of political skill and contacts, and the kiln-like summer climate of the San Joaquin Valley desert.

Another subsidy example from the history of California water: Nature subsidizes California's capitalist society through groundwater, in addition to all the other money subsidies flowing from Sacramento and Washington. Unique in its diversion of surface water using dams, canals, pumping plants, and hydropower generation, California also extracts its groundwater—*especially* its groundwater—to bring economic value to land and to the human-raised products of the land. In normal years of surface-water abundance, groundwater is the source of 35 to 40 percent of California's water supplies, but during droughts is as much as 60 to 65 percent of water use.

Nature's groundwater subsidy to San Joaquin Valley irrigated agriculture expanded. By the early twentieth century, development of groundwater resources (and not grand, monumental dams and curvaceous, sweeping aqueducts) was expected to be the primary source of water for irrigated agricultural production in southern California and the San Joaquin Valley.[1] Several factors enabled the Valley's rapid growth in this period: abundant land; plentiful, good-quality groundwater; and technological synergies spawned by the invention and diffusion of centrifugal pumps, hydropower generation, and alternating-current transmission methods. While the San Joaquin Valley floor was cloaked in land and water monopoly under the Miller & Lux cattle corporation, south of the San Joaquin River, the eastern Tulare Lake basin fairly bustled with hardworking farm families finally obtaining land and water that had eluded them when the focus was on getting surface water to land. Extracting water from underground made these lands valuable too.

The San Joaquin Valley made up the southern two-thirds of the Central Valley and would-be settlers now saw a vast, potentially arable land. By 1912, the Valley was estimated to have some 7.5 million acres in cultivation, though only about 1.7 million acres were irrigated (Mendenhall et al. 1916, 10).

The San Joaquin Valley's northern third contains four well-endowed rivers: the Stanislaus, the Tuolumne, the Merced, and the eponymous San Joaquin. Its southern two-thirds have only three relatively large rivers: the Kings in the north (draining what is today Kings Canyon National Park), the Kaweah toward the middle (draining modern-day Sequoia National Park), and the Kern in the south. These rivers and smaller creeks (among them the Tule and the White) flowed into other terminal lakebeds such as the Tulare in the north, and Buena Vista and Kern Lakes to the south. When these lakes flooded on occasion, they drained north to Tulare Lake, via Buena Vista Slough (Alevizon and Vorster 1998, 2–44 to 2–51; Preston 1981, 29–30). During the last Ice Age and even before European contact, the southern San Joaquin Valley in the spring would have appeared from the air as a vast network of lakes knitted together by chains of riparian wetlands, all fed by Sierra snowmelt or foothill rainfall and runoff.

But after settlement, surface flows in the Tulare Lake basin were widely believed insufficient to irrigate all the acreage its farmers desired. Nature's largest subsidy to California comes from its groundwater. Except for the south and west sides, abundant, high-quality groundwater was available in most parts of the San Joaquin Valley, a second factor in its rapid agricultural development (San Joaquin Valley Water Committee 1929, 4).

While no estimates were made by the California Conservation Commission on the total capacity of the geologic strata to store water in any of the Central Valley basins, *it was assumed* to be a lot. In its 1913 report on San Joaquin Valley groundwater resources, the commission saw the need to increase surface storage *and* use of groundwater to achieve full usage of available water resources (State of California 1913). Of course at that time, the matter of surface storage for both power production and consumptive use was legally contested. Until resolved through the California Supreme Court's 1926 *Herminghaus* decision and the 1928 passage of Proposition 7 by the California electorate (see chapter 7), groundwater would be the primary water resource that enabled expansion of irrigated agriculture.

The Conservation Commission recognized the presence of relatively shallow water tables as vital to lucrative cropping strategies for farmers. Vineyards and citrus orchards could gain competitive and profitable advantage by pumping groundwater for irrigation, especially on the Valley's east side lands and some areas near the trough of the Valley. There was so much groundwater that in the early twentieth century some areas had still-untapped artesian (spontaneously flowing) well opportunities to supply future irrigated agricultural development along the bottomlands of both the Tulare Lake basin and the San Joaquin River basin (Figures 5.1–2; Mendenhall 1908; Williamson et al. 1989, Fig. 17).

These artesian districts were areas where water was under pressure from overlying geologic strata with underground flow from upper elevations to the Valley trough on the east side. Newly drilled wells released that pressure, causing the water to flow effortlessly to the surface. The only obstacle for a diverter in using such an easy and bountiful well effectively was capping, storing, and controlling the flow so that it was available when needed and not wasted.

Geologist W. C. Mendenhall reported 522 artesian wells in the San Joaquin Valley in 1916. Southern California south of the Tehachapi Range had another 3,000 (Mendenhall 1916, 31, Table 4). He further estimated that groundwater beneath the Valley's surface would gain widespread use, "and by their use hundreds of thousands of acres now arid and unproductive will be brought to yield handsomely" (Mendenhall 1916, 34).

Mendenhall estimated that there were some 4,300 square miles of San Joaquin Valley lands where two-thirds of the artesian waters were "sufficiently pure" for use in irrigation (Figure 5.1). He recommended cost-minimizing strategies to help ensure farming success from groundwater development: if a farmer possessed junior surface water rights, he should use that irrigation water first, since its delivery by gravity cost little or nothing; then use the artesian groundwater, where available, only to supply crops later in the irrigation season. Such wells delivered groundwater at minimal cost, especially in dry years. He recommended growers cultivate primarily high-value, reliable market crops that, when sold, justify the high up-front expense of drilling a well and pumping groundwater. Vineyards and citrus orchards were favored for the ability of their fruits to repay the cost of irrigating them with groundwater and still yield a profit to the grower.

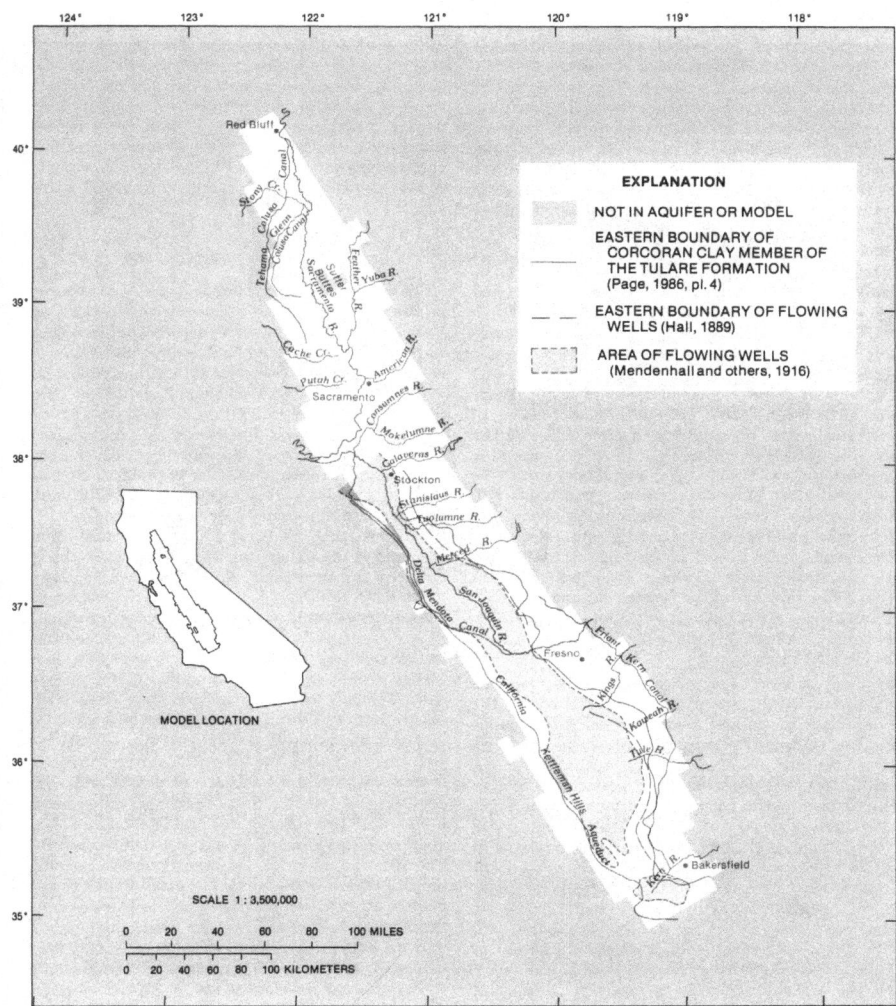

FIGURE 5.1. Areas of predevelopment artesian (flowing) wells, late nineteenth and early twentieth centuries, in the San Joaquin Valley. Source: Williamson et al. 1989: Fig. 17; original map data from Mendenhall 1908.

But there was a fly in this ointment. Sparing artesian usage until later in a season conserved the pressure that made it costless. But the more artesian wells are drilled in close proximity to the same source, the greater the rate at which the "head" or flow pressure is released from underground. As the density of wells increases, spontaneous artesian flow decreases, like a balloon deflating from air loss. The underground pressure driving water to the surface dissipated faster, a process Mendenhall also acknowledged.

FIGURE 5.2. Horse-drawn cart beside artesian well, Kern County, California. Photo by Carleton E. Watkins circa 1880–90. Source: Library of Congress.

When the number of wells drawing the artesian supply is greatly increased in any particular neighborhood, the wells interfere and the yield to each is lessened. When the maximum acreage is dependent on artesian flow under these conditions, the installation of pumping machinery may become necessary in order to insure the continuance of an adequate water supply. (Mendenhall 1916)

Water would still be there, but it would take energy for pumps to extract it.

As seen in the thirty-six-year map sequence in Figure 5.3, San Joaquin Valley irrigation emerged by 1886 first on the alluvial deltas of the Kings, Kaweah, and Kern Rivers. (A small, irrigated area in Kern County between Bakersfield and Delano was due to development of the Calloway Canal.) With this rapid growth of irrigated agriculture came equally rapid construction of hydroelectric power plants and the invention and use of alternating current transmission and long-distance distribution systems. Historian James C. Williams provides a similar sequence of maps showing the spread of the hydropower transmission grid between 1900 and 1925 (Williams 1997, 168–98, Figs. 9.1–3; also Vincent 1925, 568, 570, 572–74).

Looking back on the first quarter of the twentieth century, Pacific Gas and Electric Company vice-president W.G. Vincent Jr. recalled the explosive growth electricity transmission enjoyed in California. In 1900, there were 700 miles of

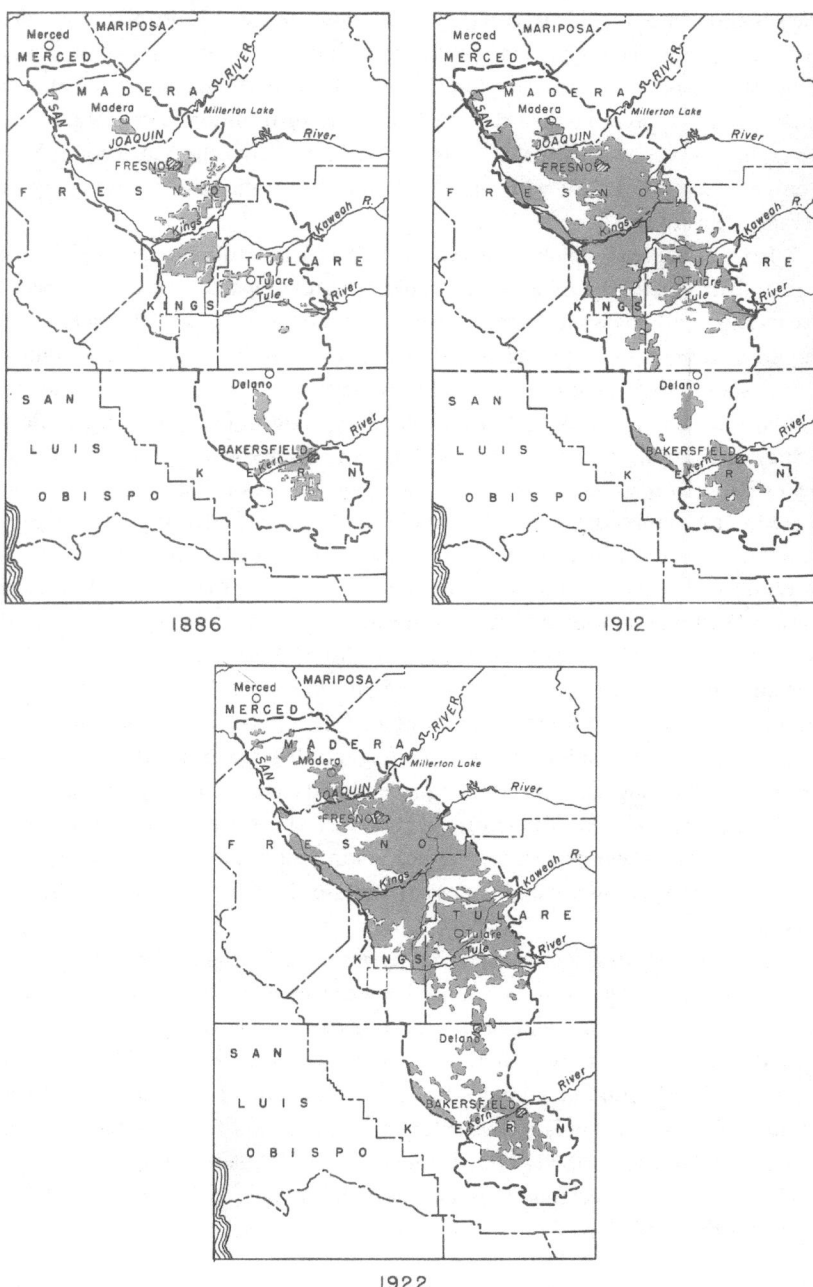

FIGURE 5.3. Development of irrigated acreage in San Joaquin Valley: 1886, 1912, and 1922.
Source: USDOI 1962.

transmission lines capable of carrying 10,000 volts or more in twenty-one unique lines. By 1925, Vincent reported that California's electricity system operated 9,000 miles of transmission lines carrying voltages of 20,000 to 220,000 volts and that 10,000-volt lines were by then classified merely as distribution lines, not transmission. His maps show that major transmission lines served the San Joaquin Valley from 1910 on, coincident with the expansion of irrigation in the valley by that decade (Vincent 1925).

Irrigation spread rapidly between 1886 and 1922, as settling farmers took advantage of hydroelectricity to power groundwater pumps, just as hydropower was also expanding to urban development elsewhere in California. These techniques for lifting water from the depths centered on Fresno, northern Kings, and Tulare Counties.

A state Department of Public Works report issued in 1927, authored by consultant and University of California, Berkeley, irrigation engineering professor Sidney T. Harding, documented declining groundwater levels in the San Joaquin Valley between 1920 and 1925. Harding was born in Massachusetts, spent his boyhood in Texas and Kansas, and then graduated from the University of Michigan in 1905 with a degree in civil engineering. Prior to joining the faculty of the University of California, Berkeley, in 1914, he worked on irrigation projects in various capacities in Washington, Montana, and California. His arrival at Berkeley united him with civil engineer Bernard Etcheverry with whom he partnered on many projects. Together they fostered water-related engineering ideas with many talented graduate students, who went on to populate positions throughout California and the West (Online Archive of California 2014). Throughout his career, Harding maintained extensive consulting contacts, advising federal and state agencies as well as private clients on practical and disputed matters of water-resource development. Almost every important water project or adjudication in California and neighboring states called on his expert advice and counsel. (Professor Harding will reappear in chapters to come.)

Harding reported to the state that by 1925, areas around the rural community of Wasco in central Kern County had seen depth to groundwater fall 20 to 30 feet. Nineteen twenty and 1924 had been particularly dry years, and the dry period extended back to 1917. In Tulare County, where some of the first groundwater pumps had begun operation in the early 1900s, groundwater depths had fallen up to 30 feet around Lindsay, and between 15 and 20 feet from the Earlimart area along the Southern Pacific rail line through Tipton to Tulare. Groundwater depths fell between 5 and 10 feet in the Visalia area on the alluvial soils of the Kaweah River in the northern portion of Harding's study area.[2]

* * *

The problem of groundwater overdraft revealed the dark side of proprietary individualism: the possibility that unrestrained competition among individual landowners for a vital resource could destroy access to that resource for most–a literal race to the bottom of the aquifer. As one early-twentieth-century civil engineer, Clarence Johnston, diagnosed it,

> The danger in irrigation matters never begins with the community, or the State. It has its birth in the greed of one or two who, through the weakness of supervision in behalf of the public, are able to get what they are not entitled to, whereby enriching themselves at the expense of their neighbors. (Johnston, n.d., 689; cited in Wiel 1928b, n. 106, 272)

In other contexts—quota systems for petroleum deposits, for example—destructive competition was controlled or eliminated by pro rata division of pumping rates among monopolistic combinations, or oligopolistic control among a few principal corporate actors in an industry.

Were there alternatives to monopolistic combination and restraint of extraction in the context of individualized groundwater use? The California Supreme Court offered one twenty years before groundwater overdraft began to affect the San Joaquin Valley in its landmark groundwater decision in a southern California case, *Katz v. Walkinshaw*. But before exploring this decision, some background on groundwater law is in order.

There are generally two kinds of groundwater recognized in California law: water flowing in defined subterranean channels (such as lava tubes, which are rare, or flow beneath the bed of a known river channel), and water that percolates from the surface to the water table. Generally, groundwater moves slowly compared to rivers, since it must eke its way through pores between grains of sediment or cracks in rock. Those pores can vary widely in size. When sand grains are large, pores tend also to be large, and water can flow quickly. When underground strata are primarily made of clay (whose particles tend to lie flat), water may hardly pass through at all.

Water flowing in defined subterranean channels is generally treated as analogous to surface water by California courts (and today by the State Water Resources Control Board). Groundwater, or "percolating water," was largely unregulated until just recently by the state of California, though there is considerable case law governing disputes over proprietary rights in percolating water.[3]

English common law (earlier noted as the founding legal framework of California at statehood) treated groundwater the same as minerals or rocks in the soil—when used in England: the proprietor owned water from the surface down to the center of the earth.[4] Owners could take as much of the resource as they wanted from beneath their land, with little or no consideration for neighbors. American jurists, however, adapted the common law, and that case law and legal methodology came to California when it adopted English common law in April 1850.

Thus, in California, groundwater was not recognized as a stationary mineral, but a liquid that flowed beneath the surface. This flow behavior could cause conflict and legal injury among neighbors drawing from the same source. The American legal innovation, according to Harding, in a book he wrote in the 1930s, was that each owner is entitled to use groundwater from his land subject to the limitation that such use does not interfere unreasonably with the similar rights of others to the same resource—also known as the "non-injury rule."[5]

Adverse use, as the name implies, means a use that is "without license or permission," according to *Black's Law Dictionary*. Adverse use helps describe those innovating mill owners back east (discussed in chapter 3) who dammed a river or stream to create the head they needed to drive water wheels and power mill operations. The rule of adverse use in California is five years: if neighbors on your stream fail to challenge your adverse use of water within five years, your adverse use can ripen into a "prescriptive right."[6] In fact, Henry Miller acquired some of his San Joaquin River rights through prescription. Riparian, overlying, or appropriative rights can be lost or reduced from adverse use and application of the rule of prescription. It can enable anyone to divert or pump water for an economic use, as the legal phrase is sometimes put, "as against all the world." If such pumping went unchallenged, adverse users could secure their own rights to the groundwater reservoir.

As a groundwater reservoir becomes more developed with more overlying owners and appropriators extracting, groundwater levels can fall, like a clamor of teenagers thrusting straws into the same chocolate milk shake, each sucking equally hard. Each may obtain a good, chocolatey flow at the outset, until such time that the glass is soon drained. Draining the aquifer is the primary risk of unregulated, fully competitive groundwater pumping. Once drained, the aquifer may take years, if ever, before water accumulates again in extractable amount. In the meantime, overlying right holders have incentive to demonstrate that their use of groundwater might be large, and appropriators have incentive to pump harder in order to maximize their prescriptive rights to groundwater through use adverse to the overlying water rights holders. When such legal principles are applied to a dynamic groundwater system, they are the very expression of the capitalist ethos.

* * *

And yet, in urbanizing southern California, through a case of groundwater competition, the California Supreme Court suggested a different outcome was possible. This case was about a community's interest in its flowing artesian wells.

Marcus Katz's artesian well stopped flowing without warning in his yard on July 27, 1899. He and his wife Leah lived at Third and E Street in San Bernardino, and their well had served them faithfully (according to subsequent court records) for more than twenty years. They were used to receiving up to one inch of flow (one inch is about one-fortieth of a cubic foot per second) whenever they used it—the flow you might get from a typical campground spigot.

Almira Allison also owned property in San Bernardino with an artesian well not far from the Katzes at Sixth and E streets. Residing there more than twenty years herself, Allison's well had constantly flowed at a rate of about one inch until it too suddenly failed on July 27. Rachel Tyler (living at Second and C streets) and William McDonald (at Fourth and D streets) suffered similar interruptions of their one-inch flowing artesian wells on July 27.

It seems Mrs. Margaret D. Walkinshaw, residing at First between C and D streets in San Bernardino, uncapped her nine wells that same day. Walkinshaw lived south and downslope of the neighbors whose artesian wells failed. She had called in a young handyman, Charles Reber, to uncap wells on her property and turn the water into a ditch across her property connected to a system owned by the Riverside Water Company.

Compared to her neighbors' controlled, one-inch-flow artesian wells, Walkinshaw unleashed a relative torrent from underground. An engineer from the Riverside Water Company testified later that he had visited and measured Walkinshaw's flow. He found 100.2 inches of flow on July 29; 97.6 inches on August 1; 102 inches on August 18; 116 inches a week later; 116.2 inches on September 9; and 114.5 inches on September 26.[7]

The Katzes, Allison, Tyler, and McDonald jointly filed suit in San Bernardino County superior court on September 18, 1899, to stop Walkinshaw's torrent. Apparently, they prevailed on the court to require Walkinshaw to cap her wells, which occurred on October 10, three weeks later. In subsequent testimony at trial, each of the plaintiffs and seventeen other witnesses (who had lost flow in their wells in and around San Bernardino) reported the flow in their wells restored on or about October 11.[8]

Begun on May 10, 1900, the trial concluded nine days later with trial judge John L. Campbell granting Walkinshaw's motion for "nonsuit"—meaning that the plaintiffs failed to make a legal case or bring forward sufficient evidence to prove their accusations against Walkinshaw. Her attorney, Byron Waters, was skeptical that the water source for all the parties to the case was in any way shared among the plaintiffs or among the plaintiffs with Walkinshaw, and that the water source had neither name nor stable description "so as to distinguish it or identify it from any other stream."[9] Katz, Allison, Tyler, and McDonald appealed to the California Supreme Court on June 13.

Evidence in the record suggests (though not conclusively) that Margaret D. Walkinshaw was a stalking horse for private water companies arranging prescriptive diversions of artesian groundwater for export to distant communities in the region.[10] For example, Riverside Water Company already tapped artesian flows from the upper Santa Ana River watershed to Riverside and other growing communities in the Santa Ana River basin east of Los Angeles at the time, alkali lands upslope of San Bernardino.

Rachel Tyler's son, Emery, went to see Walkinshaw's wells pumping two blocks away with Almira Allison's son Charles. While there, he later testified that Walkinshaw

> went into a long harange [sic] extending over 20 minutes or half an hour as to how the old settlers in this town were treating her by commencing an action against her, when the Riverside Company, wealthy people were sinking wells around the neighborhood, and she couldn't understand why they should pick on her, unless it was because she was poor and a widow, and that we would have a better case; she told me to the effect that we jumped on her because she could not defend herself."[11]

Her motive to help Riverside may have been pecuniary, but the trial's transcript does not reveal any specific quid pro quo; yet somehow her defense was provided for throughout the trial, appeal, and eventual rehearing before the state supreme court.

Walkinshaw's counsel, Byron Waters, briefed the state supreme court that some artesian supplies were developed from lands that are essentially desert, but that were nonetheless "water-bearing." "This land," he asked the state court to notice, "is sought for and purchased by parties, corporations, and communities having these interests in hand solely for the purpose of developing water thereon to be conveyed as a water supply at a distance." Nearly all of San Bernardino County lands, continued Waters, "are of such class and of little value; that no one would think of sinking a well on the land with a view of bringing water to the surface and using it on such land itself" (Waters 1902, 40–42).

To show this was not unique to San Bernardino Valley, Waters drew the justices' attention north to the San Joaquin Valley. California's largest system of artesian wells was believed to occur in northern Kern County, near the southeastern shore of Tulare Lake. "[N]early all of the largest artesian wells," Waters wrote in late 1902, "are put down upon alkali land," the kind of arid desert lands William Brewer dreaded while with the California Geological Survey forty years prior. Three systems of artesian wells were developed for Kern County irrigation by Haggin's corporate offspring, the Kern County Land Company, and by Miller & Lux and another company, Cox & Clark. Waters continued,

> [A]nd in hardly any case can it be said that the water which flows from the artesian wells, or is pumped from other wells, is used on the land upon which the well is situated, nor is its use limited to what would be called an artesian belt or a saturated district, but the water is taken to localities where artesian water cannot be obtained, sink a well as deep as you may. (Waters 1902)

The City of Riverside, Gage Canal Company, Temescal Water Company, and the City of Los Angeles (which would subsequently acquire and export Owens River water to the San Fernando Valley), all of which depended on groundwater, were also vitally interested in issues raised in *Katz v. Walkinshaw*.

Walkinshaw had prevailed at trial with the declaration of nonsuit. Once the California Supreme Court reversed on appeal in 1902, however, the case became a cause célèbre for speculative water developers and monopoly water users alike.

* * *

The motion for nonsuit turned on the question of whether the Katzes, their allies, and their attorney, C. C. Haskell, had properly identified their source of water. Each plaintiff identified their water sources as artesian wells from "an underground natural flow and stream of water" and said that Walkinshaw "wrongfully and without any right, by means of wells and excavations . . . tapped the said underground stream and drew off and diverted the water thereof and did thereby prevent any water from flowing into and through any of the aforesaid wells of the plaintiffs." They alleged Walkinshaw had uncapped her wells so that underground flow could be "conducted to and used on other lands at a distance from and not riparian to said stream. . . ."[12] Throughout the trial, witness after witness testified to having lost all artesian flow on July 27 when Walkinshaw opened her wells, only to see flow return once her wells were capped. Yet no one identified a river or stream with a name attached to their water source, nor did they say it ran in a definite bed or channel with banks or sides. Walkinshaw's motion for nonsuit, crafted by her attorney Waters, maintained that the plaintiffs and their witnesses were talking about a legal chimera instead of a stream. The entire San Bernardino Valley basin was an artesian belt, he told the judge at trial, driven by percolating water, rather than a "stream" with a bed or channel.[13]

To expert witness F. C. Finkle, a civil engineer in private practice from Redlands, it could be seen both ways. Finkle's testimony takes up more than half the trial's transcript, describing hydrogeologic and hydraulic concepts, with lengthy explanations of local conditions. He had thirteen years of experience in southern California (largely in the San Bernardino Valley) practicing civil engineering. "[P]ractically all of my experience has been in the hydraulic branch of the profession," he told the trial court. Before entering private practice, he worked for the East Riverside Irrigation District and the City of San Bernardino where he was city engineer.

Finkle made the case for the defense that in fact water percolated underground throughout much of the San Bernardino Valley from the great alluvial fans gathered at the base of the mountains above. "The artesian belt is fed . . . principally in two ways," he testified, "by the underflow of all the various ravines and canyons and streams which enter the valley" on one hand. Water is also absorbed in the valley "from rainfall upon that surface, and by flood water discharged from the mountain canyons upon that surface, which enters it as if going in through a filter."

Once water reaches the artesian belt, said Finkle, it entered a netherworld constrained on the west by a large granite dyke that blocked it and directed the water flow to the southeast toward San Bernardino along the general path of Lytle Creek. On the east side of the valley there was another underground structure that pushed the water west toward San Bernardino, and in places like Warm Creek this subsurface flow reached an open riverbed of surface flow. The alluvium filling the basin was a vast admixture of gravel, sand, rocks, and very fine sediment.[14]

The water in this environment became artesian by filling voids in alluvium. Entombed under impermeable lenses of clay or fine sand sediments, the water came under pressure from other water upslope, continuing to flow downward, and looking always for the path of least resistance: sometimes flowing toward narrows where coarser sands, rocks, and gravels pushed the water to daylight in open streams; oozing out elsewhere as springs; or, if human well-digging allowed, through artesian boreholes from which water flowed unaided to the surface for use in homes, farms, and businesses.[15]

So far, Finkle described percolating water. But in cross-examination, and recross, he repeated that "it all moves in one direction which would tend to give it the characteristics of a stream, at the same time it moves—it percolates through the interstices. It moves down the inclination, practically at right angles to the contour of the valley." And while he could not locate any particular underground stream in the San Bernardino Valley, Finkle opined, "[T]he only way I could figure out a stream in the valley would be to say that *the whole thing is a stream.*"[16]

Whatever its hydrogeologic basis, Finkle's expert testimony was a victory for both sides: he convincingly described the basis for percolating water flow in the San Bernardino Valley, which seemed to offer support for the defense's motion for nonsuit. But he also accounted for why the *Katz* plaintiffs perceived their artesian wells as providing a continuous stream of flow: it was due to pressure being applied naturally to underground water from upslope as well as from a defined valley-wide geologic structure that gave shape to the basin and defined the sides of a "stream," broadly construed, though he acknowledged he was not speaking strictly of a "legal stream."[17]

Later he said pointedly of the San Joaquin Valley that he had been to Bakersfield, Visalia, Tulare, and Fresno where there was abundant fill between the Sierra and the Coast Range, where there was surface flow and artesian flow. "I think that the existence of artesian water bearing strata are explainable upon the same theory as the artesian basin here," he told the trial court.[18]

* * *

California Supreme Court Justices Jackson Temple and Lucien Shaw authored successive, unanimous opinions on *Katz v. Walkinshaw* that in California landowners possessed "overlying rights" to groundwater that are part and parcel of their landed real property; but this right was limited to a reasonable and "correlative" share of the water in the common pool of the basin in which it occurred. The evolution from a common law interpretation under Justice Temple to California's "correlative" doctrine under Justice Shaw emanated from specific events surrounding *Katz*.

Justice Temple authored the first *Katz* decision. He found that the common law doctrine view of groundwater owned by the overlying landowner was, essentially, limited by the noninjury rule: overlying owners may not use groundwater to such an extent they harm their neighbors. His opinion was based primarily on case law drawn from English courts and eastern American courts (including Pennsylvania, New York, and New Hampshire). He completed the opinion in November 1902 and died shortly thereafter.

Justice Temple observed dryly, "[T]he analogy between the right to remove sand and gravel from the land for sale and to remove and sell percolating water is not perfect." Quarrying sand or gravel from one's land does not remove any from a neighbors' land, while extracting groundwater in large quantities is likely to do so. Justice Temple wrote,

> If the water on his lands is his property, then the water in the soil of his neighbors is their property. But . . . [b]y pumping out the water from his lands he can perhaps deprive his neighbors of water for domestic uses and, in fact, render their land valueless. In short, the members of the community have a common interest in the water. It is necessary for all, and it is an anomaly in the law if one person can for his individual profit destroy the community and render the neighborhood uninhabitable.[19]

Justice Temple's opinion guaranteed dismay among private owners of water rights. As we have seen, the turn of the twentieth century was a crucial time for Californians' expanding access to electric power, groundwater pumps, and thereby, expansion of irrigated agriculture. Within a few weeks of his decision, petitions for rehearing the case poured in from attorneys representing southern California water companies and from Miller & Lux in Kern County. They asserted that Justice Temple's opinion gave short shrift to the nonsuit issue (Short 1902, 14–15) and that the rest of his opinion was important enough but simultaneously so vague that a broader airing of legal issues must be addressed by the court.

In the wake of Justice Temple's death, the California supreme court granted a rehearing in *Katz v. Walkinshaw* to consider the issues of the case "more fully, and by the aid of additional arguments as might be presented by persons not parties to the action, but vitally interested in the principle involved." *Katz* posed a question, wrote Justice Shaw, who was assigned to author the second *Katz* opinion of the court, "that is novel and of the utmost importance to the application to useful purposes of the waters which may be found in the soil."[20] The parties contributing amicus briefs to the court included six southern California-based private water companies, and the cattle, land, and water giant from the San Joaquin Valley, Miller & Lux.[21]

At the time, Justice Shaw was new on the California Supreme Court. Born in Indiana in 1845, of Scottish and English descent, he received his law degree from Indianapolis Law College in 1869 and practiced in Indiana until 1883, when Shaw and his law partner relocated their firm to Fresno. When his partner returned to Indiana, Shaw moved to Los Angeles, where he was elected to a judgeship in county superior court for two terms before his election to the state supreme court in November 1902. His official eulogy states that "the most vital and constructive contribution of Judge Shaw is found in the long line of decisions in which he expounded the law governing rights to the use of waters—a subject of ever-increasing importance in the semi-arid region of California." Of *Katz v. Walkinshaw*, the eulogy notes, "Judge Shaw laid down the rules governing the rights of owners of land overlying a common supply of percolating water, and this decision has ever since been regarded as the foundation of the law of California on this difficult subject." *Katz* was among the opinions he wrote in his first year as a California Supreme Court justice.[22]

Miller & Lux's attorney, J. S. Chapman for Houghton & Houghton, argued to the court that "it had become a rule of property" in California long before Justice Temple's *Katz* opinion, "that there are no correlative rights as to underground waters" and that "a landowner has an absolute property in and dominion over all waters percolating in the soils owned by him *usque ad infernos*" (Chapman 1903, 55).

C. C. Haskell, attorney for the plaintiffs, argued this point directly in replying to the rehearing briefs of the southern California water companies and Miller & Lux. He alleged that the larger context was that Walkinshaw diverted her water to benefit lands elsewhere and that speculators such as Riverside Water Company were carrying away San Bernardino water to other places. The vast San Bernardino Valley reservoir, he contended

> is being actively exhausted, if not absolutely destroyed. . . . The testimony shows that . . . when the supply is sufficiently reduced there is nothing to prevent these water corporations with millions of money [*sic*] at their command from . . . converting the entire artesian basin into an arid desert. When Riverside, Colton, Bloomington and East Riverside Irrigation District, all takers of water from the artesian basin, have driven their tunnels 150 feet below the surface and have destroyed this rich agricultural valley for all useful purposes, there would be nothing to prevent a more powerful corporation with more capital from driving a tunnel 200 feet beneath the surface and taking this water to the arid lands north and east of Chino and drying the orange orchards of Riverside and other communities dependent upon the water supply. The defendant contends that . . . any one may capture it who can. That might gives right. (Haskell 1900, 79–81)

It was the same process legal scholar Morton Horwitz identified among competitive mill owners on eastern streams prior to the Civil War. Haskell wrote that the defendants' friends "ask not only to be permitted to take this water without limit, or restraint for themselves, but that every other person shall have the same right, who has the strength, to take it from them—a destructive rule which only secures present benefit without regard to future disaster." And he concluded that the protection of present and future property values for cities and towns throughout the San Bernardino Valley depended on "having some rule of law established that shall give stability and permanency to investments." His argument was entirely consistent with the vested property-oriented legal viewpoint then prevailing (Haskell 1900, 82).

Taking up the briefs for rehearing *Katz*, Justice Shaw found a "misconception of the extent to which the common law is adopted [in California] and a failure to observe some of the rules and principles of the common law itself." He added, "[T]he true doctrine is, that the common law by its own principles adapts itself to varying conditions and modifies its own rules so as to secure the ends of justice under the different circumstances. . . ." Justice Shaw summed up that adaptability in this way:

> Whenever it is found that . . . the application of a given common-law rule by our courts tends constantly to cause injustice and wrong, rather than the administration of justice and right, then the fundamental principle of right and justice, and which its administration is intended to promote, require that a different rule be adopted, one which is calculated to secure persons in their property and possessions, and to preserve for them the fruits of their labors and expenditures.[23]

Shaw then recounted the arid conditions of "the southern half of California, especially below the Tehachapis," noting the deficiencies of surface-water supplies relative to abundant land (a noteworthy observation ten years prior to the California Conservation Commission's 1913 report) and that "it is clear also that the difficulties arising from the scarcity of water in this country are by no means ended, but on the contrary, probably just beginning."[24]

But applying the absolute ownership rule (*cujus est solum*, the idea that landowners own everything in their soils including corporeal water) sought by Walkinshaw and her attorneys "will tend to aggravate these difficulties rather than solve them," Justice Shaw argued. The logic of applying *cujus est solum* posed a serious danger to California groundwater.

> [I]f any property right in [percolating] water is recognized, the task must be abandoned as impossible, and those who have valuable property acquired by and dependent on the use of such water must be left to their own resources to secure protection for their property from the attacks of their

more powerful neighbors, and failing in this must suffer irretrievable loss; that might is the only protection.[25]

Granting Walkinshaw absolute ownership of percolating water in land threatened to give wealthy landowners incentive to acquire more land and water, forcing small landowners to defend themselves directly and without benefit of recourse to the courts (i.e., "left to their own resources to secure protection of their property" from attacks by neighbors).

In revisiting Justice Temple's *Katz* opinion, Justice Shaw may have found compelling Justice Temple's observations that "the members of the community have a common interest in the water" and "it is an anomaly in the law." They point to the need to use the common law rationale to adapt water law in California. By petitioning the court to apply *cujus est solum* to California groundwater, the *amici curiae* ("friends of the court") who sought the rehearing of Justice Temple's *Katz* opinion as a result got more than they bargained for from the new justice. "It is apparent," he wrote in the decision,

> that the parties who have asked for a reconsideration of this case . . . will be constantly threatened with danger of utter destruction of the valuable enterprises and systems of water-works which they control, and that all new enterprises of the same sort will be subject to the same peril. They will have absolutely no protection in law against others having stronger pumps, deeper wells, or a more favorable situation, who can thereby take from the unlimited quantities of the water, reaching to the entire supply, and without regard to the place of use.[26]

Viewing this specter of water-market anarchy among water users overlying the same groundwater basin—one in which they would collectively fail to protect their own individual interests in percolating water—Justice Shaw may have found the reason he needed to invoke adaptation of the common law to "varying conditions" such as California's, "where the differences are so radical as in this case, and would tend to cause so great a subversion of justice, a different rule is imperative."[27]

There ensued what some might disparage as "judicial activism," even though it justified stability for property values. Consistent with Justice Temple's previous opinion in the case, Justice Shaw applied "reasonable use" to the California situation because it "affords some measure of protection" for landowners using groundwater with respect to each other. His application of "reasonable use," however, did not stem from a largely economic motive, as Horwitz suggested for eastern U.S. water cases. Instead, Shaw sought to apply reasonable use under common law principles to solve *collective* water supply allocation and use problems. His "reasonableness" acknowledged and made a place in California water law for the common interest of overlying landowners using groundwater from the same basin. They had "correlative rights" with respect to each other. Analogous to riparian right holders along rivers and streams, overlying right holders had no priorities one over another, unlike appropriators. They had to share the resource. And like riparian right holders, the overlying landowners' correlative rights were paramount in the underground water supply; appropriators were limited to whatever surplus might exist year-in and year-out. Reasonable use and correlative share would be the bases by which each overlying owner's destructively competitive water use could be restrained. Thus,

> Disputes between overlying landowners, concerning water for use on the land, to which they have an equal right, in cases where the supply is insufficient for all, are to be settled by giving to each a fair and just proportion.[28]

Two decades later, and having been confirmed subsequently as Chief Justice for the California supreme court in the interim, Shaw looked back on *Katz* without regret, observing,

> The geological formation of the land, its topographical characteristics, and the aridity of the climate produced conditions so different from those of the countries from which our common law rules were derived, that the well-known rule that the ownership of the soil in fee gave absolute title to all beneath the surface, including such subterranean water supplies, was held unsuitable to our conditions. In this the court followed the fundamental principles on which the common law is founded, rather than the rules for technical application to special subjects adopted for practical use in the different conditions prevailing in the countries from which we derive that law. (Shaw 1922, 459–60)

By supreme court fiat, private landowners in the same groundwater basin in 1903 could become part of a collective relationship—a commons, let's call it—concerning their underlying groundwater usage if they chose to exercise it. This collective relationship could not be arbitrarily imposed; the *Katz* court merely defined the rule by which basins and landowners could apportion their property in water use and thereby protect themselves and each other. But they would have to act to create it, to ask the court system to adjudicate their competing demands. Because of the level of interest in groundwater management in rapidly urbanizing southern California, the *Katz* decision would have profound importance (a story ably told by William Blomquist, 1992). And Justice Shaw's reliance on reasonable use doctrine would show up again in key supreme court decisions, mostly after his death in 1923.

* * *

State Engineer Paul Bailey reported euphemistically to the legislature in 1927 that the San Joaquin Valley had an "imperfect water supply." The northern half of the Valley (essentially that drained by the San Joaquin River and its three major tributaries, the Merced, the Tuolumne, and the Stanislaus) had good prospects for securing water supplies with storage reservoir projects. But in the southern half, from the Kings River south to the Kern, supplies were deficient. "Here more than four-fifths of the mean flow of the streams is now in use although no reservoirs have been constructed," wrote Bailey. Groundwater supplements farmers' irrigation supplies, he stated, and the Valley "has enjoyed an attractive source of water easy for individuals to develop." Artesian wells were largely gone, replaced now by pumping.

However, the water table for southern San Joaquin Valley communities was falling, and "experience is demonstrating that these underground supplies are not sufficient for the full development of the overlying lands so that at some point" groundwater use will exceed its annual replenishment from rainfall and snowmelt percolating into the arid Valley's alluvial fans.

Katz v. Walkinshaw notwithstanding, from the autumn of 1921 through the autumn of 1929, average depth to groundwater in the upper (southern) San Joaquin Valley fell from 35 feet below ground surface elevation to 55.4 feet—over 20 feet. The worst area, Sidney T. Harding reported separately, was around Earlimart and Delano in southern Tulare County, not far from Tulare Lake's bed (California Department of Public Works 1931b, 422, Table 165). Harding warned that greater overdrafts loomed because large areas of potentially irrigable land were still undeveloped in Kings, Tulare, and Kern Counties (California Department of Public Works 1927a, 9). The problem was systemic, rooted in California's system of water rights for groundwater in which "each overlying land owner has an equal right to secure ground water in proportion to his needs," wrote Harding. "Additional development would only result in an increase in the rate of lowering [the water table]," he said. "Such additional development has occurred in the past whenever the prospect of favorable crop prices has resulted in an increased demand for irrigated land" (California Department of Public Works 1927a).

Harding believed the limits to continued exploitation of southern San Joaquin Valley groundwater were economic, not physical. If economics dictated the outcome, then only the strong groundwater users would survive, as Justice Shaw and attorney C. C. Haskell foresaw two decades earlier in *Katz*. Letting economics dictate use of groundwater threatened permanent economic stagnation and community impoverishment.

Harding timidly suggested that a hypothetical power could mandate groundwater pumping for the common good to reduce pumping lifts and pumping costs.

> Fully as large permanent usefulness from a ground water supply could be gained by limiting the draft to the amounts which the available supply could maintain without overdraft and lowering. Such a limited draft would enable

all pumping to be practiced with smaller lifts and greater profit. Under our existing principles of rights to the use of ground water where each owner of land overlying a source of ground water supply has an equal right to participate in its use, there is no means by which the draft can be limited to the supply, as in all areas in the Southern San Joaquin Valley outside of some of those served by canals[,] the ground water is insufficient to supply all of the overlying areas. (California Department of Public Works 1927a, 10)

"Fully as large permanent usefulness . . . ": what we today would likely call "sustainability." But by what power or authority would demand be limited to a sustained yield in a groundwater basin as large as the San Joaquin Valley? Harding did not elaborate. But he traced the problem to the competition among overlying owners who possessed "equal rights" to pump California groundwater and the initiatives of "appropriators"—individuals and water companies who wanted to pump groundwater for use on "distant lands."

Bailey's 1927 report had called for imports—in effect direct subsidies in the form of water itself—to the southern San Joaquin Valley, the Tulare Lake basin region.

> There are now about half a million acres in the southern San Joaquin Valley supporting prosperous communities, that are either overdrawing their underground supplies or are approaching this condition. These areas are constantly growing larger. Their available surface supplies are already put to full use. Therefore, new water from some outside source is essential for continued growth and prosperity. Without it, the level of the underground waters upon which the southern half of the valley is so dependent, must permanently recede over extending areas until the profit in farming is entirely consumed in pumping the irrigation supplies to the ground surface.

Bailey openly described California's tragedy of the commons in the southern San Joaquin Valley. "The complication in the approach to exhaustion of the water supply in the southern San Joaquin Valley is of state-wide concern for there is no simple means of relief," he wrote, adding, "There is no way to stop the sinking of new wells. All the overlying lands have the legal right to pump from the underground sources if they choose" (California Department of Public Works 1927b, 34–35).

Adding new reservoirs in an area that gets an average of 5 to 10 inches per year (see Figure 1.1) at the valley floor elevations might help, but "little new water would be created thereby" because so much of the surface streams were already committed to prior rights. Such reservoirs' main use would be to control existing supplies for later use, not to increase supplies generally.

Areas of the northerly San Joaquin River basin (from Merced to Modesto) were not available "because there are areas of deficient supply close at hand to the few regions of surplus." Bailey urged the legislature to look to the Sacramento and Trinity River basins as "the most accessible region of surplus." In particular, he argued that the Sacramento River flows that were currently used to "maintain navigation" north of Sacramento would then be diverted at the south Delta for use in the San Joaquin Valley.

Bailey envisioned a complex, cascading "exchange" of waters from the three main Central Valley watersheds—the Sacramento Valley, the Delta, and the San Joaquin Valley—in order to defray the southern San Joaquin Valley's water shortages and force Nature to subsidize the latter's growth trajectory. The Sacramento River would provide supposedly surplus water to supply Delta water exports. In turn, these exports would be "boosted up the main channel of the San Joaquin by a series of pumping plants, each one pumping the water over a low dam to the higher level of the pond behind it." The dams would themselves be collapsible during winter floods and could be compatibly designed to accommodate commercial navigation locks to allow ship traffic up the 160-mile San Joaquin corridor (California Department of Public Works 1927b, 36). Then these waters would be used in "exchange" on San Joaquin River basin agricultural fields, enabling export of water from the San Joaquin and Kings Rivers farther south to Tulare and Kern Counties to address the groundwater overdraft problems there.

To accomplish the last of the cascading river basin exports, Bailey then proposed new storage facilities for the upper San Joaquin River at Temperance Flat (a project never developed, but that is back under consideration eighty-five years later) and at Pine Flat on the Kings River. From Temperance Flat, water would be diverted just downstream at the Fresno County hamlet of Friant into a "Friant-Kings River" canal for delivery into the Kings River, where thirsty agricultural diverters awaited. From Pine Flat, Bailey also proposed that Kings River water would be diverted down a proposed "Kings River-Earlimart" canal that would cross the Kaweah and Tule Rivers before ending in the Tulare Lake area at the town of Earlimart.[29]

Other than these engineering concepts for the Central Valley and some reservoir projects put forward for urbanizing southern California, Bailey's report was short on specifics. Despite his brevity, he made clear to the legislature and the California public that the limits of groundwater and surface-water supplies were in sight, even though not all of the San Joaquin Valley's lands were developed. Failure to address Nature's misallocation of resources to California's landscape foretold economic disaster for the southern San Joaquin Valley's Tulare, Kings, and Kern Counties, he argued.

Harding's suggestion of regulating the groundwater commons—perhaps through adjudication—went unheeded. Bailey's suggested resolution to this tragedy of the commons was to obtain supplies from somewhere else like the Sacramento River basin—to "pour water on the problem" as the joke about California's preferred solution to water problems goes—rather than engage Californians on fundamental matters of efficient water allocation and use amid conditions of scarcity and intense and growing competition.

Their diagnoses were by no means lone cries in the wilderness. A committee of San Joaquin Valley agricultural elites in 1929 admitted to the state legislature that the Valley's success exploiting its own water resources was undercutting itself.

> Up to a certain point the two factors, abundant underground water close to the surface, and abundant cheap electric energy, made possible within the past twenty years a great agricultural development and sustained it, no matter how deficient the annual rain fall or stream run-off. Indisputable facts now show however that that point has been reached and far exceeded. The annual draft on the underground water supply now exceeds and has for several years exceeded any possible replenishment of that supply. The supply from the surface streams is utilized more completely than in any other area of the state. (San Joaquin Valley Water Committee 1929)

Echoing Bailey's 1927 report, the committee extrapolated to the legislature its view of the logical outcome of continuing overdraft of groundwater.

> There can be but one result and that result is now in plain sight. Steadily falling levels in the underground basin, vast expenditures by landowners in deepening wells and installing enlarged pumping equipment in their endeavor to maintain their crops, and finally . . . the reaching of an economic limit where further efforts cease and farms are abandoned, are facts now existent in the Southern San Joaquin Valley Counties. They are more acute and more tragic now in some areas than in others because of diversity in local water conditions; but their import is all too plain, and they point to but one conclusion. The present agricultural development of these counties cannot be maintained, and no sustained future development is possible unless additional water in great quantity is imported into these counties as soon as possible from regions having a water surplus. (San Joaquin Valley Water Committee 1929)

The state's Department of Public Works documented these falling levels for an eight-year period from 1921 to 1929 (California Department of Public Works 1931b, 359, Table 139).[30] Figure 5.4 shows the groundwater units that had the most significant water shortages in the 1920s, stimulating state water planning to alleviate "deficiencies." The upper San Joaquin Valley (from the Madera area north of the San Joaquin River south to the Bakersfield region and most areas in between of Tulare and Kern Counties) saw a cumulative depletion between 1921 and 1929 of about 3.6 million acre-feet, an annual average of about 452,000 acre-feet (California Department of Public Works 1931b, 359). The year with the greatest deficiency of supply

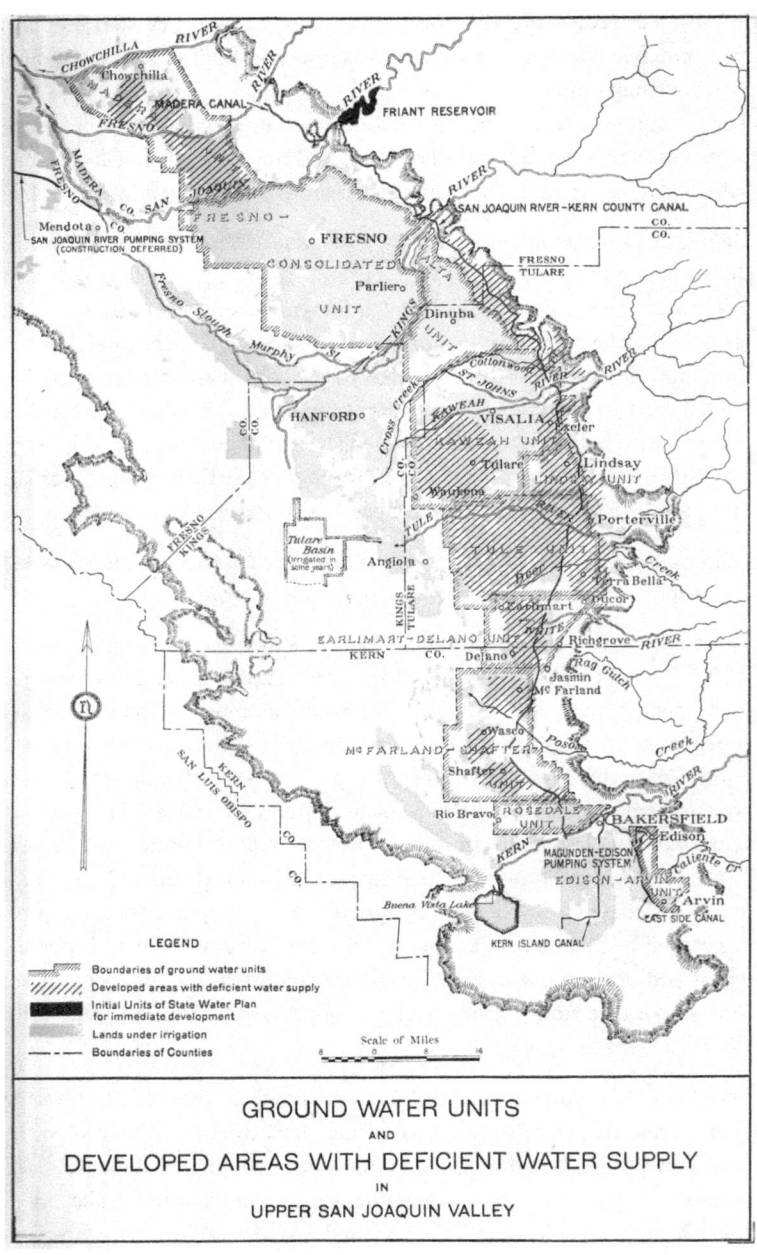

FIGURE 5.4. Groundwater areas and developed areas with deficient water supplies in upper San Joaquin Valley, 1931. Source: California Department of Public Works 1931b.

in the region was 1929, when demand exceeded available supplies in the region by 680,000 acre-feet (California Department of Public Works 1931b, 372).

Agricultural elites in the San Joaquin Valley could not imagine living within their hydrologic means and along with state engineer Paul Bailey essentially admitted that the collective use of groundwater—mostly by individual proprietors in the San Joaquin Valley, on preferred terms of unfettered hydrologic competition by proprietary and corporate landowners alike—did not add up. Yet where water supplies did not match their dream of putting all available land into agricultural production, we can see the early steps toward the "market vacuum" for water wherein government and Nature's subsidies contort and garble market signals. (There may be good or bad political reasons for subsidies, but they inherently interfere with and distort market price and cost signals.)

In Kern and Tulare Counties, pumpers preferred not to view their groundwater as a commons, contrary to the view encouraged by the State Supreme Court in *Katz*. Instead, they saw themselves as owners of absolute private, individual, vested property rights, even though the competitive reality in the raw data and their daily experience of falling water tables in the 1920s and early 1930s suggested such a proprietary regime would not last.

NOTES

1. On the water resources of the Sacramento Valley, San Joaquin Valley, and Southern California, see State of California (1913, 143–71, 188–229, 241–327). See also Mendenhall et al. 1916.

2. See California Department of Public Works (1927a, b). Changes in groundwater depths interpreted from Map 3, "Lowering of Ground Water for the Five Year Period 1920–1925 in Southern San Joaquin Valley."

3. California passed the Sustainable Groundwater Management Act in 2014.

4. *Cujus est solum, ejus est usque ad infernos,* goes the Latin distillation of the principle described in Harding (1936, 95).

5. Harding (1936, 95) notes the earliest such case affecting groundwater was Bassett v. Salisbury Manufacturing Co., 43 N.H. 569 (1862). His Latin translation of the principle was *sic utere tuo ut alienum non laedus.*

6. "That an action to enforce the right to water can be barred by five years' adverse possession we consider settled in this state," Evans v. Ross, 67 Cal. 19 (1885), based on Union Water v. Crary, 25 Cal. 504 (1864) and Davis v. Gale, 32 Cal. 26 (1867), 35. Cited in Hutchins (1956, 298).

7. Transcript on Appeal at 12, folios 45–46, *Katz v. Walkinshaw Transcript on Appeal,* 141 Cal. 116 (1903) filed July 6, 1900.

8. Analysis of *Transcript* in author's notes.

9. *Transcript,* at 74, folios 293–294.

10. The California Supreme Court case materials I reviewed contained no documentation of such a relationship, but Riverside Water Company was acknowledged to have developed artesian wells elsewhere in the San Bernardino Valley basin before the incident with Margaret Walkinshaw. Walkinshaw's lead attorney, Byron Waters, wrote to the California Supreme Court: "The City of Riverside, or what is known as the Colony of Riverside is supplied . . . in great part with water taken from artesian wells. Those wells are situated in San Bernardino

County and on the opposite side of the Santa Ana River from Riverside, the water flows from the wells into ditches and flumes, and is taken some fifteen miles across the land of other parties before any of it is put to beneficial uses. . . . In addition to this, the *domestic* water system of the City of Riverside is supplied wholly with water which flows from artesian wells; these wells are on the same side of the Santa Ana River as is Riverside, but the water is taken through a pipe system some seven or eight miles through or over the lands of other parties, and finally disposed of to the citizens of the City of Riverside for domestic purposes." (Emphasis in original.) See Waters (1902, 39–40). Accessible at the California State Archives, Sacramento, California.

11. *Transcript* at 61, folios 244–49.
12. *Id.* at 8–9, folios 32–33.
13. *Id.* at 73–74, folios 290–93.
14. *Id.* at 27.
15. *Id.* at 21.
16. *Id.* at 38.
17. *Id.* at 39.
18. *Id.* at 38.
19. Katz v. Walkinshaw, 141 Cal. 140 (1902).
20. *Id.* at 116, 120.
21. *Id.* at 116.
22. Eulogy of Justice Lucien Shaw, 220 Cal. 781, 785–86.
23. *Katz*, 141 Cal. at 124.
24. *Id.* at 128.
25. *Id.* at 128.
26. *Id.* at 133.
27. *Id.* at 133.
28. *Id.* at 136.
29. See map of "Coordinated Plan" in California Department of Public Works (1927b, between 26 and 27).

30. According to the California Data Exchange Center and a water-year classification system employed by the State Water Resources Control Board, these eight water years (1922–29) contained the driest year on record for the San Joaquin River basin at that point (1924) as well as one wet runoff year (1922), two above-average years (1923 and 1927), two below-normal (1925 and 1928), one dry (1926), and one other critical year (1929). Accessed December 27, 2015, http://cdec.water.ca.gov/cgi-progs/iodir/wsihist. These years were likely selected because they contain what was at the time a representative spectrum of water years (from critically dry to wet). The years were recent for the public's recollection and therefore participation in understanding the hydrology and water-supply problems the department was analyzing and evaluating.

Chapter 6

District, Rule, Decree

MARKET FAILURE—a structural mismatch between supply and demand for a resource or commodity—resulted once monopolistic corporations such as Southern Pacific Railroad and Miller & Lux gripped California's land and water markets. But monopoly of land and water was not the sole cause of market imperfection. The San Joaquin Valley's experience showed that Nature is not uniform in providing geography, resources, and climate of equal benefit to all places.

In California's case, geography and climate could impede irrigation and water distribution. Irrigation itself entails turning water out at some optimal point of diversion along a river, or pumping it from underground, for delivery through a gravity-fed canal whose proper alignment and slope could be deduced from the landscape by survey. Mendota Pool was an especially good point of diversion; but not all diversion points or canal routes are created equal, and good ones are therefore scarce. Topography and geology further dictate costs irrigators must pay to spread water to land where Nature had not otherwise intended. Yet failure to properly engineer water distribution to meet everyone's needs often reflected a failure to find that optimal canal route or foresee all other potential costs. When costs mounted—or perhaps as failures to foresee such costs grew—would-be irrigators understandably questioned whether they could afford to pay. Wealthy monopolists like Miller & Lux might afford them (although Miller & Lux did not necessarily have to), but most individual farmers or landowners could not. The gap between what private irrigation developers and their customers could and would afford on one hand, and costs imposed by the landscape on the other, could only be bridged by turning to government for action and relief.

Before 1880, few Californians would have endorsed the idea of having the state or federal government involved with private water rights and resource development. But buffeted by recurring economic depression punctuated by drought; thwarted by land and water monopolies; and humbled by the array and magnitude of costs involved in irrigating, Californians reconsidered this position at the end of the nineteenth century. They began building a movement for state involvement in water rights and water development before the ink dried on Justice McKinstry's 1886 decision in *Lux v. Haggin*. By the first decade of the twentieth century, the California water market failed to provide enough surface water to supply broad settlement of the land and meet the water rights claims by those who gained a foothold there. And as we saw in the previous chapter, there was also doubt about groundwater's efficacy.

In the aftermath of *Lux v. Haggin*, Californians *organized* collectively to acquire and develop more surface water locally. For this effort, the California Conservation Commission in 1913 offered the nostrum, "An ounce of monopoly-prevention is worth a pound of monopoly-cure" (State of California 1913, 19). Such local attempts often caused conflicts of their own when some residents and landowners declined to participate in irrigation development schemes. Later, as it became clear that just organizing new irrigation services was not enough, others sought to *rationalize and regulate* water rights, and then to *plan* for a coordinated, statewide water development project. Each step of organization, regulation, and planning required new laws and more government involvement.

Newly organized irrigation districts, as "subdivisions of the state," were to provide their service areas with irrigation facilities and water, based on new appropriations of water. Some had difficulty coping with inexpert farmers filling leadership roles. Other districts were merely speculative ventures that failed during economic depression in the 1890s and early 1900s. Still others survive to this day. Subsequent legislation expanded the variety of water agencies that could be created in response to geographic, land-ownership, and political or economic preferences of the parties wishing to organize them. To ensure they weren't simply speculative, the legislature designated the state engineer to evaluate them for soundness as business prospects. Today, there are hundreds of water and irrigation districts in California governing local water-resource storage and distribution.[1]

Equally important, many of them became fiscal and fiduciary vehicles for ensuring repayment of bonds for financing dams, canals, and irrigation- and municipal-distribution facilities. Private corporations could not raise the requisite security for bonded capital to build water facilities or were plagued by cost overruns once begun. The new districts' taxing powers within their service areas were granted by the state legislature to meet that financial security requirement. As such, irrigation and water districts blurred the line between public and private: public taxing and bonding authorities were underwriting irrigation service to individual farmers and landowners. Because of this rather unique identification of the irrigation privilege with public use, the proliferation of districts eventually provided sufficient tax base and financial strength to support the federal Central Valley Project, and later the State Water Project.

State involvement directly regulating water rights emerged from both *Lux v. Haggin* and the spread of special irrigation and water districts. The California Water and Forest Association, a group of corporate, political, and educational leaders, led efforts to get state government to regulate water rights. Initially, the association raised funds to hire the U.S. Department of Agriculture (because of its expertise in irrigation practice and technology) to investigate water rights throughout California. On the San Joaquin River, one investigator reported that the ratio of over-appropriation reached about 172 acre-feet of water claims to every acre-foot of actual water that flowed there on average. By 1914, twenty-eight years after *Lux v. Haggin*, voters passed the Water Commission Act, giving the state a role regulating new water right applications. Older riparian and pre-1914 water rights were grandfathered and became vested.

This period of ferment in water issues also saw the Water Commission Act foster "adjudications"—where water right holders could seek to end water conflicts by obtaining court decrees based on the best available evidence of water use in a river reach or a groundwater basin. Adjudications began almost immediately and continued into the early 1940s, as the state planned for the Central Valley Project. The CVP, the state's first coordinated water system contemplated in its water plans of the 1920s and 1930s, took as an article of faith that there was obvious surplus water for capture in storage and diversion to areas where supplies were considered deficient. But of course there were disagreements about whether a surplus existed, and if it did, its size.

* * *

O. P. Calloway, the Kern County developer whose settlement project and canal were absorbed by James Ben Ali Haggin in 1875, was hardly alone in the difficulties he faced matching surface water supplies for irrigation with abundant land for settlement. Elsewhere in the San Joaquin and the Sacramento Valleys, developers faced long odds anticipating and capitalizing on settler demand for their real estate. Many things could go wrong when it came to privately financed irrigation development. For starters, engineering costs of project design, construction, operation, and maintenance could be underestimated. Settler demand for land with water service was often overestimated, given the optimism of local real estate and irrigation boosters. The willingness of new settlers to pay user fees for water and drainage service could be exaggerated, especially if markets and prices for crops they grew were lackluster. Finally, the ability of private developers to enforce collection of charges and fees was limited. Risks were great; rewards were few all too often.

Passage in 1887 of the Wright Act brought hope throughout the state that a democratization of surface-water irrigation would enable local economic development to take root, that problems of community-based irrigation development could be overcome, and with it the grip of monopolists like Miller & Lux might be loosened if not broken. Behind the beneficence of irrigation lay what economists today call an "economic multiplier." The more farmers with access to inexpensive irrigation supplies, the more likely they could afford to grow higher value crops, such as vineyards, orchards, citrus, and the like. Such crops could earn farmers higher incomes than dry-farmed field and grain crops that were common then in California. Historian Alan Paterson wrote that if increased income occurred in "the anticipated community of small farms, irrigation was expected to have definite social benefits as well." Farmers flush with extra income and purchasing power would be sociable, not isolated; their towns would see greater sales of farm equipment, increased on-farm employment, and more civic and cultural engagement (Paterson 1987, 52).

The Wright Act enabled communities to form irrigation districts and design irrigation projects, obtain water rights (at that time under the California Civil Code previously discussed), issue bonds to finance irrigation works, condemn land for right-of-way or facility siting, and levy water rates and property taxes to cover the costs of district construction, operation, maintenance, and debt service. Holding an election took as few as fifty landowners living within an area that could be irrigated to petition their county board of supervisors. The board would then hold hearings as needed to clarify and modify boundaries and then schedule an election on the district proposal among all eligible voters within the area to be served—which could include cities and towns. If approved by a simple majority of the electorate, a second election was held to seat a five-member district board to govern the newly organized district (Paterson 1987, 54). Bonds could be issued any time the district was ready with facility designs and cost estimates. And they could do all of this without anyone looking over their shoulders or checking their calculations.

The formal histories of local irrigation and reclamation districts attest to the challenges facing private developers and early irrigation district formation, though of course only those districts that survived similar challenges lived to tell their tales (Barnes 1987; Basye 2011; C. F. Davis 1984; Kelley 1989; Paterson 1987; Swain 1978; West 1924). Many others did not.

Modesto and Turlock Irrigation Districts, located along the Tuolumne River in eastern Stanislaus County, were formed under the Wright Act. Their experience illustrates what every newly formed district faced. "After sixteen years of planning, endeavor, and disappointment," irrigation engineer Frank Adams reported to the U.S. Department of Agriculture's Office of Irrigation Investigations in 1905, the Modesto Irrigation District "had so far met the problems of finance and construction as to be ready to deliver water to the farms of the district. The problems presented at this juncture, however, were new to the people of these districts." The District financed, undertook, and completed a canal from LaGrange Dam where the Tuolumne exits the Sierra foothills. "[A] hundred or more widely separated farms" were ready to receive water deliveries from the canal. Suddenly the detailed questions and problems mushroomed, wrote Adams. Thus,

> How much water was it going to be necessary to deliver to each farmer for each acre of alfalfa or other crop irrigated? How often, and by what method, should this water be applied to the land? How much water was it going to be necessary to turn into the head of a 16-foot lateral to deliver the needed amount to 100 scattered acres at the lower end of this lateral? Should each irrigator receive his pro rata [sic] of the available supply as a continuous stream, or should he receive a larger volume for a shorter period? What administrative

officers and employees were going to be needed in the work of delivery and how should they be organized so that each irrigator in the district, whether at the head of the first lateral or at the foot of the last one, should receive his share of the common supply with that certainty and promptness required for successful irrigation farming in a dry, hot climate? How far was it going to be necessary to restrict the choice of individual irrigators as to time and method of water delivery so as to give that uniformity of system without which no plan of delivery would be successful? In a word, how should the district proceed to make the best use of the water it had obtained at the cost, measured in money alone, of $1,250,000? (Adams 1905, 94)

Embedded in questions about "how much water" lurked the practical matter of "head, booster, flow" that water lawyer Samuel C. Wiel would warn Governor C.C. Young about some twenty years later (chapter 7). For Modesto and Turlock irrigators, they were questions of central importance to their districts' irrigation engineering. Other questions addressed scheduling of deliveries, professional management, corporate organization, and district governance. Such questions overwhelmed farmers, few if any of whom were trained in business management, fluid dynamics, irrigation engineering, or cost accounting. But such questions had to be answered, without fail.

The Wright Act was overhauled by the legislature in 1897 when it passed the Bridgford Act to tighten petitioning and financial requirements. But economic conditions worsened, and the Bridgford Act's interest rate requirements on bonds made them harder to sell in the U.S. bond market. The political will to fix the problem seemed to have evaporated in Sacramento. To historian Donald Pisani, the Bridgford Act "virtually scuttled the district concept." Where fifty landowners were sufficient for a valid petition, now a majority of all landowners representing a majority of property valuation of irrigable lands was required before an election on district formation could be held. It also raised the electoral requirement from the Wright Act's simple majority to a two-thirds supermajority. And irrigation district supporters had not only to demonstrate that the majority of the local tax base supported district formation, they also had to design and accurately estimate the cost of irrigation works and delivery systems needed to serve the district ahead of time so that bonds could be packaged and voted on concurrent with the district formation vote. The Bridgford Act further provided an "opt out" process by which dissenting landowners could withdraw; a movement of seceding landowners could render infeasible the tax base of a fledgling district. "The Bridgford Act," wrote Pisani, "achieved its basic objective; no new irrigation district was formed until 1909."[2] In the eight years between 1887 and 1895, forty-nine irrigation districts had formed in California under the Wright Act; in the thirteen years between 1895 and 1908, no new districts were formed; and from the passage of the Bridgford Act in 1897 until 1911, just four new districts were formed (Hutchins 1923, 4, Table 1).[3]

As of 1911, only twenty-five of the forty-nine irrigation districts had issued any bonds.[4] Of the other twenty-four, eleven had been legally dissolved; twelve were simply inactive; and just one, Walnut Irrigation District near Whittier in Los Angeles County, was reported active and meeting its debt obligations (but had issued no bonds). Of the twenty-five that issued bonds, nine settled all outstanding bonded indebtedness; four exchanged new for old bonds and remained active; five more had settlements pending on their bonds, and seven were "totally abandoned, with no plan of settlement as yet seriously taken up" (Commonwealth Club 1911, 527). It was indeed a poor track record for the twenty-four years since Wright Act passage.

In 1911, the Commonwealth Club of San Francisco devoted its November meeting to the problem of marketing irrigation-district bonds. Frank Adams (who compiled the district statistics) reported to club members that "probably less than one-third of the districts that were organized under the Wright law would have passed official public inspection, such as some States have adopted and as was partly provided for by the last legislature. Of the others, a considerable number were dishonestly conceived and promoted. The remainder were either not justified or ahead of their times," but, he added hopefully, "there can be no question that more districts would have succeeded in more prosperous times" (Commonwealth Club 1911, 527–28).

Irrigation districts faced great difficulties selling bonds. One problem was that their enabling legislation mandated that the interest rate on district bonds was not to exceed 5 percent, making it difficult to compete for buyers seeking higher rates. Compounding the problem, six-percent bonds issued by out-of-state districts operating under federal Carey Act provisions had high failure rates, devaluing all such bonds and the lands that ostensibly secured them. As farmers went bankrupt during the panic of 1893, and national politics were roiled by the ascent of the populist agrarian movement, many bond buyers had been burned or knew someone who got burned. In such an atmosphere, California's lower, capped-interest bond rates were unattractive, to say the least (Commonwealth Club 1911, 554).

"Why should irrigation districts be limited to a 5% rate of interest," bond counsel Alfred T. Brock of N.W. Halsey & Company told the Commonwealth Club in 1911, "when the law allows school districts to issue bonds up to 8%?" Brock urged that the law be amended to allow district directors to set a bond rate at what they expected would be most profitable to the district and encourage competition with similar bonds around the country. At the same time, being allowed to set a competitive rate would enable districts to enlarge the market from which they could potentially raise capital (Commonwealth Club 1911, 555). (It would also help bond counsels earn higher commissions, it must be noted.) Indeed, "the investor is the person that has got to be considered in this matter," chimed in commercial banker James Lynch, because "the private investor is timid and he has a very long memory."

By 1911, much of the poor irrigation-district management that plagued bond performance throughout the West had been addressed by hiring professional engineers and business managers to manage district affairs (Commonwealth Club 1911, 558). Naturally, investors are deeply concerned with the security of their investments: how sure is one bet compared with another? The challenge with irrigation-district bonds was to assess whether "the management of an enterprise under a big corporation [is] placed in capable and experienced hands, and with an experienced staff," or a district lacking one or more of these advantages, investor William J. Dutton told the Club. All too often, he said, early irrigation district bonds were run by "farmers unfamiliar with the work, or with broad finance, and a large amount of money coming is liable to make them extravagant." He added that the talent pool of civil engineers who had designed and built irrigation systems was thin. If cost estimates and the value of issued bonds proved too low, more bonds would have to be sold, or "the work must stop, and the bond holders face the opportunity of becoming land owners" (Commonwealth Club 1911, 560–61).

Reliable water rights were key to the success of irrigation districts as well. Vested legal title to use water was the *essential basis* of an irrigation district's financial and hydraulic security. State engineer Nathaniel Ellery remarked to the club, "If we were to start irrigation projects to-day [sic] it would require litigation to determine the rights upon the streams." In his official role, he sat on a new commission (established by the legislature in 1909) to evaluate irrigation district applications from county boards of supervisors for their overall feasibility. He reviewed applications to confirm who had title to land and water. "Undoubtedly many of you know that the water rights of the State have been mightily mixed," he acknowledged. "Under the law as it stands now, anyone has the right to go upon any stream and post his notice and declare for so much water. To find out what waters have been appropriated under that method, it is necessary for one to travel along the banks of that stream and find out about those locations in that manner." Other states, he said, "have laws superior to ours." Their water rights systems were administered centrally: anyone could go to the state capitol to learn who controlled how much water or file their own water rights claim in one place. Ellery told the club it was time to correct California's water rights problem. "I think we are behind in this subject," he said (Commonwealth Club 1911, 545).[5]

* * *

Ellery's point about California's "mightily mixed" water rights invoked a study completed a decade earlier. In November 1899, some of California's most luminous elite created the California Water and Forest Association. Ten months later, the association saw membership reach 6,000, most of it from northern California. Its leaders sought to address the structural irrationalities of California's legal method for appropriating water. They clamored for statewide regulation and state responsibility for determining the validity and amounts of water claimed. Their voices were those of the Progressive Movement to reform government operations to incorporate principles of business efficiency, accounting, and analysis into the methods of governing.

The Association advocated a comprehensive survey of irrigation potential in California. Members raised $4,875 to complete the survey, even after the governor vetoed funds in 1899. The Water and Forest Association stated the need for the survey.

> [N]owhere in America are there irrigation problems more important, more intricate, or more pressing than in California. . . . We can offer, we presume, examples of every form of evil which can be found in Anglo-Saxon dealings with water in arid and semiarid districts. Great sums have been lost in irrigation enterprises. Still greater sums are endangered. Water titles are uncertain. The litigation is appalling. (Mead 1901, 10)

The Water and Forest Association requested a plan of study that would focus on the amount of water in streams; the "duty" (or use efficiency) of water in different irrigation basins; the claims upon water, collated by streams "and not by counties as now"; the nature of water-right titles; the adjudicated claims upon the waters; the amount of land now irrigated and the amount that could be irrigated; the potential for increased storage capacity in each watershed; and finally the extent to which irrigation can be expanded into new lands "by better methods of distribution and use."

The U.S. Department of Agriculture also established an Office of Irrigation Investigations (OII) to study how much irrigation was occurring throughout California and the West and devoted over $12,000 to its California study. In 1900, OII found that on many rivers throughout California more water had been appropriated year-round than existed in the flow of the rivers. The office carefully studied eight rivers.[6] On the San Joaquin, researcher Frank Soulé found that six different persons had claimed "all water flowing in the San Joaquin River" on top of claims totaling nearly 462,000 cubic feet per second (cfs). The biggest flood flow recorded at that time, Soulé reported, was about 59,800 cfs, "and therefore the claims of water . . . are nearly eight times the greatest flood flow of the river . . . and are 172 times the average flow per second, 2,680 cubic feet" based on data from an eight-year period of gauging undertaken by one-time state engineer William Hammond Hall. Of this state of affairs, Soulé observed wryly,

> As the water of the San Joaquin is not in the condition of an elastic vapor, one experiences great difficulty in understanding how all these claims could be satisfied. (Soulé 1901, 232)

This inflation of water rights claims arose because of the hands-off approach to water rights regulation California had adopted ever since statehood (the same hands-off approach that led to so much water rights litigation). It was only in 1872 that the legislature attempted to rectify matters, and then only a little. Declining calls by some irrigation advocates for the state to create a water rights office, the legislature instead amended the California Civil Code to describe the process by which individuals must seek to appropriate water. They were to post a notice no fewer than ten days in advance of when they intended to divert, and stating how much was to be diverted (often declared in a unit of measure known as a "miners inch," one-fiftieth or one-fortieth of a cubic foot per second), for how long, and for what use. They had to take the notice to their local county recorder where the notice was recorded as a legal document. The appropriator then had to diligently build the diversion works and divert the water to the use stated in the notice, and do so according to that notice. The civil code also stated that nothing in the law was intended to abridge the rights of riparian diverters, whose rights were not quantified (Soulé 1901, 228).[7]

Yet mounting water litigation, particularly in the San Joaquin Valley, but also in the Sacramento Valley and southern California, continued to prompt calls for state authority to plan, construct, and distribute water statewide. Private companies were not as efficient or as fair as people had hoped they would be. In the case of private water utilities serving San Francisco and Los Angeles, the cost of water was publicly believed to be excessive and Progressive-era movements to municipalize water supplies succeeded in these cities early in the twentieth century.[8] And as Frank Adams's 1911 research showed, public irrigation districts were in disarray.

* * *

With California's 1872 civil code system of prior appropriation, there was no objective independent party or government certification, no seal of approval, to verify that water rights claimed by appropriation were good and true. There was no oversight or verification, just a claim by a private individual, and an obscure one at that. Such claims could only be confirmed at one of the many county recorders' offices. Landowners and developers had strong incentive to inflate water right claims reported to the county recorder and in turn inflate land values for new farming plots. It could as well increase their control of water, provided they made good on their claims. For example, along the Chowchilla Canal (a conduit diverting from the San Joaquin River upstream of Mendota to the east side of the San Joaquin Valley), holding water rights and waterworks to irrigate multiplied by "at least twenty-five times the value of those [lands] in the same locality which remain unirrigated," according to Soulé (1901, 223–24).

Soulé pulled his punches against California's system for appropriating water, but his research method illustrates the system's irrationality. To study the San Joaquin, he first had to determine how many counties the river crossed to his point of study—the confluence of the San Joaquin with the Merced River. There were three counties whose recorder's offices he would have to visit: Fresno, Madera, and Merced. In sizing up the official notices, he noted he would have to make "diligent inquiry among irrigators and old residents interested and well informed as to irrigation matters."

The earliest claim he found dated to 1857. Such records, accruing even before the soft requirements of the 1872 Civil Code procedure, "were often very indefinite both as to the location of claims and the amount of water appropriated; but probably in the ordinary case the water claimed was, after use, turned back into the stream." Given the state of these records, Soulé's sighs of resignation, head shaking, and eye rubbing are easily imagined over a century later: "It would have been practically impossible, however, at a later date for another person to decide upon either the validity of the claim or the locality in which it was made, owing to the looseness of the description."

There were claims; then there was actual use. Figuring out how much water was actually appropriated on each stream was similarly difficult. His experience was typical for the other engineers collaborating with renowned irrigation engineer Elwood Mead on the California irrigation investigation. "The miners and irrigators in the early days," Soulé reported, "gave fanciful and arbitrary names to streams, gulches, and valleys, which later were changed and in time forgotten." In many other instances, smaller creeks tributary to the San Joaquin River might have the same name as tributary creeks on other rivers, including one as close by as the Kings River, part of which also flows through Fresno County.

"When, as was often the case," Soulé continued, no objectively mapped geographic information was supplied in the notice, "it was practically impossible to locate the claim unless some natural object—such as a ranch, bridge, or abandoned mine—was mentioned which happened to be known by some person questioned by us." Other streams that had been so heavily diverted that they "had sunk into the sands to disappear before reaching the main stream" had also to be investigated with local informants "whether any of their water, in times of flood, still reached the San Joaquin."

Ignorance of standard units of water measure also plagued the notices of would-be appropriators. Soulé grieved that "even in the cases of corporations appropriating large amounts," the units reported in the notices were incorrect and "often disagreeably prominent. Square inches and square feet of water were often claimed, as well as 'cubic inches' and 'cubic feet' under a 4-inch pressure [the pressure definition only applied to the "miner's inch" unit of measure]; and the powers of translation of the writer [Soulé] in endeavoring to interpret the real meaning of the appropriator were often severely taxed."

Again, claims to immense quantities of water, ridiculously disproportionate to the means stated for diverting them, were a common feature; and claims to "all the waters in the river" or to millions of miner's inches were frequently encountered in the search of the records.

Finally, unable to contain his exasperation, Soulé tells how he *really* felt about California's system of appropriating water.

> It was found to be practically impossible, except in the cases of the few existing canals, to ascertain if the water claimed had ever been used. The writer can conceive of no more difficult task for the searcher of records than to trace and pass upon the validity of almost any of the older water claims and indefinite statute prescribing the form and method of appropriation. (Soulé 1901, 229–30)

Multiply Soulé's experience by fifty-eight counties, and a twenty-first century reader may glimpse the embarrassingly tangled and uncertain world of water rights in California, appropriative and riparian, on the eve of World War I. With the basic record-keeping system of appropriative water rights in such a condition, and riparian right holders not otherwise required to quantify their rights, just fifty years after the Gold Rush, few in California had any idea who really held valid water rights or how much they could really claim, let alone what was actually used. How could anyone be certain of *any* water rights, let alone those that newcomers might hope to acquire? The question is especially *hydraulic* (in the sense of water under pressure) when one reflects on the judicial turn toward protection of vested property rights that characterized the power of corporate personhood combined with concentrated monopoly capital, and how those property rights determine the stability of return on investment in California.

In this light, Miller & Lux's commitment to shaping legal doctrine—which began about this time—was thus integral to establishing the legitimacy of what they knew to be their key asset: property value and its economic power to continue protecting those rights and values. Along the way, Miller & Lux shored up the inventory of rights for others whose property values were also dependent on California water law. Whoever could *demonstrate* the size, extent, and beneficial use of their rights to water would be more likely to retain them, regardless of public policy questions. Such asset valuation was no less true for young irrigation districts struggling to raise capital for their facilities. On the other hand, for any individual or corporation buying agricultural property, the cost of water had to include shouldering the burdensome cost of "protecting" the property right as a water right holder—particularly in fees for expert legal and engineering witnesses. When we also reflect on the faith and wealth needed to accept and make good on such risks, we can appreciate the steely resolve behind this generation's intense commitment to building dams, diverting water, and filing lawsuits that might benefit all of California—perhaps to the detriment of applying a more balanced approach to efficient water use.

* * *

Congress enacted the National Reclamation Act in June 1902, which got the federal government into the irrigation business throughout the American West. The Act created the U.S. Reclamation Service, precursor to today's U.S. Bureau of Reclamation. Many writers have ably chronicled the Act's passage and explained its politics (Hundley 2001; Pisani 1984, 1992; Reisner 1986; Stegner 1962). In existence just three years, the California Water and Forest Association published a draft bill for comprehensive water reform in late 1902, after the federal law had passed. The WFA appointed a commission (more like a task force) of leading lights, including Elwood Mead; Frederick Haynes Newell, the new head of the federal Reclamation Service; the presidents of Stanford University and the University of California; the heads of their schools' engineering departments; the sitting chief justice of the California Supreme Court; and a former state supreme court justice. All except Mead and Newell were members of the Association. Earlier in his career, Mead had revamped Wyoming's water rights administration with a model permitting system.[9]

The WFA's commission addressed the need for maps of all riparian lands, data for water volume in all streams, and information on how much water the riparian right holders were using and for what purposes. Its bill would also enable California to prepare a full list of existing (that is, what we now think of as pre–1914) appropriative water rights, with records on file with the secretary of state in Sacramento as well as with each county recorder. The proposal threw a commission at the problem too: new users would have to apply to a water rights board of engineers for rights. Claims could not be approved without meeting a long list of conditions. Since appropriative water rights increased the value of land that was previously without water, the bill would also attach these permitted water rights to the deeds on such land, meaning they could only change hands when the land was sold. The new agency created by the bill would also have the power to limit or reduce water rights if a permittee wasted water. It would have the power to adjudicate water rights in a basin or watershed, and its decisions could only be challenged in court.

At its core, the WFA's bill sought to remove some responsibility from the courts for determining water rights and place administrative responsibility with the state. Its authors hoped this restructuring would reduce court costs and attorneys' fees while increasing the efficiency with which water rights were determined in California. Historian Donald Pisani reports that the bill got much favorable attention at the end of 1902, but by December controversy erupted.

Southern California irrigation interests held a convention in Riverside to which neither members of the Association nor other supporters of the water-reform bill were invited. Speakers at the convention denounced the bill with a parade of horribles. The legislation was called "autocratic, dictatorial and nagging." Southern California irrigation companies believed the bill would "overturn the established order of civilization," reducing present irrigators to the status of "peonage" by substituting "a bureaucracy at the State capital in the place of local management." The Southern

California interests, however, ignored the administrative fragmentation, the water title uncertainty of so many other parts of California, and the excessive claims on the state's streams.

The bill died in the legislature from inattention, which Pisani blames on its being "swept up in other issues which undermined its appeal" (Pisani 1980). But there may have been more to its death than simple inattention. The WFA's draft legislation was debated in Southern California just weeks after the California Supreme Court issued its first decision in *Katz v. Walkinshaw*, the one authored by Justice Jackson Temple (chapter 5). Artesian groundwater appropriators such as Riverside, Temescal Water Company, Miller & Lux, and other *Katz amici* that were petitioning for a rehearing may have felt besieged, first, by a court decision going against them, and then by a proposal to have a state commission regulate all new surface water appropriations. This confluence of events may help account for the apparent suddenness of controversy that December.

The San Francisco earthquake of 1906 also delayed the Water and Forest Association's push for water-rights reform. Not until Hiram Johnson rode a wave of progressive Republican reform sentiment into the governor's office in 1911 did California progressives get another chance at water policy. Governor Johnson appointed the California Conservation Commission, which authored a report issued in early 1913 anticipating passage of water-reform legislation later that year (see chapter 5). Implementation slowed when another new progressive electoral innovation—the popular initiative and referendum—was invoked by interests (supported by Miller & Lux) to force a referendum before the electorate on the water-reform legislation. In the referendum, the legislation was nonetheless narrowly approved by California voters, taking effect the next day, December 19, 1914.

Overnight, the new voter-approved Water Commission Act remade the world of California water rights and cleaved appropriative water rights in two. From that day, there were pre–1914 and post–1914 appropriative rights. Pre–1914 rights were presumed vested under the new law and not subject to direct regulation. New appropriations of water were subject to state review and approval by an appointed water rights board. (While unregulated, the State Water Resources Control Board today is empowered to *investigate* prior water rights—both riparian and pre–1914.[10])

In current California water rights doctrine—only slightly changed since 1914—stream flows are first available to riparian diverters. Any surplus determined by the State Water Resources Control Board is then available for appropriation by other water rights applicants. When deciding to permit a new water right on a stream, the State Water Resources Control Board performs a water availability analysis.[11]

Advocates for reform sought to bring balance and certainty to water rights. But this addressed only who could appropriate, divert, and use water—the demand side. On the other side of the equation in 1900: how much water really flowed in California's rivers and streams, and how much could be supplied? No one knew. As the twentieth century unfolded, answers were desperately needed. Yet no one took up the thorny problem of excessive claims to water. Instead, under the Water Commission Act, these claims were grandfathered, with scrutiny occurring only on a case-by-case basis, if at all. New claims would at least be analyzed as to whether there was water sufficient for the claim and then subjected to permitting and licensing steps.

But the new California Water Commission engineers could not know how much water was truly available to appropriate, for there was little continuous flow data on which to base an analysis. Regulators, by law, could not actively regulate pre–1914 or riparian claims. Yet demand for new surface water rights seemed infinite.

Once Californians began obtaining data on actual water flows in all of California's streams in the 1920s, they learned that some 70 percent of the state's population lived south of Sacramento, while 70 percent or more of California's precipitation and runoff occurred north of that city. The agricultural corollary in the Central Valley went about like this: the Sacramento Valley was water-rich and land-short (its majestic, Sacramento River headwaters fed by bounteous volcanic aquifers and spring snowmelt from the southern Cascades and Modoc Plateau). Meanwhile, the San Joaquin Valley was land-rich (with several million acres of cultivable land), and yet its river basins produced just 10 to 12 percent of total Central Valley runoff through the Delta. Moreover, south of the San Joaquin River, only the Kings River ever saw any of its runoff ever escape to the ocean, and not in most years.

Bulletin 4, issued by the state in 1923, advocated that the state invest continuously in the collection and analysis of stream-flow records. "Reliable estimates," State engineer Paul Bailey wrote to the legislature, "can only be made from uninterrupted records of many years' duration." Fifty years' worth of hydrologic data went into *Bulletin 4*, but Bailey warned further,

> It is urgent that provision be made for the continuance of stream gaging [sic] records at least as extensive as in the past, and some increase be made in appropriations for this work if possible. The construction of all the great hydraulic works on which the future wealth of this state depends, must be designed in accord with those records of stream flow. It is important that they be continuous and on all streams. (California Department of Public Works 1923, 18)

The state's new data compilation for the whole of California showed average overall runoff dating back to the early 1870s was about 72 million acre-feet annually.[12] In the wettest years, California might see runoff as much as 2.75 times that average, or about 198 million acre-feet, while the "least seasons" were about three-eighths of the average annual amount, or about 27 million acre-feet statewide. California's precipitation, runoff, and consequent water supply varied wildly. But that volatility could be tamed and turned to advantage by essentially skimming the state's floods, wrote Bailey.

> The waters of lesser floods . . . may be caught by storage works constructed in the mountainous regions and be detained for later release to supplement the waning natural flow in the streams. By such detention of the flood waters for subsequent use, the erratic run-off may be equalized and made available to man at times convenient to his special purposes. (California Department of Public Works 1923, 31)

Equalizing the state's runoff meant catching winter storms in upstream reservoirs for later distribution during the dry summers. This was the basic hydrologic strategy the state put forward in 1923 and it remains in place today. But the plan went well beyond a simple formula to capture water in the north and ship it south, from areas where rainfall, snowpack, and runoff were abundant to areas where it was not.

According to this data-infused deconstruction of California water resources, Nature had utterly failed Californians' designs for the Central Valley. Humans thus resolved with not a little hubris to equalize Nature's endowments for the Central Valley.

* * *

When the Water Commission Act took effect, it dealt not only with acquisition and regulation of water rights, it also addressed how the commission itself would determine and contribute to the resolution of disputes. Up to that point, California had never legislated regarding the adjudication of water rights (Chandler 1913, 149). The Act positioned the commission as a "referee" for the "ascertainment of the relative rights to the various claimants" along a stream or water body.[13] While court decrees had been issued for adjudication among multiple parties in California, many other cases involved disputes between just two parties, allowing other latent disputes to fester. The San Joaquin River court cases often instigated by Miller & Lux exemplify such water conflicts "flooding the courtrooms."

The new Water Commission was a beehive of hydrologic and hydraulic expertise concentrated in state government. Its enabling act authorized it (on petition of claimants) to determine water rights and navigate complexities for a fraction of the costs to individual claimants suing each other over and over. This seemed especially important given the tangle of water right claims California had amassed since statehood.

While adjudication is a form of litigation—a judge is asked to determine and enforce rights to stream or aquifer once and for all—the Act's authors intended to move beyond iterative (and socially and economically wasteful) litigation. Under the Act, "the findings and conclusions of the commission, after being filed in the proper court and confirmed by its judgment, would finally determine in one proceeding rights which, without such a procedure, would be settled only by a large number of expensive and vexatious lawsuits" (State Water Commission 1917, 44; State Water Commission 1921, 34–36)." After ten years of working with the new law, state engineer Edward Hyatt boasted in 1924,

> When the rights on a stream are established and known, as by an adjudication ... the question of proper utilization of water on a given stream is practically solved. It has been long ago demonstrated in every other Western State that this method means complete success, and is the only method which can bring success. (Hyatt 1925, 134)

The first large, surface-water adjudication under the Act came on the Stanislaus River, initially addressing eighty-one claims in a 1922 decree. The commission compiled its determinations and completed a second adjudication on the river in 1929. The Stanislaus decree resolved claims among irrigators, power companies, mining interests, and residential water users (State Water Commission 1921, 37–38). Of the process, the commission proudly reported,

> This proceeding has demonstrated the efficiency and economy of this procedure as compared with the ordinary court process, and has the advantage of an impartial investigation and finding by the state itself, followed by a review of the courts allowing for correction of error or oversight by the Commission. (State Water Commission 1921, 38)

All of the water rights resolved on the Stanislaus in 1929 were pre-1914 claims. Some dated to the early 1850s (San Joaquin County Superior Court 1929).

With amendments to the Act in 1921 and 1929, the legislature settled on two paths by which adjudications could proceed: one, when a court referred a case to the commission for determination of water rights (Section 24), and the other when the commission itself initiated a proceeding under Sections 25 through 36. Both processes ultimately would return to a judge for final determinations and to set up permanent watermaster service (in which an expert engineer was authorized to distribute water according to terms of the decree and to enforce them). Both processes would take advantage of the economies of scale available from commission experts in processing adjudications.

By 1940, the Water Commission had twenty-five cases for which it had determined rights and for which the original referring court subsequently entered decrees. Another seven "statutory" adjudications initiated by the commission had entered into court decrees by then as well. The commission's record was rather specific geographically. Thirteen of the referred cases and one statutory case came from Modoc County alone. These decrees all applied along creeks tributary to the Pit

River, the Sacramento River's largest tributary north of the Feather River. Another seven referred cases came from Shasta County, most of which were either tributary to the Pit or to the upper Sacramento. A historical hypothesis, beyond the scope of this book, is whether any or all of these adjudications came in response to the state's plans to dam and store water at the Kennett site northeast of Redding on the Sacramento. The last of the Modoc and Shasta decrees were entered by 1940 when Shasta Dam was still under construction. It is possible these decrees were defensive actions, though State Engineer Edward Hyatt noted in 1924, an extremely dry year, that drought was also a likely factor (California Department of Public Works 1940a, 37–39; Hyatt 1925).

The Act was also concerned with distributing water as called for in the decrees it enabled through the aforementioned watermaster service. A 1940 state pamphlet described the qualities of a good watermaster in administering a decree: excellent administrative skills, impartiality, and competency since year-to-year water "is transitory, a vital necessity, often inadequate in quantity to serve all." Given daily and seasonal fluctuations of rivers, streams, and aquifers, a watermaster must also be expert and exude confident authority in the administration of the decree.[14]

In 1940, the state reported on its experience with the cost of adjudication. Water users covered by decrees split the cost of administering them with the state. Overall, the cost of decrees ranged from $0.35 to $2.00 per acre. However, the Division of Water Resources anticipated that the upcoming Butte Creek adjudication would cost "considerably less than the $0.35 minimum noted above." This was for resolving eighty-five separate claims on that creek, whose watershed covers about 300 square miles (California Department of Public Works 1940b; 1942, 7). The costs of each adjudication, borne at the outset by the Water Commission, were paid up front by the commission but were recaptured through assessments on the land involved for watermaster service (Hyatt 1925, 134).

Still, actually solving water problems in a pragmatic and permanent way was rarely in the interest of claimants. Up to this point, the Central Valley was just large enough—and just afflicted enough with real and feared monopolies—to make settling disputes with one's neighbors daunting and elusive.

NOTES

1. DWR (1994) reveals thirty-nine unique general district acts and 121 special district acts authorizing agencies and districts that provide water supply as at least part of their missions. The UC Riverside Water Resources Collections and Archives maintains a searchable list of URL links to 316 districts and agencies online at http://webarchives.cdlib.org/a/CAWaterDistricts/sites. In the 1970s, Goodall et al. (1978) identified more than 1,000 water districts over a ten-year period to give a snapshot of how water was governed at the time.

2. Pisani (1984, 277–78) quotes a despairing George Maxwell, an irrigation enthusiast in 1898: "No bank in California will loan on an acre of land in any irrigation district. No man who is informed as to existing conditions will purchase property or make investments in an

irrigation district unless it be as speculation—gambling on the chances of knocking it out. Home seekers shun the irrigation districts as though they were cursed with the plague. The system hasn't a friend left except those who are bondholders, or a few who are getting cheap water at their neighbor's expense."

3. Perhaps this impasse also contributed to the surge in groundwater irrigation development and electricity transmission networks during this period, a hypothesis for investigation by a historian other than me.

4. Bonds are a contract for a loan of capital from wealthy individuals or syndicates of wealthy people, managed through securities brokers, bond attorneys, and money managers, to a district. The loan provides funds up front to purchase and develop dams, pumping stations, canals, or other public facilities. In return, the district issuing the bonds promises to make regular and routine payments of interest according to a schedule. At the end of the bond term the full principal is repaid to the bondholders. Failure by the district to pay either interest or principal on the bonds is considered a default, a breach of the loan relationship with the bondholders, and the facilities built with the bond proceeds may be taken over by a party representing the bondholders, or the financing of the district may be restructured under more secure terms for the bondholders. In either case, default is a risk but never the desired outcome when bonds are issued and purchased. Bonds are typically categorized according to their level of security. The dams, canals, and irrigation laterals of the agricultural districts up and down California's Central Valley were backed by the general-fund budget of the district as a whole (that is, "general obligation" bonds), or by specific revenues from user charges from the operation of the hydraulic works in the district. Different types of districts were empowered to issue one or both types of bonds.

5. As an item of interest, his name now adorns a City of Los Angeles reservoir on upper Lee Vining Creek near Tioga Pass in Yosemite National Park (Browning 1991, 64; Gudde 1998, 121).

6. The rivers were the Susan, Yuba, Cache Creek, Kings, San Joaquin, Salinas, Los Angeles, San Jacinto, and Sweetwater.

7. California Civil Code Section 1415 stated: A person desiring to appropriate water must post a notice, in writing, in a conspicuous place at the point of intended diversion, stating therein:

1) That he claims the water there flowing to the extent of (giving the number) inches measured under 4-inch pressure.
2) The purpose for which he claims it, and the place of intended use.
3) The means by which he intends to divert it, and the size of the flume, ditch, pipe, or aqueduct in which he intends to divert it.

A copy of the notice must, within ten days after it is posted, be recorded in the office of the recorder of the county in which it is posted.

8. Spring Valley Water Company's monopoly reign in and through San Francisco is described in Brechin (1999) and Righter (2005) and the reign of the Los Angeles City Water Company is described in Mulholland (2000, Chs. 3, 8). See also Hope and Sheehan (1983, 32–33).

9. *Water and Forest* (1902) lists California Water and Forest Association advisory council members, the most notable of whom include J. B. Lippincott, the consulting civil engineer who worked closely with Fred Eaton and William Mulholland to secure Owens River water for Los Angeles about this time; Benjamin Ide Wheeler of UC Berkeley; W. H. Mills, benefactor of Mills College; former State Supreme Court Justice John Works of Los Angeles; David Starr Jordan of Stanford University; Will Green of Colusa County, himself a large landowner in the

vicinity of the original Central Irrigation District, later the Glenn-Colusa Irrigation District; and Frank Soulé of UC Berkeley.

10. There is inevitable disagreement over how far the board's authority reaches in adjusting such rights. But in 2015, the SWRCB expanded its scrutiny of both riparian and pre–1914 water rights when it issued a "drought information order" that stated "there may be unlawful diversions of stored water by riparians or pre–1914 appropriative water right claimants in the Sacramento and San Joaquin River watershed and Delta." The board issued the order because it needed "supporting documentation for the claimed water right including the property date and the date of initial appropriation," as well as information from claimants on water usage under those rights. See also Light v. State Water Resources Control Board, 226 Cal. App. 4th 1463 (2014).

11. This was the hierarchy of water rights at the time. Later California Supreme Court decisions, principally the Mono Lake Decision in National Audubon v. Superior Court, 33 Cal. 3d. 419 (1983), place flows to protect instream beneficial uses such as fish and other aquatic organisms ahead of all other consumptive diversions, with water rights following the historical hierarchy of riparians, then pre–1914 appropriators, and finally post–1914 appropriators. The state has yet to apply this hierarchy universally however.

12. To refresh the reader, an acre-foot equals about 325,828 gallons of water, or the amount of water covering an acre of land to a depth of one foot (that is, 43,560 cubic feet).

13. California Water Commission Act, 1913 Statutes Chapter 586, § 24, reprinted in State Water Commission (1917, 29).

14. There were still eight decrees entered after the long drought ended in 1934 (see chapter 9), four of which were from Modoc County and two from Shasta County (California Department of Public Works 1940a, 12; Hyatt 1925, 134).

Chapter 7

A Lawsuit Is a Poor Match for a Dam

THE 1916 REPORT of the State Water Problems Conference itemized three "particular evils of the riparian doctrine": "uneconomic use" (since "of necessity, only a small portion of the irrigable land is riparian, large areas of land, if this doctrine is strictly enforced, would be deprived of water for irrigation"); "insecurity of other rights to water" because of the paramount status and high economic value of riparian rights; and "securities made uncertain" (State Water Problems Conference 1916, 53, ¶159 and 160).

To its authors, the only way to counteract these "evils" was by resort to "adverse use" in order to acquire prescriptive rights usurping riparian use (in essence, attempt sustained theft of a riparian neighbor's water). Yet the possibility was too great that unspecified but apparently fearsome riparian right holders would successfully challenge the attempt to procure prescriptive rights before the statutory five years of adverse use was achieved. Such a strategy "is too uncertain and risky, however to be depended upon," cautioned *Water Problems'* authors.

Water Problems further alleged that "not infrequently . . . appropriators of water for nonriparian land have expended large sums in building reservoirs and other diverting works only to be enjoined from using the water after such works were completed" (State Water Problems Conference 1916, 53, ¶161). Its authors gave no examples, but they may have had *Katz v. Walkinshaw* in mind.

The final evil of "securities made uncertain" meant,

> [T]he existing condition comes very near paralyzing all water development in the state. Securities issued by companies desiring to develop hydroelectric energy, or to divert water for irrigation; bonds of irrigation districts; and in fact, any securities based upon any use of water, run the risk of attack at any time until, by operation of the statute of limitation, or by prescription, the rights to such water have become perfected. As water becomes more valuable, and the riparian proprietors obtain a clearer understanding of their rights, it becomes increasingly difficult to develop any of the water resources of the state. (State Water Problems Conference 1916, 53–54, ¶162)

This parade of horribles, attributed to riparian right holders, smoldered for a decade until Christmas Eve 1926, when the California Supreme Court's decision in *Herminghaus v. Southern California Edison* struck like lightning in the Central Valley, touching off a blaze of long-seething invective against riparian water right holders.[1] In the San Joaquin Valley where Amelia Herminghaus and her siblings had originally brought suit against Southern California Edison (SCE), the power company spawned by Henry Huntington (nephew of Collis P. Huntington, one of the original Southern Pacific "robber barons"), journalists and newspaper editors added disinformation about *Herminghaus*. Despite a publicly available judicial record showing that riparian doctrine consistently held sway over appropriation in California, the editor of the *Stockton Independent* claimed,

> In this state, riparian interests have been modified to some extent by the doctrine of prior appropriation and a more recent act sought to establish the further principal [sic] of beneficial use. In other words, the greatest use had the greatest claim upon the water. This principle now has been rejected by the Supreme Court.[2]

To fan the flames of discontent over *Herminghaus,* Madera-area attorney Sherwood Green, an anti-riparian advocate, addressed the advisory council of Sun-Maid Raisin Growers at the Hotel Fresno a few days after Christmas in 1926 on the subject, "Who Owns Our Streams?" The *Fresno Bee* reported,

> "The supreme court's decision in the Herminghaus case is one of the most severe blows administered to the state since the decision in the Lux-Hagen [sic] case in 1886," Green said.

The *Bee*'s reportage garbled both the riparian and appropriative doctrine. The appropriative doctrine was treated as "everyman's" water right—"being his to use or release in any amount reasonably necessary to his undertaking"—an idea more closely associated with the traditional common law idea of absolute ownership and rejected as inapplicable in *Katz* twenty-three years earlier.[3]

C.A. Barlow, then president of the California State Irrigation Association, called the *Herminghaus* decision "legalized robbery of the people of California." Barlow added in a press release picked up by the *San Francisco Chronicle*:

> "[T]he recent decision of the Supreme Court that a riparian right owner has a bona fide title to water and can place it to use or let it run to waste as he may see fit is a serious menace to the future life and development of the State of California.
>
> "The decision may be in the letter of the law," he continued, "but as a matter of right no man should have any title to water that he does not put to beneficial use. This interpretation of riparian rights would forever make impossible the co-ordinated conservation of the waters of the State."[4]

The *San Francisco Chronicle* reported later in January, 1927, that *Herminghaus* sowed doubts about the feasibility of combining flood control and water storage for power and irrigation in the Sacramento River basin, as proposed in state engineer Paul Bailey's newly released state water plan.[5] Using reservoirs for flood control and using them to store water for irrigation or power generation are opposing purposes. Reservoirs must be managed to make room for late-winter and spring flood flows, while at exactly the same time, dam operators hope to increase storage for summer irrigation demand and electricity needs for groundwater pumping and refrigeration.

Herminghaus also reminded the state engineer that he and his department of public works had somehow to acquire the water rights to construct the ambitious array of reservoirs and canals envisioned in his new $358 million plan. And some even interpreted *Herminghaus* to mean that building dams for flood control and public safety was precluded, since high flows could be among the "usual and customary flows" of any river in California and therefore part of the riparians' claim to their own legally reasonable use.

Herminghaus trial court judge J. E. Woolley retired between the conclusion of the *Herminghaus* trial and the state supreme court decision.[6] He wrote the *Byron Times* (eastern Contra Costa County) to take exception to its characterizing his trial court decision and that of the state supreme court as "highly radical." "The fact of the matter is," wrote Judge Woolley, "the attorneys for the Edison Company advanced for the first time the proposition that storing of water for the development of power is a reasonable exercise of a riparian right.... Far from being radical," accepting the power company's reasoning "would have completely overturned the doctrine of riparian rights..., thus seriously jeopardizing *vested property interests,* which results would have been productive of endless litigation."[7]

Also forgotten in the post-*Herminghaus* hyperbole was the court's observation that taking water for a public use such as power generation, flood control, and even irrigation, could in fact be done; the owner whose water rights would be invaded merely had to be compensated by the public entity taking the water rights. Such an elemental part of American jurisprudence, and a constitutional principle since adoption of the Bill of Rights, was ignored in much of the feverish rhetoric of the *Herminghaus* aftermath.

Nor was the California Supreme Court intimidated by public outrage. Despite turnover on the bench, on September 1, 1927, the court rejected the Fall River Valley Irrigation District's anti-riparian suit against the Mount Shasta Power Company on grounds similar to those in *Herminghaus*.[8] Clearly, the court adhered to precedent in the absence of legislative leadership or public initiative.

Before Fall River concluded, however, the politics of *Herminghaus* continued at a boil. The court rejected a plea by Southern California Edison to rehear the case in late January 1927.[9] That decision was appealed to the U.S. Supreme Court, which also refused to hear the company's appeal.[10] By early February that year, Governor C. C. Young convened a conference of power, irrigation, and municipal utility interests to discuss what legislative actions should be taken, and proposed legislation was sent to the legislature in mid-February.[11] A hastily drafted bill presented constitutional amendments to declare all waters under state control and to define and limit riparian rights. The bill would also have empowered the legislature to create a new state water commission (atop the one created in 1914 to administer water rights) appointed by the governor to hear and determine water rights claims and claims for compensation.[12]

In the febrile anti-riparian atmosphere during the first few months after *Herminghaus* was issued, one attorney for East Bay Municipal Utilities District managed to describe the essence of the decision.

> [T]he Edison Company must condemn in an appropriate proceeding the riparian rights of the Herminghaus interests to the extent that it interferes with the same and pay the damages which will be assessed in that action. It may then proceed with its development untrammeled by any claims from this group of land-owners. This damage is the difference in the market value of the tract with riparian rights as they now exist and what that market value will be with the stream regulated as the Edison Company proposes to regulate it.[13]

Both despite and because of its controversial reception, the *Herminghaus* decision in late 1926 ushered in the end of an era in California water law. A new era was dawning in which the state's residents—at least those paying attention to water issues—would come to rethink water rights and water resource development, both locally and statewide, as matters of reasonable use.

On two points, the *Herminghaus* court brought clarity if not resolution: first, surface-water users needed to use water *reasonably;* second, if electric utilities or other public agencies were to confiscate water rights claimed by others, they must compensate vested title holders for the value of what was taken. On the first point, the court found that nothing in state law compelled riparian water use to be reasonable with respect to the claims of appropriators along the same river.[14] (Analogously, *Katz v. Walkinshaw,* as we saw in chapter 5, applied reasonable use among the overlying rights holders to a common pool of groundwater but also did not require use to be reasonable with respect to groundwater appropriators.) Despite this lack of iterative legal accountability among *all* water users in California, the *Herminghaus* court's stance on reasonable use held the kernel for amending the state constitution to make the concept of reasonable use applicable to all water rights under state law.

* * *

Amelia Herminghaus and her siblings owned 18,000 acres of riparian land in Fresno and Madera Counties, much of the property extending along banks of the main channel of the San Joaquin River for about 20 miles where the river forms the county line. Their holdings included lands adjacent to Mendota Pool (Figure

4.2). The family used water for "many past years" to irrigate their lands. The San Joaquin's flood flows also coursed through their property over twenty natural slough channels that crisscrossed the landscape as it left the Sierra. Several minor channels drained to Fresno Slough. Some of these did so year-round, others more ephemerally, only to make their way back to Mendota Pool from the slough. Other such sloughs with higher elevation beds carried the larger flood events across Herminghaus property to Fresno Slough, thence to Mendota Pool.

The Herminghaus family's stance against Southern California Edison (SCE) owed much to the influence of Miller & Lux. Historian M. Catherine Miller found through archival research that until 1921, the family had shown little interest in their San Joaquin River lands, collecting rent largely as absentee landlords. According to Miller, they "had shown more interest in protecting their land from flooding than in protecting their right to water" (M.C. Miller 1989, 90). They resided in Los Angeles, not the San Joaquin Valley. One of their tenants was Miller & Lux. In particular, Catherine Miller found correspondence between the company and the family dating to 1913 indicating that Miller & Lux "rented this land as much for the control of water it provided as for the value of the feed" the water stimulated (Miller 1989). In 1921, the company, represented by its omnipresent attorney Edward Treadwell (whom we met in chapter 3 as Henry Miller's biographer), contacted P.H. Bottoms, Amelia Herminghaus's son-in-law and business manager, informing Bottoms that the family's water rights were valuable and "possibly the most obstructive to reservoir development on the river." Historian Miller attributes to this contact the germ of the family's demand for compensation in the coming court case with SCE.

The utility company wanted to expand its hydropower empire in the upper San Joaquin River basin to store water to generate electricity. That power would ultimately be consumed in the Los Angeles region.[15] SCE had already constructed a number of reservoirs and generating stations in the previous decade. The specific controversy grew from SCE's desire to add reservoirs at what are now Florence and Shaver Lakes. Florence Lake is situated on the South Fork of the San Joaquin above Huntington Lake, while Shaver Lake was to be built on Stevenson Creek at a lower elevation. Miles of tunnels drilled through Sierra granite would connect these reservoirs, ensuring that every drop of rain and snowmelt reaching them would have many opportunities to generate electricity as it descended from the highest Sierra elevations through SCE's tunnels and turbines.

But before tunnels could be completed to Florence Lake on the South Fork by SCE construction crews, and before new power generation could begin, the Herminghauses sued to stop SCE from proceeding with diversion and storage, claiming that their riparian rights would be damaged and their land values harmed by the hydropower developments.

Previous SCE projects had encountered the riparian rights of Miller & Lux, a downstream neighbor to the Herminghaus family along the San Joaquin River

(Figure 4.2). The two companies had reached agreements in which SCE would store waters from the winter and spring snowmelt for release to generate power during the irrigation season to benefit Miller & Lux lands downstream in summer and fall.[16] But confronted with the Herminghaus situation, SCE declined to offer any compensation or storage for later use. SCE wanted the court to ignore the Herminghauses' rights, arguing that its proposed use represented a far higher use of water than did the family's.[17] Harkening back to early-nineteenth-century eastern mill cases, SCE believed its higher value—more economically efficient use of water—merited special treatment.

The *Herminghaus* case contained in part a sideshow of two aging, practiced legal rivals in state water law: Edward Treadwell and James F. Peck. Treadwell, long an attorney with Miller & Lux, was on the Edison team. He was now in private practice, having been relieved of his Miller & Lux duties five years after Miller's death in 1916. James Peck, a longtime adversary of Miller & Lux, represented Herminghaus family interests. His past clients included western Stanislaus County customers of the San Joaquin & Kings River Canal & Irrigation Company (the Miller & Lux subsidiary) in largely unsuccessful suits that sought more equitable water rates and rights to the San Joaquin.[18]

Treadwell's arguments on behalf of SCE echoed the riparian-versus-appropriation politics that *Lux v. Haggin*'s parties employed and which were often replayed in the various San Joaquin River cases between 1900 and 1915: the Herminghauses allegedly wasted vast amounts of flood water letting it run on grasslands adjacent to the river where they (or their tenants) ran their herds. In Treadwell's narrative to the court, prior appropriation was again the water right of economic development and opportunity—the water right of entrepreneurial capitalists, industry, democratic opportunity, and technological progress. He portrayed the family's insistence on receiving "flood" flows of the San Joaquin River (in addition to flows at other times of year just to irrigate and overflow their estate) as a profligate and selfish method of water use—and therefore unreasonable.[19] Its continuance would crimp the ability of SCE's new power plants to generate power at the most profitable times of year for the benefit of a growing California economy.

Peck and his team countered that the "flood" flows were part of the "usual and customary flows" of the river, (because snowmelt in the spring and early summer could cause flooding on a regular basis). As a riparian owner for 20 miles, the family was entitled to receive the water unimpeded. Noting the many relevant precedents for riparian rights in California case law since statehood, Peck urged the court to stand on precedent (invoking the legal principle of *stare decisis*).

There was an earlier case, *Miller & Lux v. Madera Canal & Irrigation Company* from 1909, with facts from the nearby Fresno River that closely fit those of *Herminghaus*. In *Madera*, the canal company argued that Miller & Lux was not entitled to higher flows and the cattle company's riparian water rights should be restricted to lower flows: just as mill owners had argued for the industrialization of New England rivers, the provision of canal and irrigation services in its service area would stimulate broad-based economic development. The *Madera* court rejected this position. Riparians were entitled to the usual and customary flow of the river passing by their banks, regardless of whether that flow was high or low, and as even earlier in *Lux v. Haggin*. (In *Madera*, Treadwell was then part of Miller & Lux's victorious legal representation.)

The state supreme court decided the *Herminghaus* case on a 5–3 vote with Justice John E. Richards writing the majority opinion.[20] Born in 1856 in Santa Clara County, Richards graduated from the University of the Pacific in Stockton in 1877 and took his law degree from the University of Michigan in 1879. He practiced in San Jose with the prominent firm of Moore, Lane & Leib, crediting his time there with imbuing in him a "great love of the law and legal research. . . ."[21] He had served eleven years as an appellate judge, later in his career, when Governor Richardson appointed him to the state supreme court in 1924. *Herminghaus* was among the first decisions he authored in his time with the high court. He died in 1932.

James Peck's argument for *stare decisis* swayed the *Herminghaus* court. Justice Richards cited *Madera* favorably at least three times and *Lux v. Haggin* once. "Wild irrigation," characterized by Treadwell himself a few years later in Henry Miller's biography (see chapter 3), was more or less sustained in Richards's *Herminghaus* opinion as characterizing a reasonable use of the usual and customary flow of the San Joaquin River. But the case raised issues beyond the riparian-appropriative duality.

For the sake of equalizing electricity generation throughout the year, the SCE dams at Florence and Shaver Lakes would impound waters from the San Joaquin River and prevent higher flows from reaching Herminghaus lands. Justice Richards agreed with trial judge Woolley and the Herminghauses that these higher flows were part of the "usual and customary flows" of the San Joaquin. Because these flows are "parcel to the land," Richards opined that continuous deprivation of waters to the family's lands by SCE was sufficient to demonstrate damage, deprivation "of a valuable part of the riparian's estate."

> The flow of natural water over land is a continuous source of fertility and benefit; and its withdrawal is followed by consequences which are perpetually injurious to the freehold. . . . It is not true, therefore, as claimed by appellants, that the water of a natural stream may be taken away from land for a great number of years, and then turned back, without any permanent injury to the land.[22]

Justice Richards directs our attention to the ecological importance of water flowing in river channels and across floodplains that riparian water rights kept intact: flood waters passing over land replenishes fertility, recharges groundwater, and benefits Nature as well as human economic activity. The rejuvenating properties of flood events—spreading silt and nutrients from an upper watershed to a lower floodplain—has long been recognized across the world, perhaps most notably in Egypt's Nile River valley, which owed its fertility to the Nile's annual flooding. The *Herminghaus* plaintiffs and Justice Richards merely affirmed a well-known and ancient truth—albeit one that was unpopular in 1920s California—about the virtues of flooding the landscape when Nature offered the opportunity.

The court recognized that even in a capitalist society, Nature provides economic assets and services through the spontaneous service of flooding, a facet of water ecology that can make human property both economically productive and valuable. This relationship is at least partially protected by riparian rights. But, wrote Justice Richards, when such an injury occurs between an appropriator and a riparian, the riparian is entitled to restrain the appropriator's diversion to the extent it deprives the riparian of the usual and customary flow of water that is or may be beneficial to his land. He added ominously that the riparian "is not limited by any measure of reasonableness" to the appropriator as a matter of current law. Echoing *Lux v. Haggin*, he reminded SCE and its many allies that "public policy is at best a vague and uncertain guide, and no considerations of policy can justify the taking of private property without compensation."[23]

In the view of the court's majority, SCE sought the Herminghaus water properties without paying for them, a violation of longstanding constitutional principle. Although as a public utility SCE could assert that the water was for public benefit—the generation of electric power for a large region of central and southern California—the U.S. constitutional prohibition against taking property without just compensation should still apply. Thus, if the value of these new power uses was so great, SCE could afford to compensate the Herminghauses.[24] Eminent domain was the solution for obtaining private property to serve public purposes, said the court.[25]

Richards's finding damned SCE's refusal to compensate the Herminghauses just halfway through the opinion. Treadwell and the other Edison attorneys had marshaled other arguments. As Judge Woolley wrote to the *Byron Times*, SCE claimed a right to create storage on its lands because it owned riparian frontage on the San Joaquin River; and if that reasoning wasn't acceptable to the court, SCE also claimed a right to create storage there with an appropriative claim it had filed under the California Civil Code and the California Water Commission Act of 1913 (as well as a Federal Power Commission license for the intended project).

SCE's claim to create storage because it owned the Big Creek property as a riparian parcel was audacious.[26] Justice Richards greeted the claim by reciting the bundle of rights that customarily accompany riparian access to the use of water.

> [Southern California Edison Company] is entitled to the reasonable use of said waters and of the ordinary and usual flow thereof for such customary

and domestic uses as inhere in riparian owners along similar streams, and for irrigation of their said riparian lands. Being an upper riparian owner along said stream and the tributaries thereof, it is entitled to the benefit of whatever reasonable waste or diminution of said waters occurs during and in the course of the reasonable exercise of its riparian rights therein. In addition to the foregoing usual and customary uses of said waters, the appellant [SCE] is entitled to make appropriate use of the same for the development of power and electrical energy.[27]

But the trial court found, and Justice Richards agreed, that the riparian right does not include the right to divert *and store* a quantity that amounts to the "usual and ordinary flow" of the river. Doing so, "for periods and to an extent . . . would practically effectuate a withdrawal of said waters from a large portion" of the Herminghaus lands "during the period in each season when they are benefited by its flow and overflow, especially in and through those slough and channels which are wont to convey such waters to the plaintiffs' higher lands." The trial court rejected the riparian claim to store water, stating that it was "not sustainable as a matter of law."

SCE asked the court not to review the facts of their proposed operation of their hydropower reservoir but to reconsider the matter of law. The company put before the court a series of cases from other states "wherein a qualified right of an upper riparian proprietor to impound the waters of a stream has been recognized." Justice Richards noted they referred "in the main to a mere temporary detention of water by dams during periods of scant flow in order to [sustain] the uninterrupted operation of mills or water-wheels which would otherwise be insufficiently supplied with their usual and expected quantum of water required for their continued activities."[28]

The cases did not match with the facts in *Herminghaus*, wrote Richards:

> the defendants [SCE] frankly admit that their proposed plans . . . hold in contemplation the retirement of said waters for long and indefinite periods of time; in fact, admit that as to certain of said reservoirs the sequestration of the portion of the said waters stored therein will be cyclic; and . . . their ultimate return to the river would depend not at all upon the claims and asserted rights of lower riparian owners to the usual, natural, and ordinary flow of said waters, but altogether upon the will and convenience of the defendants in their proposed utilization of said waters for power production.[29]

Excusing SCE from its riparian obligations (among them, to participate in a commons with other riparians along the same stream), wrote Justice Richards, "would put an end to the whole doctrine of riparian rights, not only as to these plaintiffs and all other lower riparian owners similarly situated, but also as to the defendants themselves." To decide thus would give the green light to upstream riparians to build dams and monopolize control of rivers throughout California. It would destroy the riparian commons, should corporations such as SCE use a riparian right to store river flow for power production.

There remained SCE's appropriative claim to store the water on Big Creek. Justice Richards restated that Herminghaus riparian rights trumped the appropriative claim because of their right to the usual and customary flow of the river. In rebuttal, SCE contended that portions of the Water Commission Act limited Herminghaus riparian rights and enabled SCE to store "unlimited amounts" of water on the upper San Joaquin River. SCE's attorneys pointed to Section 11 of the Act, which stated that if there were waters not put to useful or beneficial purpose on riparian lands for up to ten consecutive years after passage of the Act, then those waters were presumed to be available for appropriation by other water users. Justice Richards rejected this interpretation of Section 11 as irrelevant to the facts in *Herminghaus*: the waters applied to Herminghaus lands had replenished fertility of its grasses and other vegetation usable by their cattle, a recognizable beneficial use, and were not available for appropriation.

Treadwell and his SCE legal team further argued that Section 42 of the Act also called for use of no more than 2.5 acre-feet of water in the irrigation of uncultivated areas of land not devoted to cultivated crops. To Justice Richards and the court majority, Herminghaus lands used water from riparian access "in the annual production of crops or cattle." Though on uncultivated lands, it was an entirely reasonable use of water, regardless of the amount. During the 1920s, state water-use researchers had fanned out across the Central Valley to determine the "duty of water" for many crops throughout the Central Valley and found the water needs of different crops highly variable.[30] Richards determined that the legislature's assignment of a 2.5 acre-foot per acre "duty of water" was arbitrary and therefore unlawful: "To concede this would be to concede to the legislative department of the state government the arbitrary power to destroy vested rights in private property of every kind and character."[31]

Legions of *Herminghaus* critics were outraged at this seeming frontal attack on a measure thought to require greater efficiency of water use. The perception, if not the reality, that appropriative rights had achieved supremacy over riparian rights was probably due to the rapid growth of irrigated agriculture in the Central Valley and the rapid arrival and expansion of hydroelectricity from mountain "installations" serving the cities of the Central Valley and the coast. Justice Richards and the court majority dashed that perception and with it the "duty of water" section of the Water Commission Act that seemed to demand accountability for monopolizing water wasters. Yet, irrigated lands had increased from 60,000 acres in 1870 to 1.45 million acres in 1899 and 4.2 million acres by 1919.[32] Though Justice Richards ran the table for riparian interests through SCE's arguments and upheld the constitutional obligation of public entities to compensate taken property justly, irrigated agriculture had in fact expanded.

* * *

To longtime water rights lawyer Samuel C. Wiel of San Francisco, the heated aftermath of *Herminghaus* may have seemed a once-in-a-lifetime teaching moment. How often had such a clear opportunity appeared to educate the California public about water rights as a unique species of property law, as instruments of economic and agricultural development, that most profoundly affect communities throughout the state? Never, though he had lectured on water law from time to time at UC Berkeley across the Bay from his San Francisco office.

Born July 24, 1878, Samuel Charles Wiel was the last of the four sons of Lewis and Henrietta Wiel, Prussian immigrants in the late 1860s or 1870s. Their sons were born in Maryland, though Lewis and Henrietta reported them in San Francisco to the 1880 census, once they were there. Other biographical data on Samuel Wiel is sparse, suggesting he preferred to protect his privacy and let his law practice and legal writings speak for him. But a biographical index card from the California State Library reveals he was educated in San Francisco and at the University of California, earning his law degree in 1902 from Harvard Law School. By 1905, he published the first edition of his two-volume *Water Rights in the Western States;* and in 1911, it was already in a third edition. He signed his numerous law review articles, "Samuel C. Wiel, San Francisco, California." According to his *San Francisco Chronicle* obituary in March 1951, he was the son of California pioneers and had resided at the Fairmont Hotel.

Upon learning the results of Governor Young's hastily called water conference in early February 1927, Wiel wrote him immediately to express profound legal and scientific concerns regarding the direction in which legislative proposals were heading. Governor Young, California's last progressive Republican governor, had just been elected in a landslide in November. Wiel subsequently published their ensuing correspondence, as well as that with some of the leading water rights attorneys in California (many of whose clients were riparian water right holders, of course) in the San Francisco legal newspaper, *The Recorder.* Wiel also compiled the correspondence as a political pamphlet intended for easy distribution with the unassuming title "Rights to the Use of Water in California" (Figure 7.1).

Wiel designed his pamphlet to evoke the formality of a ballot title, a legally solemn, politically important document. He asked, "Shall constitutional amendments in the interest of the extensive mountain installations manipulating the streams at their sources forbid the courts from recognizing the rights of large numbers of people in the valleys below them, and so thoroughly that not a single landowner in the State with land bordering a stream will be safe from loss?" By "mountain installations," he meant the hydroelectric power plants and dams with

> # Rights to the Use of Water in California.
>
> Correspondence between
> GOVERNOR YOUNG
> and SAMUEL C. WIEL, of the San Francisco Bar, one of the leading authorities in the West upon the law of waters; LUCIEN SHAW, formerly Chief Justice of the California Supreme Court, who formulated the doctrine of underground waters; WARD CHAPMAN of Los Angeles, authority upon Southern California water conditions, and H. M. WRIGHT of San Francisco, formerly United States Master in Chancery, who tried the Spring Valley rate cases.
>
> Shall constitutional amendments in the interest of the extensive mountain installations manipulating the streams at their sources forbid the courts from recognizing the rights of large numbers of people in the valleys below them, and so thoroughly that not a single landowner in the State with land bordering a stream will be safe from the loss?

FIGURE 7.1. Rights to the Use of Water in California (pamphlet cover), by Samuel C. Wiel, 1927. Courtesy of University of California, Riverside, Special Collections, Water Resources Collections and Archives.

generators owned by private utilities such as SCE and Pacific Gas and Electric Company. "Lower levels" meant water right holders (many of them riparians) positioned downstream of the mountain installations. Did people want monopolies established through dams at the headwaters of major rivers that would prevent riparian landowners from diverting their rightful "usual and customary flows"?

The pamphlet today reads like a cross between Tom Paine and a water lawyer's closing statement in court. It states that *Herminghaus* "resulted in a definite movement on the part of the water power and other mountain installations to procure the submission to the people of constitutional amendments having the effect of A GENERAL RELEASE OF THE CORPORATIONS from obligation to compensate valley landowners along streams for damage to the value of their lands caused by interference with the stream sources" (Wiel et al. 1927, emphasis in original). At the outset of the agitation by *Herminghaus* opponents, Wiel wrote, one proposal sought to abolish all riparian water rights dating back to statehood and to nullify all pro-riparian water right court decisions. The pamphlet's introduction urges that "EVERY LANDOWNER BORDERING A STREAM in any county of the State write to the Governor, and also to his Senators and Assemblymen, and let them know that he expects a vote of absolute protection," for their vested property rights (Wiel et al. 1927, 3, emphasis in original).

In writing to Governor Young, Wiel offered that, first, the governor should bear in mind that riparian water right holders were many: "They are the farms and residences scattered over the State along the banks of streams," and California was cut everywhere by rivers and streams, from the coastal and mountain forests to the driest desert region. "Your conferees," Wiel warned politely, "obscure the great numerical extent of people that your conferees have against them."

Second, Wiel feared that the stampede to build mountain installations would lead to wholesale drying up of all watercourses in California, though he did not say so directly. Instead he argued from science and law. The conferees underestimated water itself, he asserted. The path of water in streams must overcome geography through "inertia, seepage, and evaporation on the way, and these mean the pressure of enough water in addition to the consumptive amount to create an hydraulic force for the journey." The increment of water needed to maintain flow just to get amounts intended for consumptive use was not "wantonly wasted," as the governor's conferees asserted. This increment, Wiel said, was in fact the river's "head," its hydraulic force doing naturally the work of delivering what water right holders claimed (whether riparian or appropriative).[33] He requested that Governor Young consider "what would happen from its removal."

> There can very evidently be no water supply with its head cut off. . . . Since supply cannot arrive merely by wings, the head, the booster, or hydraulic force is necessarily the most essential purpose of all, if lower uses are to be allowed anywhere. . . . [M]uch difficulty would be spared in all dealings with streams if the natural relation of head or booster to water rights were not so surprisingly misapprehended. The necessity for enough water over the consumptive amount to furnish a "push-it-to-him" force is an elementary consequence of distance from the source, character of country crossed, and flatness of slope, increasing as they decrease. I believe you will feel satisfied that in calling this wanton waste, your conferees go too far. By recognizing this law of hydraulics, universal and imperative by nature itself, the Herminghaus case has done nothing but keep its touch with sanity where your conferees, by their resentment of it, are indulging in the fantasy of resenting Providence for the way it created the Elements.
>
> [T]here is no doubt that the law must adjust its provisions to its powers. The possibilities for legal measures for streams are limited by natural factors—a fixed source and motion therefrom—which cannot be changed by us. (Wiel et al. 1927, 4)

It is not every day that an open letter appeals to a sitting governor's sense of fluid dynamics. What Wiel described to the Governor was practically the same concept as engineer Frank Adams had noted as a key problem for new irrigation districts serving their customers: how much water was needed to deliver what would be needed for flow all the way to the end of the lateral ditch, or in Wiel's case, the user at the mouth of the stream (the "push-it-to-him" force)? The question is as valid for natural rivers and creeks as it is for human-built irrigation ditches and canals.

The recent Colorado River experience among the seven states dividing its waters also bore out Wiel's point. The upper-basin states of Wyoming, Colorado, Utah, and New Mexico, and the lower-basin states of Nevada, California, and Arizona arrived at a compact in 1922, based on what by 1927 became evident as an inflated and unrealistic quantity. The lower-basin states, especially California, were forced to accept a lower allocation of guaranteed water supply than in the original compact to gain Congress's passage of the Boulder Canyon Project Act in 1928 (Hundley 2009, 273–75; 2001, 211–23; McWilliams 1976, 308–16; Wiel 1923).

The Sacramento water conferees, Wiel argued, proposed to quantify riparian rights (rather than abolish them): all would have a definite quantity from the river, "while denying them the benefit of booster, head, or hydraulic force." But they misunderstood *what a river is*. He likened their view to "cutting links out of a sausage string," or "some elongated reservoir that wherever tapped remains replete like the magic cup in the fairy tale" (Wiel et al. 1927, 7).

Wiel adds slyly yet emphatically to the governor, "The repugnancy that 'keeps the word of promise to the ear and breaks it to one's hope[!]'" The people who have your ear on this water issue, Wiel implies, are feeding you a line. They want you to believe that downstream riparians are unaffected by the fate of source waters, which the conferees and the interests they represent would manipulate through storage. As early as 1923, Wiel had written that what belongs to a water right holder is not the water itself, but the rights to its "movement or flow."

> Ownership is in its faculty of movement, continual renewal, or flowing; and the right in the stream's source, of which we speak, is of the same incorporeal nature. It is neither land there nor even water there, but the right of having this natural faculty of motion remain uninterrupted at the highest point on the stream no less than at the lowest. (Wiel 1923, 148–49)

Wiel was stating a firm case against *cujus est solum* (he who owns the soil, owns up to the sky) for surface water, against absolute ownership of flowing surface water, relying instead on water right law's foundation on the principle of usufruct.

Remarkably, Governor Young wrote back to Wiel on February 10. He assured Wiel that he had no preconceived ideas about the best methods to solve California's water problems. But he expressed concern that the state's economic and population growth depended on expanding water use and that the state faced a "rapidly-diminishing source of underground water." He urged, "[S]omething ought to be done . . . [to] conserve and put upon the land a portion of the water which is now permitted to waste itself in the ocean. I wonder if, to this extent at least, you would not agree with me?" Young promised to give Wiel's letter further study and share the letter with knowledgeable friends (Wiel et al. 1927, 8).

Rising to the governor's challenge to propose a course of action, and certainly glad of the opportunity to debate, Wiel quickly responded on February 14. What should be done? Wiel affirmed his own belief in the regulation of water resources: "I think it is a mistake to leave riparians out of its benefits," he wrote, urging acceptance of all riparians to make possible some "good faith" approach to water rights regulation (Wiel et al. 1927, 8).

Wiel also recommended to the governor better irrigation education for farmers and more farm credit available to finance irrigation systems. But with farmers and growers still facing low prices for their crops after World War I, it made no sense to Wiel to strengthen the hands of corporations at the expense of the "individual units" that riparian water right holders embodied (notwithstanding Miller & Lux's bloc of riparian rights on the San Joaquin River, which Wiel ignored but certainly knew of; see chapter 10). "I confidently count on your agreeing" that abolishing riparian rights is "inevitably harmful," he asserted.

You need to protect riparian water rights, argued Wiel to the governor, because they help preserve the flow in the rivers and streams of California for *all water users, whether they had riparian or appropriative water rights.* Without flow—the "usual and customary flow" that riparian water rights required as a matter of law and the product of sufficient head, booster, or hydraulic force at the headwaters—how else would downstream appropriators and riparians actually receive the supplies they purported to claim?

*   *   *

Assembly Constitutional Amendment 27 made it onto the general election ballot for November 6, 1928, as Proposition 7. (See Appendix B for its text.) Earlier that year, Wiel published in the *California Law Review* a two-part legal and hydraulic analysis of the problem of the "mountain installations" affecting the "lower levels." The proposed amendment had been purged of its most objectionable provisions, he wrote, such as the abolition of riparian rights. He predicted that, if passed, the amendment would actually strengthen riparian water rights to the extent that their uses were indeed reasonable and beneficial. (That is, many such claims would not be considered wasteful and unreasonable and were indeed put to some productive use.) Further, the effect of its passage would "put the *Herminghaus* ruling into the Constitution," and the requirement that injured riparians receive compensation would have constitutional legitimacy and authority. Finally, Wiel would achieve his stated wish to the governor that riparians be subject to regulation for reasonable use.

Wiel's two articles pull together ideas he had nurtured throughout his career. As they appeared, he was about to turn 50. Read today, they are heavy at times with hydraulic analysis, driving home points for lawyers and engineers that he could not make in the same detail in a public letter to a sitting governor. From the standpoint of water, rather than being separable links in a sausage string, rivers are about losses and gains from headwaters to the sea, he wrote. This accounting included evaporation, temperature, wind, percolation into the soil, percolation from groundwater into the stream, and other return flows. Such factors affect the supply and flow of water in a stream, "a reminder," he wrote, "of much the eye cannot see." Additional factors included seepage losses and transpiration of water by plants, which occur from channels and stream banks drying out during summer months, followed by California's wet winters. Only after the seepage losses are fully paid from natural storm runoff, does a stream resume flowing. The flow in a stream is also residue of water not otherwise taken up and consumed by plant roots along the stream channel. Thus,

> A stream is, in hydraulic fact, no more than a top layer of water floating over a greater—usually far greater, wider and deeper—area of water-saturated ground. In effect it is the process of flowing over a long-winding, often wide sponge, which must be filled first.

For water flowing in a stream to pass a higher point, there must be sufficient hydraulic head to provide these natural or geological demands, as he called them, before human diversions could be met. The head "furnishes the force which in water *makes a stream*."[34]

Resentful critics charged that the *Herminghaus* court legitimized waste just so the Herminghauses could irrigate their Madera County lands with flood flows. The family's right to use the San Joaquin River included flood flows to lands fed by higher elevation sloughs that would replenish the fertility of those soils and make the land produce the grasses on which their cattle fed; ergo, riparian rights condoned waste.

Confronting this reasoning directly, Wiel argued that seepage losses are not waste. They cannot be litigated or otherwise repealed because they are at root caused naturally, an act of God. "Losses which are natural are necessarily unavoidable until such time as we can find a way of penalizing the Almighty, who is the guilty party," he quipped. The proper legal axiom, Wiel averred, is that "there can be no private blame for natural topography.... [I]f the condition complained of has resulted from natural causes, and not from the conduct of the defendant, the latter very evidently cannot be held liable" (Wiel 1928a, 185–86).

Therefore, waste consists only in man-made losses, argued Wiel, occurring after the water has been diverted to use from its natural channel. Once a human being assumes control of the water, that person may be held responsible "at least to a considerable degree, for his good or bad handling of it. That is his own conduct." Other court decisions conform to this understanding. In one Nevada decision, water running to the sea "does not itself indicate to what extent or under what conditions unappropriated water is available, if at all. Rights have been established by users from the underflow which is replenished by these very floods and these rights as well as all others prior and vested must be respected."[35]

Courts are willing to consider physical "substitutes," such as pipelines, that carry water separately from natural channels. These are sometimes called "physical solutions." (We will discuss one on the San Joaquin River in chapter 10.) Physical solutions can guarantee a specific amount of water, can avoid waste, and even provide water in lieu of monetary compensation. But such solutions, Wiel warned, do not necessarily protect the underlying head or flow that bring the solution quantity to the right holder.

In fact, rivers are misunderstood in the capitalist paradigm, Wiel was telling us. They don't conform to a fixed quantum, region, or area of property the way a plot of land or building square footage does. Echoing the sausage-string example he offered Governor Young, he wrote that anti-riparians "treat a stream as a line on a map."

> A stream is often unguardedly so thought of. A lower level [riparian diverter], having right to draw off an amount of water, should therefore have attention only for the amount to be drawn. The line to be drawn from does not, on a map, have to be itself fed in order to keep it up. Its unaided presence would be accepted as it there appears. (Wiel et al. 1927, 7; Wiel 1923)

Like the famous work by Belgian painter René Magritte of a seeming tobacco pipe entitled *The Treachery of Images* ("Ceci n'est pas une pipe."), maps of streams are not streams themselves. "Lack of acquaintance with the need of maintaining an hydraulic head gives this visual illusion wide currency," wrote Wiel (Wiel 1928a, 193).

Managing the level of consumptive use would be key to protecting the head or booster needed to support water claims along a stream. From scientific research at the time, Wiel noted that diversion for irrigation actually consumed about one-third of the supply applied to cropland. The flows that returned to the stream were about two-thirds of the original application. The other one-third was either consumed by plants metabolizing water into their biomass, evaporating it, or it percolated to groundwater before returning adjacent to the stream or going deeper to an aquifer.

But each successive consumptive use logically reduces the available flow and reaches some limit past which the head or booster may effectively disappear. It is analogous to repeatedly dividing a number by 2: you may never get to zero but you get very close, with smaller and smaller results. The need for regulation originates along such a well-developed river to ensure that upper-level diversions and stored water reasonably provide for downstream fulfillment of lower-level users' rights to return flows and sufficient movement or flow so that their claims are met.

Streams may accommodate a sequence of diversions to consumptive uses that enable a human economy to emerge and thrive, while still providing a head or booster carrying water downstream to the lower-level water users. From the standpoint of using water efficiently, Wiel argues, "that function can be fulfilled only when this succession of the benefit of it is secured the greatest number of times."

When the head or booster runs out, and lower-level water rights cannot be served, just compensation from above to below on the stream must occur, since the loss of flow or motion of the stream causes legal injury, Wiel reasoned (Wiel 1928a, 199).

The fate and availability of return flows—water that returns to the river from which it was taken—is thus key to the smooth functioning of a stream, where a system of water rights is embedded. Return flows replenish a stream, albeit with unavoidable subtractions due to the seepage and consumption losses described earlier. Through the cycle of diversion-use-return flow, Wiel argued that all water right holders had a correlative stake—riparians and appropriators alike—in the head of a stream regardless of their type of right. This was because the facts of reasonable use had to be marshaled to ensure that not only was everyone's water usage equitable and reasonable according to law but the head or flow was maintained to ensure fulfillment of all claims by order of priority (paramount riparian, senior then junior appropriators). Wiel stated that on one stream (the Santa Ana River in southern California), return flows enabled eight successive projects to use the same water within 100 miles "from mountain to sea." On another stream (the South Platte in Colorado), water was "being used over again four times and increasing." Such reuse of return flows was widely acknowledged throughout the western states (Wiel 1928b, 259, n. 83).

A key passage in Assembly Constitutional Amendment 27 on reasonable water use reads:

> It is hereby declared that because of the conditions prevailing in this state the general welfare requires that the water resources of the state be put to beneficial use to the fullest extent of which they are capable. . . ."[36]

For many Californians, including anti-riparian advocates, the phrase "the fullest extent of which they are capable" has meant that the state's constitution essentially provides a license to divert water until the rivers are dry and no water "wastes to the sea," the apotheosis of the *cujus est solum* principle of the English common law applied to modern surface water resource development. What else could "fullest extent capable" possibly mean? Yet this interpretation ignores seepage losses and return flows, and cuts off "the head, booster, or hydraulic force" of rivers and streams throughout California, a prospect Wiel opposed, not just for his riparian right-holding clients, but for what he saw as the good of all California water right holders.

Wiel argued that "fullest extent capable" meant "*putting the water resources of the State to beneficial use to the fullest extent of which they are capable . . . using* the same water over again the greatest number of times that can exist comfortably together."[37] This does not mean diverting all the water from a natural channel until no surface flow is left, but instead that reasonable diversions provide return flows to the stream sufficient to preserve its head, its hydraulic force, and its motion to convey water supplies for the next user downstream. Wiel reasoned that the more these supplies could be reasonably reused, the more likely this passage of the California constitution could be fulfilled while preserving the rights of all claimants to movement or flow according to priority. He concluded with an aphorism of efficiency: *"We have come to the time when advance must rest upon more repetition of using it over again"* (Wiel 1928b, 264–65, emphasis in original).

This "reuse" or "recycling" interpretation of ACA 27 would have to prevail because California was reaching full development of its surface water rights, argued Wiel. The essence of reasonable use would need to be synonymous with reuse of return flow and efficient water use.

* * *

During the 1920s, the state water administration planned reservoirs of its own for many montane locations. Wiel warned that these dams would face challenging legal questions about their own reasonable use, given their monopolizing, controlling locations. The new state reservoirs and their management of state-controlled water supplies needed to be planned to provide a "fair compromise" that allowed repetitive reuse of water by lower-level diverters "and thus give legal standing to the maximum number of repetitions" that still maintained river flow. This would give real operative meaning to "the fullest extent capable." To accomplish such an ideal, however, Wiel acknowledged (prophetically, it seems) that it might be necessary for prior water right holders to accommodate the rights of later arrivals.

> The prior reservoir or other project may very likely be called upon to share reasonably with later projects or submit to other reasonable restrictions in order that later development may also succeed. (Wiel 1928b, 266, 267)

To reassure defenders of appropriative water rights, Wiel states that the constitutional amendment protects all water rights, but for no more than they are entitled. He quotes Justice Stephen J. Field, of the U.S. Supreme Court (and a former Chief Justice of the California Supreme Court in the state's early days), saying that appropriators' rights must always be "exercised *within reasonable limits.*" Such rights are never entirely unrestricted, said Justice Field, for they "must be exercised . . . *not so as to deprive a whole neighborhood or community of its use, and vest an absolute monopoly in a single individual*" (Wiel 1928b, 268, emphasis in original).

Wiel brings together the strands to tie the knot: given the emphasis of the proposed constitutional amendment on efficient reuse of water, its protection of riparian water rights, and its acknowledgment of appropriative water rights, the amendment also makes a "universal pronouncement against 'unreasonable use or unreasonable method of use,' repeated several times in order to exercise 'conservation . . . in the interest of the people and for public welfare. . . .'" Combined with Justice Field's rule about lawful entitlements in water rights, the prohibitions against waste and unreasonable use, and unreasonable method of use and of diversion, Wiel believed the union of these principles would make it possible for injured parties to enforce reasonable obligations on all water users, especially "the large corporate reservoirs" of the power companies. In his view, this made the proposed constitutional amendment "an effective charter." He adds, "There seems to be good ground to believe that this may prove to be the measure's most vital feature."[38]

But, Wiel predicted, for downstream water right holders, the price of reasonable use in water law doctrine in the era of dam-building and canal diversion is eternal vigilance regarding those controlling flow from upstream—those owning and operating dams—and the financial resources they will always need to defend their rights in water properties. Thus, "[R]epeated use of the same water can have legality only when everyone in the succession has as much right to legal protection as every other—the last in succession [priority], whether last in time [as among appropriators] or last in level [as among riparians], the same as the first" (Wiel 1928b, 271).

Implementing the new constitutional amendment would mean greater state government exercise of its constitutional power to police water. The architecture of a dam anchored in its channel site invites monopoly control of the river's flows by the dam owner, much the way James Ben Ali Haggin's field man controlled the headgate at the Calloway Weir on the Kern River that fateful day in the spring of 1877. "By force of geography the aggressor is above," states Wiel.

> While the upper installation by its dam has possession of the water, the lower party never has more than the basis for a lawsuit. He has only an argument, while his opponent's dam has possession of the water; and a lawsuit is a poor match for a dam as a means by which water can be secured. (Wiel 1928b, 272–73)

Disparities were legion, in his view. Whether suit from below was brought by individual riparians or appropriators (or both) for adjudication, Wiel thought the cost of bringing hundreds to court, preparing court briefs, and acquiring and vetting expert witnesses too burdensome: "[T]he lower user may easily be too poor to go through with it . . . to say nothing of keeping a decree enforced if it were obtained." The public utility or state agency owning the reservoir will possess "the equipment for offense"—organization, capital, and expertise—to resist regulation or adjudication.

The physical presence, location, and design of dams, as well as the corporate organization of the initiating utility, confer a potential monopoly on their owners. This potential could only be checked by a countervailing monopoly or by action of government empowered to regulate that monopoly. Wiel's analysis in his day clearly suggests his progressive impulses in seeking to control the predations of corporations on California's watersheds and smaller water right holders. He pointed to a new California hydraulic regime: under the constitutional amendment, and in combination with the California Water Commission Act of 1913 (from whence the government's role in water regulation stems), the most important government activities would be "regulating the upper works, particularly the large corporate reservoirs, for the protection of lower uses of the same water over again."

On November 6, 1928, California voters passed Proposition 7 by a nearly 4 to 1 margin.[39] It failed in only one county, Humboldt on the north coast, relatively far from the Central Valley. The "yes" vote there still received about 45 percent of those cast.

NOTES

1. Herminghaus v. Southern California Edison, 200 Cal. 81 (1926).
2. "Water Rights Decision," editorial, *Stockton Independent*, December 26, 1926 (Hyatt 1927).
3. "Changes in Water Rights Laws Are Urged by Green: Attorney Says Appropriative System Should Succeed Riparian," *Fresno Bee*, December 29, 1926 (Hyatt, 1927).
4. "Barlow Scores Riparian Water Right Decision as Legal Theft," *Bakersfield Californian*, December 30, 1926, story originally by Associated Press, emphasis added. The same story, titled "Irrigation President Calls Decision 'Theft,'" also appeared in the *San Francisco Chronicle*, December 30, 1926 (Hyatt 1927).
5. "Flaws Pointed In Water Plan of Paul Bailey," *San Francisco Chronicle*, January 28, 1927 (Hyatt 1927).
6. Woolley took on Miller & Lux as a client immediately after retiring from the bench, replacing T. P. Wittschen in mid-1925. Wittschen left Miller & Lux to become the attorney for East Bay Municipal Utilities District in June, 1925, to help the District obtain a mountain water supply for East Bay Area counties. See Miller 1993, 227, n. 53).
7. "Woolley's Statement: More About Riparian Decision on San Joaquin," *Byron Times*, January 14, 1927, emphasis added (Hyatt (1927).
8. Fall River Valley Irrigation District v. Mount Shasta Power Company, 202 Cal. 56 (1927). It appears the California Supreme Court had a fluid composition during this period. T. P. Wittschen, by then an attorney for the East Bay Municipal Utility District, reported that the case "was first orally argued before the state supreme court on January 15, 1926, and re-argued on July 29, 1926. The decision of the court was issued December 24, 1926; thereafter petitions were filed for a rehearing, which were in due course denied and the judgment is now final. The California supreme court consisted of seven Justices. Five were in favor of affirming the judgment of the lower court. One dissented. One Justice did not participate. When the matter came up for rehearing four of the original five who had affirmed the judgement were against a rehearing. The other of the original five was not on the bench because of the expiration of his term of office in the meantime. Two additional Justices, who heard the matter for the first time, voted for a rehearing, as also did the Justice (Shenk) who had dissented from the original opinion"; T. P. Wittschen, "Herminghaus et al. v. Southern California Edison Company: Recent Decision of Supreme Court of California Confirming Rights of Riparian Owners Jeopardizes Construction of Storage Reservoirs—Legislative Correction is Proposed," *Western Construction News*, February 25, 1927, 46 (Hyatt 1927).

9. "After the Courts," editorial, *Bakersfield Californian*, January 27, 1927 (Hyatt 1927).

10. "U.S. Supreme Court Throws Out Edison Company's Appeal: Says It Has No Jurisdiction In Herminghaus Riparian Rights Case," *Fresno Republican*, October 7, 1927 (Hyatt 1927).

11. "Statewide Meet Set in Water War," *Oakland Tribune*, January 29, 1927 (Hyatt 1927).

12. "Amendment of State's Water Law Proposed; Herminghaus Case Decision Stirs Lawmakers to Action," *Covina Citizen*, February 17, 1927 (Hyatt 1927).

13. Wittschen, *Western Construction News*, February 25, 1927, at 48, in Hyatt (1927).

14. Herminghaus, 200 Cal. at 100–102. See also Sharp (1926, 200–201) and Miller & Lux, 155 Cal. at 65.

15. The story of the development of hydropower in the upper San Joaquin River watershed south of Yosemite is ably told by Donald Jackson (1995).

16. These agreements are summarized in California Water Project Authority (1936c, 2–4).

17. Justice Richard wrote in the *Herminghaus* decision, "There is nothing in the record herein tending in any degree to show that the defendants [SCE] herein ever offered, or would be willing to offer, to reimburse the plaintiffs for any portion of the cost, expense and outlay which would be required in order to limit the amount of water entering upon plaintiff's [Herminghauses'] land to the amount thereof indicated by the trial court as susceptible of being made reasonably adequate through such artificial means." Quoted in T. P. Wittschen, *Western Construction News*, February 25, 1927, at 47 (Hyatt 1927).

18. M. C. Miller (1993, Ch. 3, "The Power of Doctrine").

19. The California Conservation Commission in 1913 employed not just one but three photographs of lands flooded, all of them near Los Banos, with captions deploring overflow and wasted water. It was a direct reference to Miller & Lux's land and water monopoly, but also any other such riparian who claimed flood flows. State of California (1913, 27, 28, 33).

20. Concurring with Justice Richard's opinion in *Herminghaus* were Chief Justice Waste and Justices Seawell and Sullivan. Justice Shenk authored a dissent that was joined by Justice Finch. The final court vote was 4–2, with one abstention.

21. Justice Richards' Eulogy, 215 Cal. 778 (1933).

22. *Herminghaus*, 200 Cal. at 96, quoting Heilbron v. Last Chance Water Ditch Co., 75 Cal. 121 (1888).

23. *Id.* at 112.

24. Justice Richards cared little for Edison's economic reasoning justifying no need for appropriators to compensate riparians: "The argument that these waters are of great value for the purposes of storage by appropriators and of small value to the lower riparian owners defeats itself. If the right sought to be taken be of small worth, the burden of paying for it will not be great. If, on the other hand, great benefits are conferred upon the riparian lands by the flow, there is all the more reason why these advantages should, without compensation, be taken from these owners and transferred to others." *Herminghaus*, 200 Cal. at 102.

25. *Id.* at 101.

26. The issue of riparian storage raised by SCE was the subject of many *amicus curiae* briefs to the *Herminghaus* court. See Miller, 1989. Among the *amicus* briefs were Samuel C. Wiel (UC Riverside, Special Collections, Water Resources Collections and Archives, Call No. L190 H4, no. 11) and the California Department of Public Works (UC Riverside, Special Collections, Water Resources Collections and Archives, Call No. L190 H4, no. 5). The state's *amicus* brief was informed by UC Berkeley irrigation engineering professor Sidney T. Harding, whose report is archived (UC Riverside, Special Collections, Water Resources Collections and Archives, Call No. HARDING 40). James Peck's respondent's brief on behalf of the Herminghaus family is at the California State Archive in Sacramento for the *Herminghaus* case archive,

along with an *amicus* brief by the old Miller & Lux downstream legal foe, James J. Stevinson Corporation (from the confluence of the Merced and San Joaquin Rivers).

27. *Herminghaus*, 200 Cal. at 109.

28. *Id.* at 111. Surmised word missing from original.

29. *Id.* at 110.

30. State Water Commission (1917, 67–69), quoting researcher A. Griffin, an engineer with the South San Joaquin Irrigation District, found the duty of water a complex measurement. California Department of Public Works (1930a, Tables 67 and 68) show widely varying duties of water for rice and general crops for 1924 through 1928. They ranged from 5–6 acre-feet per acre in the Sacramento Valley for rice to 2–3 acre-feet per acre in the Delta for other crops. Gross duty of water did not take account of return flows to neighboring streams after the initial application.

31. *Herminghaus*, 200 Cal. at 118.

32. Liebman (1983, 60, Table 2.8, citing data from Harding 1960).

33. This period clearly stimulated Wiel's thinking and writing on what, exactly, a river is. Beginning in the 1910s, he perceived the growing irrationality of anti-riparian advocates as they sought to jettison riparian rights in favor of a naïvely dangerous conception of how rivers actually operate. Wiel (1923) rooted his legal critique in hydraulic analysis.

34. Wiel's cited authorities (1928a, 184–85) include an important U.S. Geological Survey water-supply paper; the California Department of Public Works, Division of Engineering and Irrigation; Elwood Mead, the influential irrigation engineer who oversaw California's turn-of-the-century irrigation investigations; and Sidney Harding's irrigation engineering colleague Bernard Etcheverry on plant transpiration along rivers.

35. Toskin v. Winzell, 27 Nev. 88 (1903) cited in Wiel (1928a, 188).

36. Originally chaptered into the California constitution as Article XIV, Section 3, this section is now titled Article X, Section 2. It is also enacted in California Water Code, Section 100.

37. That is, using water the most number of times so that its quality is not compromised and the last user on the stream is not injured either in the quantity or quality of the water existing in the stream at "the lowest level." See Wiel (1928b, 259).

38. It is entirely possible that Wiel wrote the amendment himself and got the legislature to accept it. Perhaps historians with greater research gifts than mine will determine Proposition 7's authorship.

39. There were 913,125 "yes" votes and 270,163 "no" votes. Humboldt County's yes votes totaled 4,317. Jordan (1928, 33).

Chapter 8

Junior and Senior Partners

IT IS SAID THAT NECESSITY is the mother of invention, and crisis a spur to action. Between 1920 and 1934, drought, growth, and legal impasse were spurs to government action on water in California. After forty years in which riparian doctrine ruled state water law, the seven years from the *Herminghaus* decision in December 1926 through passage of Proposition 7 in November 1928 to the electoral victory of the Central Valley Project Act in December 1933 saw unparalleled changes by the state to its water laws and institutions. Those changes enabled construction of a massive new hydraulic system over the next two decades.

Inaction was part of this era's legacy as well. Having granted more claims to use water than naturally flowed in state rivers, California did nothing to stem their continued growth. An excess of such claims fueled water demand, helping to stoke shortage fears that could ignite in overt conflict during droughts.

Surface-water rights were monopolized throughout the San Joaquin Valley, most dramatically by Miller & Lux, almost since statehood. Politically unwilling and unable to positively legislate a water rights system for itself, California relied instead on the courts to define and elaborate riparian and appropriative doctrines as a dual system of rights—the "California doctrine" (Holsinger 1936). This yielded unending conflict, as well as confusion in the public's grasp of water law principles. Yet even as monopoly of surface-water rights flourished, irrigated agriculture spread on the strength of groundwater usage and development of hydropower energy to lift water to the surface (Treadwell 1928, 2–3).

Katz v. Walkinshaw repudiated *cujus est solum* (absolute individual ownership) in favor of correlative rights among overlying groundwater users. *Katz* explicitly established reasonable use among correlative users in a basin as the legal solution for groundwater commons tragedies in California. Its author, Justice Lucien Shaw, wrote the decision to protect the resource and those using it. Many basins throughout California subsequently sought the benefits of *Katz* through adjudication.

But judicial fiat only goes so far. Dead to California water doctrine in the wake of *Katz,* the *cujus est solum* philosophy of absolute property ownership in water lived on in the hearts and minds of many citizens, reflecting a defining belief in California as a land of democratic opportunity and entrepreneurial risk-taking, despite the monopolized reality. Ironically, that belief contributed to a tragedy of the groundwater commons in the San Joaquin Valley.

The California Supreme Court countenanced a doctrine for surface waters that placed riparian water rights paramount over appropriative rights. Despite obvious signs that irrigated agriculture throughout the state flourished and expanded from the 1870s through the 1920s, it galled some Californians that riparians could legally intimidate appropriators (except those, like Miller & Lux, who benefited from that advantage).

Politically, passage of the 1914 Water Commission Act was only a partial innovation in acquiring new water rights through state-administered appropriation. The Act made new water rights more legible, more quantifiable, and more visible to the public, but only for applicants acquiring new rights after December 19, 1914. Older claims were left to stand in regulatory shadows without a unifying system to collate and list them to avoid future conflicts. Pre-1914 water rights were still largely found in each of the fifty-eight different county recorder offices. Decrees and negotiated settlements were in the records of county superior courts, which is to say, all were nearly as illegible and hard to read as unquantifiable riparian rights. New and old rights were seldom correlated with hydrologic realities to give officials and the public a clear picture of the economy of California water.

Samuel C. Wiel stated the need to Governor Young in early 1927 for an approach for surface water—similar to groundwater—that would subject riparians to the "benefits of regulation." By this, he meant having riparians be accountable to appropriators for reasonable use of water. Wiel had also pointed out that to preserve the rights of all claimants to "flow and movement" of a stream, reason and principles of efficient water use must apply to all water allocation. To him, that meant preserving the "head, booster," of flow in the stream—the continuation of gravitational flow from the headwaters to the sea that could naturally and efficiently do the work of delivery implied in the claim of each water right along the stream. Nothing in Wiel's writings suggests he ever imagined that draining rivers dry was reasonable, or that desiccation by diversion was the endpoint of lawful water-resource development. Using it to the fullest possible use meant *reuse*, time and again, among the community of users along a stream, with gravity (embodied as flow) doing the work to deliver water to each and to all lawful water users.

Despite the Water Commission Act's small victories for state regulation, state law preserved the exemption of percolating groundwater from government regulation and its legal, if not hydrological, disconnection from surface waters. Experts like Wiel and a number of scientists saw need for a unified treatment of underground and surface water as a single resource, to no avail (Wiel 1913, 1929b). While the groundwater exemption was a defeat for Wiel and his allies, it was a Pyrrhic victory for adherents to *cujus est solum,* the individual and corporate landowners who retained private control over well usage. From the 1930s down to the present, groundwater levels generally continued to fall in the San Joaquin Valley.[1]

Economically, this did not lead to changes in either water use or in state regulation. The market for water in California was failing: demand was chronically unfulfilled by supply. The collective faith pointed to continue expanding supply. As a joint legislative committee on water problems declared, "California is an empire in the making" (California Joint Legislative Water Problems Committee 1929; excerpted in U.S. Congress 1956, 192). Cheap, abundant water was believed (as it still is) to be crucial to land value and in turn to regional wealth. Landowners hoped the creation and spread of irrigation districts would democratize surface-water access. But early district formations in the 1880s and 1890s foundered on scientific, business, and engineering difficulties. Not until state supervision in the 1910s and 1920s brought greater application of expertise in planning, design, and formation was acquisition of new appropriative rights rationalized.

An important, but often unrecognized, contribution of the 1914 Water Commission Act was addition of an adjudication process and water master provisions (with subsequent legislative amendments to improve and clarify). Adjudication, at least for some, was one path toward solving local water problems. It was initiated through the California Water Commission or through court action. The Water Commission provided expertise for proper collection and consideration of evidence needed to define and enforce rights undergoing adjudication. By 1940, twenty-five (mostly small) creek basins had sought and completed adjudications, either by court reference or state initiation. Such decrees required participants to take a pragmatic rather than ideological view of water resources. Adjudication forced recognition that riparian rights were here to stay, that *cujus est solum* contained seeds of each owner's demise, and that collective action (in this case, adjudication) could save the resource for one and all, basin by basin. Many of these decrees still function today.

While it took the 1926 *Herminghaus* decision to provoke changes in the way California governed water resources locally, regionally, and statewide, the decision was also seen widely to threaten the feasibility of the State Water Plan. California's water institutions received the new "reasonable use doctrine" into state water law, approved as Proposition 7 by the California electorate in 1928. What was reasonable would depend upon the facts of each individual case. Waste was prohibited. The state's waters had to be used to the fullest extent. Unreasonable uses, diversions, and methods were also prohibited. Yet, with adoption of the new "reasonable use" legal standard by the electorate, no one knew for sure whether riparians would be held to it.

Within this shifting institutional terrain, the question arose as to how the state was going to get water rights for its coordinated water plan. The question was really three: how would the state file for water rights it did not now have? Was there really enough water, particularly in the Sacramento River basin, to support the immense transfers of water across the Delta, as contemplated in the plan? Finally, how would the state acquire the specific water rights of Miller & Lux, the largest bloc of rights on the San Joaquin River by far, and pivotal to the plan's success or failure?

* * *

Samuel Wiel's analysis of dam owners' temptations to monopolistic, aggressive behavior was in retrospect a warning of coming conflicts during the California dam-building era of the 1930s through the 1970s (and even beyond).

Controlling the technology of a dam owned by a private corporation might be handled by creation of an independent government regulator, as so many other industries and technologies had done since the 1870s. But what if the dam owner was another state or a federal government agency? If the Central Valley Project became federally owned—which it did, in 1935—what regulatory authority would the state retain over its operations? And would state or federal agency ownership change the rules of the game so as to benefit its fellow agencies through the 1927 Feigenbaum Act (Cal. Stats. 1927, Ch. 286).

Dry year after dry year unfolded in the 1920s, followed by *Herminghaus*, and the questions became urgent: how could the state acquire water rights when claims, permits, and licenses for water rights accumulated in the state's developing economy? How could the state acquire the rights it needed to move forward with complex, coordinated, statewide water development? The state was clearly a latecomer and slow mover in obtaining water rights for its own comparatively complex system. Further, once it had obtained some, its rights were likely to face larger cutbacks during droughts than those with more senior rights on the same river systems.

In 1927, the state legislature organized a joint committee of the Assembly and Senate to examine California's water problems. The committee's charge was "to make an investigation of the water problems of the state and to recommend to the Legislature of the State of California . . . some statewide policy for the conservation and use of the waters of the state" (U.S. Congress 1956, 203). It concluded from Governor Young's February 1927 conference on state water law (about which Samuel C. Wiel wrote the pamphlet discussed in chapter 7) that the state of California should immediately file for water rights "by its proper officials or by legislation" to consummate the coordinated state water plan.

Tempus fugit: the tick-tock of water rights priorities accruing to other appropriators along the Sacramento River made it urgent for the state to file for water rights. Between 1915, after the Water Commission Act took effect, and 1927, the commission had permitted 1.3 million acre-feet of new face amounts in water rights to Sacramento River water users, many of whom also had pre–1914 claims (Table 8.1).[2] As they began their work that Febuary, the legislative committee also acknowledged "that the execution of the coordinated plan would bring it in direct conflict with a most serious legal obstacle—the rights of riparian owners along the streams involved." The committee sought "relief from the doctrine of wasteful riparian rights, a doctrine set forth in the recent decision of the Supreme Court of California in the Herminghaus case and substantiated by a long line of court decisions." In the committee's view, continued adherence to riparians' control of the "full flow"

TABLE 8.1. Sacramento River Basin Post–1914 Water Rights, 1915–1927

POST–1914 WATER RIGHT HOLDER	PRIORITY DATE	WATER RIGHT FACE AMOUNT (1,000S OF ACRE-FEET)
Reclamation District 1004	Apr 2, 1915	56.0
Reclamation District 108	Jan 25, 1917	97.5
River Garden Farms Company	Jan 25, 1917	29.3
Sutter Mutual Water Company	Feb 1, 1917	21.9
Tisdale Irrigation & Drainage Company	Jul 26, 1917	12.5
Reclamation District 108	Aug 27, 1917	270.7
Oji Brothers	Jan 3, 1918	1.9
Sutter Mutual Water Company	Jan 3, 1918	265.7
Provident Irrigation District	Jan 18, 1918	40.1
Stanford Vina Ranch Irrigation Company	Aug 5, 1918	4.6
Natomas Central Mutual Water Company	Aug 22, 1918	16.2
Lomo Cold Storage	Sep 10, 1918	2.0
Meridian Farms Water Company	Sep 10, 1918	67.3
Sutter Mutual Water Company	Jan 24, 1919	19.7
Conaway Preservation Group LLC	Mar 1, 1919	43.6
Natomas Central Mutual Water Company	Mar 5, 1919	58.4
Natomas Central Mutual Water Company	Aug 27, 1919	36.7
Provident Irrigation District	Sep 2, 1919	3.4
Glenn-Colusa Irrigation District	Dec 3, 1919	28.1
Glenn-Colusa Irrigation District	Jan 14, 1920	10.8
Rancho Esquon, Inc.	Feb 5, 1920	3.7
Sycamore Mutual Water Company	Feb 9, 1920	42.5
Reclamation District 999	Feb 11, 1920	58.4
Sutter Mutual Water Company	Apr 9, 1920	1.5
US Bureau of Reclamation	Feb 17, 1921	50.2
Butte Valley Irrigation District	Feb 28, 1921	17.2
Rancho Esquon, Inc.	Oct 9, 1921	1.8
Rancho Esquon, Inc.	Mar 4, 1922	3.8
Gorrill Land Company	Mar 6, 1922	4.6
Rancho Esquon, Inc.	Jun 27, 1922	3.0
Hot Springs Valley Irrigation District	Apr 12, 1923	48.4
Sacramento River Ranch II	May 17, 1923	2.6
Reclamation District 999	Jul 18, 1924	3.9
Gorrill Land Company	Jun 30, 1925	4.5
Rancho Esquon, Inc.	Jun 30, 1925	4.6

TABLE 8.1. Sacramento River Basin Post–1914 Water Rights, 1915–1927 (*continued*)

POST-1914 WATER RIGHT HOLDER	PRIORITY DATE	WATER RIGHT FACE AMOUNT (1,000S OF ACRE-FEET)
Sutter Mutual Water Company	Jun 22, 1926	3.3
M & T Incorporated	Jul 17, 1926	5.1
Parrott Investment Company	Jul 17, 1926	5.1
Sacramento River Ranch II	Feb 17, 1927	1.8
SUBTOTAL BEFORE INITIAL STATE FILINGS IN 1927		1,352.4
U.S. Bureau of Reclamation	Jul 30, 1927	11,153.8
U.S. Bureau of Reclamation	Jul 30, 1927	3,349.9
Sutter Mutual Water Company	Jan 31, 1928	0.1
Lomo Cold Storage	Nov 14, 1929	20.3
Conaway Preservation Group, LLC	Apr 18, 1930	5.4
Natomas Central Mutual Water Company	May 28, 1931	15.4
County of Sacramento	Jun 6, 1931	2.7
Lomo Cold Storage	Mar 21, 1932	0.7
South Fork Irrigation District	Mar 5, 1934	17.0
Reclamation District 883	May 1, 1934	2.2
M & T, Inc.	Dec 1, 1934	5.1
Parrott Investment Company	Dec 1, 1934	5.1
M & T, Inc.	Feb 27, 1936	3.1
Parrott Investment Company	Feb 27, 1936	3.1
Maxwell Irrigation District	Apr 8, 1936	29.0
Glenn-Colusa Irrigation District	May 28, 1936	0.7
SUBTOTAL BEFORE SECOND STATE FILINGS, 1938		14,613.5
CUMULATED SACRAMENTO RIVER BASIN WATER RIGHTS CLAIMS, POST–1914, IN 1936		15,965.9
PERCENTAGE DUE TO STATE FILINGS FOR CVP TO U.S. BUREAU OF RECLAMATION		91%

Source: State Water Resources Control Board; Stroshane 2012.

of a stream, "if carried on without limit, would not only make the accomplishment of the coordinated plan practically impossible but would endanger the rights of thousands of California's citizens whose very existence depends upon appropriated water rights" (U.S. Congress 1956, 186).

The committee came around to Wiel's point of view (based on the *Herminghaus* decision) on riparian water rights and just compensation issues. After three days of Senate hearings in mid-February, the committee reported that "one proposition stood out amidst all the discussions, namely: that private property in water rights can not be taken without compensation. However much it might be wished that the law were otherwise in respect to the riparian doctrine, we must face it as it is." As a consequence, the joint committee recommended creating another state water-related commission to "investigate, hear, and determine claims to the use of water, to hear and determine proceedings in eminent domain for the taking of water for public use, and regulation of the distribution thereof, and to fix the just compensation to be paid for the taking of such water" (U.S. Congress 1956, 185–86).

That recommendation dealt with existing rights the state water plan needed to acquire. To obtain rights to store and re-divert water it did not yet have, the legislature approved the Feigenbaum Act that spring. It was signed by Governor Olson, April 29, and took effect on July 29, 1927.

The Feigenbaum Act separated priority ("first in time . . .") from due diligence ("use it or lose it"). This was a legal innovation of narrow scope but of the first order. It stated:

> The priority of any such application or applications shall be as of the date this act shall become effective, and such priority shall be retained over any application made by others subsequent to said date, and which may be in conflict therewith, *regardless of any requirements or provisions of the water commission act relating to diligence in the completion of applications for water or the use thereof*[.] (1927 Cal. Stats. 286, Sec. 1; reproduced in U.S. Congress 1956, 188, emphasis added)

The Act gave the State of California special status, a pass from the due diligence principle in prior appropriation, which now applied to all *other* appropriators.

On July 30, 1927, the day after the Feigenbaum Act took effect, the director of the California Department of Finance filed the Central Valley Project's initial rights applications with the state water commission. Table 8.2 summarizes key state filings for the Sacramento River, the Feather River, and the Delta that are the water rights bases for the CVP and the State Water Project (the latter of which would not be planned until the 1950s). This date became the CVP's priority date *regardless* of the state's diligence in completing this complex, coordinated water system. Thus, the state got in line for water rights it expected to exercise *someday*.[3]

Freed from due diligence requirements (and hence freed to monopolize the rights claimed for decades to come), the state's newly minted 1927 water rights applications—often referred to as "state filings"—bought time to address difficult matters slowing Central Valley Project planning: Delta salinity control; acquisition of Miller & Lux rights (and those of others) to the Bureau's Friant Dam; the grand bargain of the Exchange Contract; construction of the massive Shasta and Friant Dams and the Delta Mendota Canal; contending with PG&E's opposition to government-owned competition in hydroelectricity production and transmission from the CVP; and the threat of adjudication spreading from the Sierra foothills along the Sacramento River tributaries to the main stem river, possibly engulfing the water rights of the CVP.

TABLE 8.2. Major State Filings on July 30, 1927, pursuant to the Feigenbaum Act, eventually completed and operated

APPLICATION NUMBER	APPLICANT/ ASSIGNEE	FACILITY	FACE AMOUNT OF RIGHTS (ACRE-FEET)	SOURCE OF WATER
A005625	DOF* /U.S. Bureau of Reclamation	Shasta Reservoir	11,153,752.50	Sacramento River
A005627	DOF /U.S. Bureau of Reclamation	Trinity Reservoir	2,336,375.30	Trinity River
A005628	DOF /U.S. Bureau of Reclamation	Tracy Pumping Plant	3,349,943.80	Old River, Trinity River
A005629	DOF/Cal. Dept. of Water Resources	Lake Oroville and pumping/generating facilities	5,882,229.00	Feather River
A005630	DOF/Cal. Dept. of Water Resources	Lake Oroville and pumping/generating facilities, plus Delta Water Facilities, including North Bay Aqueduct, California Aqueduct Intake, Clifton Court Forebay, Banks Pumping Plant, San Luis Dam, and other related facilities to the California Aqueduct.	1,393,563.50	Feather River, Italian Slough, Sacramento River Delta channels

*DOF is "Department of Finance," the original agency filing for state water rights.

Source: State Water Resources Control Board's Electronic Water Rights Information Management System (eWRIMS), accessed 2010; compiled by author.

* * *

While the Feigenbaum Act assured the State of California's place on the list of prior appropriators on major Central Valley rivers, the Joint Legislative Committee also appointed a "Legal Advisory Committee" to work in the summer and fall of 1928 on "the compensation issue" stemming from *Herminghaus*. In *Herminghaus*, Justice Richards's opinion had upheld the plaintiff family's right to compensation from Southern California Edison Company for the planned taking of its riparian flood flows along the San Joaquin River. The compensation issue, then, was how to deal with paying riparian right holders for their property in water. Among the attorneys appointed to the legal advisory committee were Edward F. Treadwell and Samuel C. Wiel.[4] Wiel recalled that the committee chair, Assemblyman Byron S. Crittenden, "presented, as the premise to be developed, that when public improvements damage private landowners the damage must be compensated. The works concerned nowadays are the public utility developments—giant reservoirs particularly for water power, city supply, and irrigation districts. They have created a new situation. Formerly it was private controversy."

The questions posed by the legislators included what constituted damage, what benefits might offset damage, and what would be the means of assessing damage and arranging compensation? "The attorneys present, speaking in turn," wrote Wiel, "accepted this point of view until shortly before the meeting ended," at which point Treadwell, who had spent his career with Miller & Lux, and after his departure arguing water law from both sides of the street, objected that the politicians should not determine the line of thought investigated by the attorneys. Instead, as Wiel described Treadwell's appeal to the legislators, "[T]he attorneys should sit separately and decide the line of thought for themselves" (Wiel 1929a, 197–98).

During the summer and fall of 1928, Treadwell and Wiel appear to have shaped much of the committee's recorded debate.[5] In the end, Treadwell prevailed. Surely ever mindful of the role of his former client, he argued for "the removal, by some method, of the claim to the flow of the entire stream, and the claim of right to use it by methods that are generally considered to be wasteful." If any lawyer knew the legal ins and outs of the waste of water, and possessed the silver tongue with which to argue them, it was Treadwell. He had argued both sides of the issue first on the Fresno River, then on the San Joaquin. (And he would later coin the phrase "wild irrigation" in Henry Miller's biography; see chapter 4.) With the Legal Advisory Committee, he seemed to relish the role of defining and solving the problem he himself had done so much to establish during his lengthy law career, most of it in Miller & Lux's employ.

Treadwell examined several options raised in the committee's mandate: the taking of flood and freshet waters; exercising police powers to impose reasonable limits to claim full flows of a river; using the state's interest in navigable waterways to limit diversions by riparians seeking full flow of a river; and applying eminent domain as the process to arrange compensation for riparian water right holders.

He dispatched the taking of the flood and freshet flows from riparian right holders because, unlike the case in small coastal watersheds where the Coast Range mountains often do not rise to elevations high enough for winter snow accumulation, the San Joaquin River watershed's floods and freshets were "predictable." That river's prodigious snowmelt would come down each spring from April to as late as July. Such flows were therefore part of the "usual and customary" flow of the San Joaquin River, despite their large variation in volume (Treadwell 1928, 3–4).

As for the exercise of government police power against riparians, Treadwell told his legal colleagues it would founder on the political views of the court justices deciding such cases. As court compositions changed, decisions in such cases would oscillate between invoking and revoking the police power regarding eminent domain and compensation. The police power would involve taking someone's property, not unlike "zoning," the newly emerging legal form of land-use regulation. On this, however, Treadwell allowed that the legislature could act to limit riparians' use of water to what they needed economically and no more (Treadwell 1928, 5–6).

Treadwell felt too that reliance on the state's interest in protecting navigable waters would be of little help, since the courts would not recognize rights to navigable waterways held by California. While some states legally asserted such a right, Treadwell observed that this was not the case here. If California tried to assert them against a riparian's claim to full flow of a stream, the state's new constitutional amendment would likely stand in its way.

That left eminent domain and just compensation. "This principle is so elementary," Treadwell said, "that it is needless to enlarge upon it, and the only suggestions that this committee could make would be with regard to the procedure by which the property might be condemned and compensation fixed" (Treadwell 1928, 9). He reminded his colleagues that these procedures included pursuit of takings cases in superior court where property damage would be decided by jury, or by an "administrative proceeding" or "tribunal" that would focus on damage claims lodged by riparian right holders, take evidence, and provide binding decisions on damages.[6]

Formerly, as counsel for Southern California Edison, Treadwell had opposed compensating the Herminghaus family (see chapter 7). Now he argued that compensation was a Trojan horse for adjudication, and it was impossible to compensate a riparian for the value of water excess to his or her needs without quantifying an otherwise correlative water right. The only way to do that, he reasoned, was through "an investigation of the entire stream and the needs of all parties upon it." This would be impracticable and expensive for each individual condemnation proceeding, "and this would be true whether the proceeding was before the court or before an administrative body" (Treadwell 1928, 11).

Making riparian rights legible, quantified, and available to analysis and planning, must happen, Treadwell said, if so many of California's water conflicts were to be solved. Even the idea of compensation would depend on it. If Proposition 7 passed in the fall, he claimed, then

> my plan for the judicial determination of the quantity of water "reasonably required for the beneficial use to be served" becomes a necessity.[7] In other words, a mere abstract limitation on the right without it defined in any tangible manner would be of little use to persons seeking to acquire the surplus [of any stream]. If condemnation of the surplus is necessary [for the state's project] such a determination of the amount of water reasonably needed becomes essential, and the condemnation could take place in the same proceeding. (Treadwell 1928, 15–16)

Samuel Wiel objected strenuously that it was necessary to quantify riparian rights or the amount of the surplus of the stream. He denied that eminent domain was a slippery slope to adjudication. In a separate report to both the Legal Advisory and Assembly committees, he presented a compensation plan (confusingly labeled a "conditioned permits plan") in which the processing of takings claims lodged by riparian right holders could be handled by the existing California Water Commission, rather than a new "tribunal" or by courts, as Treadwell suggested.[8]

Wiel also disagreed that the economic value of a riparian's water was unknowable. Upon receiving applications filed for new appropriative water rights, he reasoned, the commission would provide public notice of the application. When riparians protested such new appropriative water rights applications, as was their right under the Water Commission Act, dismissal of the protest and issuance of the water rights permit sought by the applicant would be handled routinely by estimating the economic value of the loss from the new appropriation. Damage to the land value would be measured by the appraised difference in value before and after the water was taken. Issuance and exercise of the new water rights permit would be conditioned on payment of the required compensation (hence his "conditioned permit" plan label). This approach, he felt, could both lower the administrative cost of addressing compensation by having the Water Commission handle it and reduce the over-appropriation of water rights administratively and systematically. In his minority report, he referred to such over-appropriation as "the unbalanced issuance of water rights permits, unbalanced for lack of a check."

Wiel's system sought to reconcile water rights with available river flows by actually determining whether there was enough water in a stream to support the permitted diversion, thus establishing the presence or absence of injury to other water users. If injury was detected, compensation to riparians and subsequent voiding of their water rights could relieve demand pressure on water resources, hopefully while preserving the head or flow of the stream. In proposing this plan, Wiel was almost certainly aware that the Joint Legislative Committee had reviewed and considered Elwood Mead's *Bulletin 100* from 1900 in which the U.S. Department of Agriculture Office of Irrigation documented the over-appropriation of water along the San Joaquin River. The joint committee called their legislative colleagues' attention "to some of the important reports which have been filed with it, which may be of value to other members should they desire to study them," and listed Mead's report among them.

If each new water right application to the Water Commission retired old water rights through compensation for injury, Wiel reasoned, it would go a long way toward preserving the river's flow and its ability to deliver water as much as possible through the natural service of gravity, or hydraulic head. He ridiculed Treadwell's proposal to compensate solely for the "surplus" over the diversions needed by riparians because it was unknowable and because in most cases would yield such small amounts. The hydraulic head to be preserved in Wiel's approach required running water. That flow was a natural delivery service provided by gravity and by which other water right holders could also exercise their claims. Thus, Wiel argued that what could actually be diverted as "surplus" without harming the head was probably not a large quantity. To presuppose both the water rights needed for coordinated statewide development *and* compensation to riparians would probably result in small, economically infeasible projects (Wiel 1928c, 62–78; Wiel 1929b). Compensation, therefore, should be part of solving over-appropriation, Wiel argued to both committees, as opposed to determining Treadwell's alleged "surplus."

> The present excess is in issuing permits unaccompanied by compensation. To go on extending power [to divert] would therefore be the reverse of the necessary direction. The need is simply to insert compensation into the current [bureaucratic] machinery at the point where cognizance of [damage to water rights] it most aptly arises. (Wiel 1928c, 60)

Wiel's approach to compensation certainly offered a solution to a vexing structural problem: the over-appropriation of rivers and streams throughout California (Table 8.3). But it was not necessarily part of the Legal Advisory Committee's charge. It appears the committee attorneys saw their charge more narrowly: finding the best mechanism for compensating Miller & Lux and any other riparian water right holder that dared to challenge California's massive 1927 appropriative water rights filings in support of its water plan.[9]

The attorney committee swung to Treadwell's agenda, preferring to use much of his September remarks as the body of its late October 1928 majority report to the Joint Legislative Committee on Water Problems in California. "I concur," wrote Samuel C. Wiel tersely with his signature at the end of the attorneys' report, "in such parts of the foregoing report as are consistent with a separate report filed by me herewith." Which was to say, not a lot.[10]

Wiel hindered his own case. His report—representing a minority that apparently consisted of himself—is marred by a fawning, complex, even hasty writing style that obscures his compensation plan ideas from his primary audience: fellow attorneys and busy state legislators. His plan has two names for the same idea and sprawls across fifteen pages of annotated sections (out of nearly eighty total pages). Yet a few months later, he published it in just two uninterrupted pages in the *California Law Review*. Despite enlisting expert assistance from Stanford and Berkeley

TABLE 8.3. Central Valley Water Right Claims Compared with Median River Flows as of 1927

FLOW LOCATION	ESTIMATED MEDIAN ANNUAL FLOW, 1895–1927 (ACRE-FEET)	ESTIMATED CONSUMPTIVE RIPARIAN AND PRE–1914 WATER RIGHT CLAIMS (FACE AMOUNT IN ACRE-FEET)
Sacramento River near Freeport	22,510,000	47,883,000
San Joaquin River at Vernalis	6,069,600	16,125,000

Source: State Water Resources Board 1951; Stroshane 2012; aggregation of flows estimated by author.

geologists to bolster his arguments about the unknowability of stream surpluses, Wiel failed to get legislators' attention for his alternative to over-appropriation. Treadwell's criticism of the inevitability of adjudication was apparently more persuasive. Wiel's proposal to use the change in land value to determine compensation got around Treadwell's focus on determining a stream's surplus, but his turgid presentation and tardy submission doomed his argument to obscurity. And with an agricultural depression in full swing, the idea that new water right applicants could or would pay much more than an administrative fee for filing may also have been a political nonstarter.

Yet, the Legal Advisory Committee's own majority recommendation concerning limited compensation to obtain "surplus" from riparian-dominated rivers also went on the shelf to collect dust, along with Wiel's proposal to deal with over-appropriation.

* * *

State Engineer Paul Bailey's 1927 update on the state water plan, *Bulletin 12*, promised a new supply from the Sacramento Valley to the San Joaquin. "The coordinated plan," he wrote confidently, if abstractly, "proposes to correlate the conveyance of a new supply into the southern San Joaquin Valley with the development of water for local needs throughout the length of the two valleys. In this way the new supply may be obtained with full protection to established properties."

After "serving its purpose" in the Sacramento Valley maintaining navigation flows, said Bailey, Sacramento River water would enter the Delta estuary to be diverted to the mouth of the San Joaquin River. It would then be "boosted up the main channel of the San Joaquin by a series of pumping plants, each one pumping the water over a low dam to the higher level of the pond behind it. These dams," Bailey continued, "would be collapsible so that they would not obstruct the channel during flood season. They would be so located that, if desired, locks could be constructed along side them that would make the San Joaquin River navigable for a distance of 160 miles from its mouth." The dams and pumping system would also capture runoff from lower San Joaquin Valley sources for continued use later (Figure 8.1).

The San Joaquin River, meanwhile, would be diverted into a canal at Friant Dam for delivery to the Kings River area, and another canal from Pine Flat Reservoir on the Kings would shunt water south to the Tulare Lake area of southern Tulare and northern Kern Counties (California Department of Public Works 1927b, 36–37).

Such a pumping system plan for the San Joaquin River was overly complex, however, and state engineers soon rethought it.[11] *Bulletin 25*, issued by the state in 1930, described "exchanges of water" that would make the Central Valley Project legally and operationally possible. This exchange, wrote state water planners, would substitute water from Kennett (the reservoir that became known as "Shasta")

FIGURE 8.1. Proposed San Joaquin River Pumping System: fourteen dams between the Delta and Mendota area to accommodate the exchange of Sacramento for San Joaquin River water diverted at Friant Dam to Tulare and Kern Counties. Fortunately this devastating project was replaced in the 1940s by the Delta Mendota Canal, completed in 1951. Source: California Department of Public Works 1927b.

releases via the Delta in lieu of waters stored in and exported from Friant reservoir (California Department of Public Works 1930b, 179). Shasta waters would substitute for San Joaquin River flows no longer received for diversion at the Mendota Pool because those flows would be exported from the San Joaquin River at Friant Dam. A Madera Canal and a "San Joaquin River–Kern County canal" would distribute Friant-held waters north and south (California Department of Public Works 1930b, 97, Table 17).

An additional west-side canal from Mendota to Kern County would draw water from Mendota Pool not needed by Miller & Lux's descendants for delivery along 100 miles of canal south to Kern County on the west side of the upper San Joaquin Valley. (This canal reach would later be realigned and subsumed into the California Aqueduct and the San Luis Canal.)

Bulletin 25 acknowledged that in California such ambitious exchanges or substitutions of water supplies had never been attempted.[12] State water planners claimed that court decisions in Idaho, Utah, and Washington favored water substitution and tentatively offered, "[I]t is believed a substitution of water is legal, whether the opponent be a riparian owner or an appropriator."[13]

Bulletin 25 also broached the idea that the riparian rights and "appropriations of early priority" from "a large area of grass and pasture lands" along the San Joaquin—another thinly veiled reference to Miller & Lux—be purchased in order to "release the waters thereby acquired for storage in Friant reservoir and diversions therefrom northward to Madera County lands and southward into the areas of the San Joaquin Valley lying south of the San Joaquin River." In the view of the state water planners, this purchase (which included snowpack "floods and freshets") would "eliminate the riparian vendor as an objector to such a transfer" of the rights from its diversion at Mendota to its storage at Friant—much the way that Wiel would have had riparians compensated by newly filed appropriators.[14] While identifying specific rights by which it could obtain a legal source for the export of San Joaquin River water to Tulare and Kern—that is, the "large area of grass and pasture land"—*Bulletin 25* disclosed no details of the purchase and exchange deal to be worked out. As it turned out, that was years away. But purchasing the flood flows for the grasslands in that area would give Friant reservoir and its diversion canals a supply—mainly in wetter years but not in drier years, when Miller & Lux's senior appropriative rights on the San Joaquin would be most useful to the project. The specific rights involved in "exchange of existing supplies for an imported supply" were not disclosed in *Bulletin 25,* even if they were understood in 1930.

Despite passage of Proposition 7 in 1928, state water planners continued to fear riparians' power to challenge projects proposed by appropriators after *Herminghaus.* And of course such projects included those of the State of California. One feared outcome was that vested riparian right holders would require compensation from appropriators—the very issue identified by the Joint Legislative Committee in 1928–29 (and as confronted in Wiel's proposed compensation plan). In effect, riparians still had legal and economic power to prevent appropriators from moving forward. Unreasonably high demands for compensation might make certain projects uneconomic. The water planners wrote in *Bulletin 25,*

> The riparian doctrine presents a serious obstacle to the operations proposed, whether by storage or exportation, and that the State Water Plan is

fundamentally nonriparian in character.... They enjoy the right to enjoin nonriparian usage and prevent seasonal storage. Unlimited by any rule of reasonableness as against diversion to or usage upon lands other than those riparian to the source, entitled to an injunction without a showing of damage and empowered to prevent storages for release at periods of scant flow, these paramount proprietors, though the owners of relative small acreages along the stream, may restrict usage to said acreages, though the water produced by the stream, if properly husbanded, would supply not only all that they can reasonably use, but also an abundance for nonriparian usage. That such is the law of riparian right has been recently affirmed by the Supreme Court of California in [*Herminghaus*]. (California Department of Public Works 1930b, 178)

This passage somewhat gratuitously dismisses the Herminghaus estates as "small acreages," forgetting their 20 miles of stream bank frontage.

The state cautioned that there was no guarantee that case law ensuing from Proposition 7 would trump the precedents supporting riparian control of rivers that were upheld in *Herminghaus*. Further, "the constitutional amendment in question must face a determined challenge and be construed by the Supreme Court of the United States in reference to the 'due process' clause of the federal constitution before its validity or effect will be definitely established. Reliance upon the police power [with either *Herminghaus* or Proposition 7] therefore is uncertain."[15]

In the absence of a systematic study of the reality of this risk, it appears there was really only *one* fearsome entity: Miller & Lux. This riparian had a huge bloc of water rights to the San Joaquin River and still possessed formidable, if dwindling, corporate power owing to its hydrologic assets. Even with the onset of the Great Depression and the collapse of Miller & Lux's share of the beef market, it remained difficult for state officials to acknowledge that their vituperation against the *riparian doctrine* was mainly aimed at Miller & Lux representatives during the 1930s—a sort of muscle memory from decades of collective rhetorical exercise. Yet it tarred all riparians. Moreover, Miller & Lux still controlled the senior *appropriative* water rights of the San Joaquin & Kings River Canal & Irrigation Company.

Bulletin 25 also addressed groundwater. It found an average seasonal supply deficiency of about 387,000 acre-feet affecting about 400,000 acres in the upper San Joaquin Valley. The maximum annual deficiency was about 680,000 acre-feet in 1928–29, the first full year of the 1928–34 drought.

The "logical source" to address this deficiency was the San Joaquin River, close by. A canal designed to use gravity could transport imported surface water from Friant to eastern Fresno, Tulare, and Kern Counties. The average annual San Joaquin supply from "surplus and 'grass land' rights" was estimated at 601,000 acre-feet, which would cover many if not most lean years (California Department of Public

Works 1930b, 164). *Bulletin 25* estimated that, had Friant Dam and its Madera and San Joaquin–Kern County Canals been in operation in the 1920s, instead of a 2.5 million acre-foot deficiency, the upper San Joaquin Valley (with San Joaquin River imports of 3.9 million acre-feet) would have a net groundwater recharge of about 1.36 million acre-feet (California Department of Public Works 1930, 165, Pl. XI).

* * *

Compensating Miller & Lux was going to be a big, fearsome bill. A 1936 appraisal by three widely respected civil engineers valued the company's water rights at $2.45 million ($41.3 million in 2014 dollars).[16]

What would the bill be for? How much access to water, and from where, would result from these upcoming negotiations? The water rights for the San Joaquin side of the state plan involved rights on the San Joaquin River upstream of the Merced River confluence—both riparian and pre–1914 appropriative rights.

In its prime, Miller & Lux (and some smaller nonaligned entities) had acquired and held an estimated 1.46 million acre-feet of combined riparian and appropriative water rights along the San Joaquin River. Table 8.4 summarizes pre–1914 and riparian rights on the San Joaquin River. It is distilled from a series of California Water Project Authority reports produced between 1936 and 1939 (California Water Project Authority 1936a–c, 1937a–f, 1938, 1939a–c). Overall, the major water rights holders there claimed about 1.75 million acre-feet in riparian and pre–1914 appropriative claims. Often the cattle company's rights were described as extending to "all of the San Joaquin River." Table 8.4 suggests it was nearly so. Miller & Lux canals included Gravelly Ford, Aliso, Lone Willow Slough, Columbia, San Joaquin and Kings River Canal, Firebaugh, Main, Outside, Blythe, Helm, and San Luis.[17]

This portion of the San Joaquin River and its water rights were the focus of two efforts during the 1920s. First, came an attempt to form a Madera Irrigation District (whose committee members had acquired the Friant Reservoir site) to supply Madera County with irrigation water. Later there was an attempt to form a more region-wide San Joaquin Water Storage District. Both attempts forced the communities of the upper San Joaquin River into protracted litigation and negotiation with Miller & Lux and its canal company as its grip on the local economy weakened.[18] Ultimately, negotiations failed when Miller & Lux repeatedly refused to quantify its rights. Miller & Lux saw quantifying rights as tantamount to limiting them in the face of intensifying regional competition for water. Frustrated by this recalcitrance, Madera Irrigation District officials finally withdrew from negotiations in mid-1930, opting to drag Miller & Lux to court in an eminent-domain proceeding. As it also liquidated its herds and lands, Miller & Lux finally submitted to quantification of its water rights, a defensive action at that point in the corporation's deterioration. So began the test of the dead hand of Henry Miller (see chapter 4).

TABLE 8.4. Riparian and Pre–1914 Appropriative Water Rights on the San Joaquin River

SAN JOAQUIN RIVER IRRIGATION USES	POINT OF DIVERSION	OTHER DESCRIPTION	AMOUNT OF WATER RIGHTS
Friant to Gravelly Ford right holders	Nearly 200 diverters or groundwater pumpers proximate to San Joaquin River	Rights of most of these landowners were eventually acquired by USBR*, but some of those not immediately acquired by 1939 became plaintiffs in *Rank v. Krug*, a suit by riparian and groundwater water right holders in this area against Friant Dam. Case decided in federal court in 1950. The court acknowledged that these water right holders collectively used about 200,000 acre-feet per year in this area of the San Joaquin River. This was the section of river that received releases from Friant under state water right decision 990. Below Gravelly Ford, however, the river dried up through to the confluence with the Merced River. The San Joaquin River Settlement Agreement (2006) put continuing riparian releases to these water right holders at 116,741 acre-feet in most water years.	116,741
San Joaquin River Exchange Contractors rights	USBR* diverts these flows at Friant Dam into Madera and Friant-Kern Canals	Subject of a water rights exchange contract with USBR (U.S. Congress 1957). Originally "cropland" rights owned by Miller & Lux on which permanent and other crops were cultivated with highly reliable senior appropriative and riparian water rights. The Exchange Contractors, having provided USBR with an easement for use of these rights, receives in their place flows from Shasta Reservoir via Jones Pumping Plant near Tracy and the Delta Mendota Canal. (Estimated at 817,000 acre-feet in the USBR Purchase Contract with Miller & Lux.)	840,000

TABLE 8.4. Riparian and Pre–1914 Appropriative Water Rights on the San Joaquin River (*continued*)

SAN JOAQUIN RIVER IRRIGATION USES	POINT OF DIVERSION	OTHER DESCRIPTION	AMOUNT OF WATER RIGHTS
Tranquillity & James Irrigation Districts—Fresno Slough	Riparian diversions along Fresno Slough above Mendota Pool	Diversions were subordinated through case law to Miller & Lux rights and allowed only when San Joaquin River reached 1,360 cfs, and then the districts could take just 12 percent up to a maximum of 140 cfs along Fresno Slough. Estimated face amount for these districts obtained from California Water Project Authority (1936c, Table 5).	29,300
USBR purchase rights from Miller & Lux, Inc.	Friant Dam, re-diverted at Madera and Friant-Kern Canals	Subject of a water rights purchase contract with USBR, and appraised at this quantity of water (Etcheverry et al. 1936; California Water Project Authority 1936c). Originally grassland and "uncontrolled" riparian flood flows. Grassland flows were pre-1914 appropriative rights of the Miller & Lux canal company; "uncontrolled" flows were riparian rights associated with lands adjacent to the San Joaquin River owned by Miller & Lux cattle business for grazing.	623,200
Chowchilla Farms	Chowchilla Canal, east side San Joaquin River above Mendota Pool	Subject of a water rights purchase contract with USBR for appropriative rights via Chowchilla Canal and under appropriative and riparian rights through Blythe Canal. These rights were acquired for storage at Friant Dam and diversion into Madera Canal (California Water Project Authority 1937e).	49,300
Lands between Chowchilla Farms and Stevinson lands	Between Chowchilla River and Merced River along east side of San Joaquin River	Subject to water rights purchase contracts with USBR, including lands of Bloss, Hatfield, Crane, Turner, Erreca and Hansen (California Water Project Authority 1937f). In 1936, subordinate only to prior appropriative, prescriptive and contractual rights held by Miller & Lux and associated companies.	40,281

TABLE 8.4. Riparian and Pre-1914 Appropriative Water Rights on the San Joaquin River (*continued*)

SAN JOAQUIN RIVER IRRIGATION USES	POINT OF DIVERSION	OTHER DESCRIPTION	AMOUNT OF WATER RIGHTS
Edison Securities	Riparian at confluence of Fresno Slough and San Joaquin River	Subject of a water rights purchase contract with USBR for uncontrolled overflow riparian rights from the San Joaquin River and associated sloughs upstream of Mendota Pool, along south bank (California Water Project Authority 1938). Edison Securities purchased these riparian lands from the Herminghaus Estate in January 1928.	33,127
Stevinson Canal/ East Side Canal	Riparian and pre-1914 appropriative diversions upstream on San Joaquin River from Merced River	Unclear whether USBR entered into a water rights purchase contract with Stevinson. Stevinson's diversion rights were considered subordinate to Edison Securities and Miller & Lux (California Water Project Authority 1939a, 18), and Stevinson instead was able to arrange a supply of water for its lands via the Merced River from Merced Irrigation District under the Stevinson Contract. East Side Canal appropriation from the San Joaquin River was found to average 14,268 acre-feet, while residual riparian rights to the San Joaquin averaged 5,900 acre-feet.	20,168
TOTAL PRE-1914 AND RIPARIAN WATER RIGHTS, UPPER SAN JOAQUIN RIVER			1,752,117

*USBR: U.S. Bureau of Reclamation

Sources: Etcheverry et al. 1936; California Water Project Authority (1936a–c, 1937a–f, 1938, 1939a–c); Miller 1993; Stroshane 2012; U.S. Congress 1957.

San Diego judge Charles G. Haines was brought to the San Joaquin Valley to render a more impartial decision on Miller & Lux's rights. He completed his decree in 1932 (Fresno County Superior Court 1932). The "Haines Decree" specifically recognized Miller & Lux rights in detail and subjected those rights to evidentiary rules (that is, witnesses providing sworn testimony, susceptible to cross-examination under penalty of perjury). The decree became the quantified legal basis by which the California Water Project Authority—and later the U.S. Bureau of Reclamation—would recognize the scope and value of the Miller & Lux water rights in the river.

Miller & Lux's water rights were finally made visible for state water planning (California Department of Public Works 1952, 57; Fresno County Superior Court 1932; Miller 1993; Minasian 2016).

During the economic depression of the 1930s, the state of California obtained narrow statewide voter approval of the Central Valley Project Act but was unable to sell bonds to finance the project. Through an emergency appropriation in a congressional rivers and harbor bill in 1935, the federal government took over the Central Valley Project, with the U.S. Bureau of Reclamation named to run it. At this point, "Miller & Lux filed pro forma protests and assertions of its rights and promptly entered into negotiations" with the Bureau of Reclamation between 1935 and 1939 (M. C. Miller 1993, 173). While the California Water Project Authority continued to plan aspects of the project, the Bureau assumed the lead role, since it had capital, expertise, and—given its role in creating jobs and stimulating the economy—the ability to fulfill public hopes for the project. So, instead of the senior Miller & Lux water rights partnering with the state of California for the CVP, the cattle company now had the Bureau of Reclamation as its junior partner.

The Bureau also purchased the Friant reservoir site from the Madera Irrigation District through a separate purchase agreement in the late 1930s.[19]

In entering that partnership, Miller & Lux granted the Bureau an easement to the cattle company's most senior, pre-1914 appropriative water rights in exchange for a supply "of like amount" from the Sacramento River via the new Delta Mendota Canal. The canal would traverse a high contour of the western San Joaquin Valley from Tracy to Mendota Pool. This arrangement became known as the "Exchange Contract" and created the hydrologic security that enabled construction of Friant Dam and Millerton Lake to store up to 520,500 acre-feet of water annually. Friant Dam supplies could then be diverted into the Madera Canal for delivery northwest of Friant to the Madera and Chowchilla irrigation interests and south to Tulare and Kern Counties in the southern (upper) San Joaquin Valley. In this way, the Bureau's Friant facilities acquired or borrowed about 1.6 million acre-feet of pre-1914 water rights for export when flood flows could be captured and diverted.[20] These exports have generally not reached the Delta or San Francisco Bay since the early 1950s, except in such flood events as occurred in January 1997.

Two agreements between the U.S. Bureau of Reclamation and Miller & Lux and its corporate descendants were executed in July 1939: a purchase agreement (USDOI 1939a) and an exchange agreement (USDOI 1939b; amended contracts USDOI 1956, 1968). Through the purchase agreement the Bureau acquired title to "all waters of the San Joaquin River in excess of flows as specified," with simple, monthly average flow schedules attached (i.e., "overflow" rights derived from Miller & Lux's "overflow grasslands water rights"). The exchange agreement, on the other hand, gave the Bureau the right to all waters of the San Joaquin River "if, as, and when" the Bureau were to import waters equivalent in quantity and quality to those that the Miller & Lux affiliates were otherwise entitled to receive from the San Joaquin River. That is, Miller & Lux's (or now, the Exchange Contractors') reliable rights to San Joaquin waters were exchanged when equivalent firm deliveries from the Sacramento River via the Delta Mendota Canal were available at Mendota Pool.

Since then, how often has it happened that the Bureau failed to deliver the substitute supply from Shasta to Mendota Pool? Twice: 2014 and 2015. There have only been seven years between 1977 and 2015 in which the Exchange Contractors have seen less than 100 percent of their substitute allocation from Shasta delivered at Mendota Pool.[21]

The criteria for deliveries to the Exchange Contractors included: defining a critical year as a water year in which "full natural inflow" to Shasta Lake beginning February 1 is 3.2 million acre-feet or less, or total accumulated deficiencies below 4 million acre-feet in the immediately prior water year or successive prior years exceed 800,000 acre-feet (U.S. Congress 1957, 605).

In years when these conditions do not apply, deliveries to the exchange contractors are to be 100-percent reliable at an amount not to exceed 840,000 acre-feet. But when water years become "critical," the Exchange Contractors' substitute supply may be 650,000 acre-feet without triggering a requirement that the Bureau release water from Friant Dam into the San Joaquin River to make up the shortfall. No matter how bad a drought gets for the Central Valley Project, the Exchange Contractors are to be served, whether from Shasta, Friant, or both.

The Exchange Contract reaffirms the status of the most senior Miller & Lux affiliates' water rights to the San Joaquin River, while enabling both of California's massive water transfers from north to south: (1) San Joaquin's basin to Tulare and Kern Counties, and (2) the Sacramento's basin to the San Joaquin's. The legal and hydraulic pivot of this exchange is today still Mendota Pool; Friant Dam for decades has been operated "if, as, and when" the Delta Mendota Canal delivers sufficient flows. The Exchange Contract continues the Exchange Contractors' status as the most powerful water rights holders in the San Joaquin River basin. In dry years, they have the power under the established law of the Central Valley Project to prevent export of surface water to Tulare and Kern Counties from Friant Dam, should deliveries from Shasta and the Delta Mendota Canal fail.

The Bureau's post–1914 water rights claims amount to 8.3 million acre-feet in the San Joaquin River basin. This is a lavish exaggeration on both the Bureau's and the State Water Board's parts. Some originated as state filings under the 1927 Feigenbaum Act. All are unchecked by the continuing reality of over-appropriation. And yet the Bureau remains a junior partner to the controlling senior rights of the Exchange Contractors in the San Joaquin Valley. And during drought, Friant and Madera Canal contractors have seen this system deliver supplies at or near zero.

NOTES

1. Eventually, Central Valley Project deliveries to spreading basins from the Friant-Kern Canal helped slow the overdraft of groundwater in Tulare and northern Kern Counties but did not end it, as mentioned in chapter 5.

2. The concept of "face amount" quantifies a water right, enabling different water rights to be compared on that basis. It represents the total volume that could be realized by full extent of the right's exercise. Water rights may be composed of a flow rate (often expressed in cubic feet per second), a storage quantity, and a season of use. The face amount is essentially the flow rate times the total amount of time in the season of use, plus (or limited to) any storage capacity.

3. As things worked out, it took decades before these applications received operational permits, while the diligence requirement continued to be postponed. Today, state water regulators apply great deference to the agencies of the coordinated, statewide water development system (that is, the Central Valley Project and the State Water Project) because of the Feigenbaum Act appropriative water rights. But that is another story.

4. The other attorney members of the Legal Advisory Committee were chairman Henry E. Monroe (president of the San Francisco Bar Association), Fred G. Athearn of San Francisco (one of whose clients was Pacific Gas & Electric Company), Louis C. Bartlett (former city council member from Berkeley), William B. Bosley of San Francisco, Spencer Burroughs of the state's Division of Water Rights of the Department of Public Works in Sacramento, A. L. Cowell of Stockton, and Homer J. Hankins of San Francisco.

5. My search of the California State Archive, California State Library records, and the Water Resources Collections and Archives at the University of California at Riverside, Special Collections, revealed no surviving formal documents of the legal advisory committee—such as meeting agendas and minutes.

6. Treadwell (1928, 10) acknowledged that "some have suggested that the matter be handled by the present Division of Water Rights [of the Department of Public Works], while others have suggested that the Division is too closely connected with the program of the state to take these waters to be deemed an impartial tribunal, and for that reason they have suggested that a new commission be created for this particular purpose."

7. Treadwell is quoting Proposition 7 language here.

8. Wiel authored two more law review articles in early 1929 that dealt with aspects of *his* presentations to the Legal Advisory Committee but were not included with its final report to the joint committee. The two 1929 articles built on his two-part essay in the *California Law Review* from early 1928 (see chapter 7). On one hand, they provided details of his proposed plan for compensating riparian water right holders in order to preclude their enjoining the state's appropriations. On the other, Wiel deepened his analysis of the legal implications from hydraulic science concerning the question whether it was even possible to anticipate a surplus from rivers, as assumed by Treadwell, bringing a geologist to the committee to address the question. He also completed a separate report for the Legal Advisory Committee, which he submitted four days after the committee's report went to the Joint Legislative Committee. His minority report is Wiel 1928c; see also Wiel 1929a, 1929b.

9. It is possible that Wiel was even on the cusp of suggesting that his compensation plan might demonstrate less actual need for a system like the Central Valley Project—an interesting subject for a "what if" history of California water.

10. Wiel's "separate" report was omitted from the official records compiled by northern California congress member Clair Engle in his *Central Valley Project Documents*. Copies of

Wiel's report are available at UC Berkeley's Main and Bancroft Libraries and at the University of California at Riverside, Special Collections, Water Resources Collections and Archives.

11. There was no thought disclosed in *Bulletin 12* as to consequences downstream for the Delta. Nor were potential consequences for groundwater recharge or for migratory salmon and steelhead populations, which at the time thrived in the San Joaquin River. These fish species had used Central Valley rivers for at least the last 15,000 years. Commercial and sportfishing industries, and subsistence fishing by California Indians and poorer contemporary immigrants depended on them (Hollowell and Hollowell 2010). Fourteen dams and pump lifts might have doomed spring-run Chinook salmon on the San Joaquin River to earlier extinction and extirpated what natural aquatic and terrestrial habitat remained along the San Joaquin after eighty years of agricultural development. This project was later redesigned and relocated by Bureau engineers as a "high line canal" in 1939. Initially the new canal design was considered as an alternative approach to the San Joaquin River Pumping System. It was later renamed the Delta Mendota Canal. This new design would substantially reduce the cost of the pump lift and eliminate immediate impacts to salmon and steelhead habitat along the length of the San Joaquin River from the Delta to Mendota—at least until Friant Dam was completed in the late 1940s.

12. However, about this time the Stevinson irrigation colony downstream, near the Merced River confluence, was arranging a legally analogous exchange with the Merced Irrigation District.

13. Such substitutions or exchanges can be viewed legally as "physical solutions" to the problem of injury in water rights law. See California Department of Public Works 1930b, 180.

14. The Bureau's acquisition of post–1914 water rights, assigned from Madera Irrigation District and the state of California, was mostly to complete the transfer of its purchased rights from Mendota to its points of storage and diversion at Friant (California Department of Public Works 1930b).

15. In terms of legal practice and process, it is doubtful that the U.S. Supreme Court would be the final arbiter of Proposition 7. Water law is viewed primarily as a police power held by the states by virtue of its very specific local and regional character. Subsequent decisions on reasonable use of water in light of Proposition 7 were made in California courts (California Department of Public Works 1930b).

16. For the estimated water rights value, see Etcheverry et al. (1936, 36); California Water Project Authority (1937a, 21, Table 11); and U.S. Bureau of Reclamation News Clippings (1936–42): "$2,450,000 Deal on Water Rights for Dam Speeded: Page Says Miller & Lux Agreement Will Hasten Friant Project Work," *Fresno Bee*, April 12, 1938; "Accord Reached on Water Issues," *Bakersfield Californian*, April 12, 1938; "Page Reports Agreements on Rights for Central Valley Water Project," *Contra Costa Gazette*, April 12, 1938.

The dollar equivalency is a rough estimate of the equivalent worth of these rights in 2014, using simply the December 1936 Consumer Price Index deflator of 14.0 and the November 2014 deflator of 236.151 (Base = 1982; U.S. Bureau of Labor Statistics 2014).

17. Two California Water Project Authority reports (1936c, 9–25; 1937b) summarize the Haines cases and decree, the Miller & Lux grassland rights, riparian rights, appropriative rights, the rights of Miller & Lux neighbors upstream and downstream, and pending litigation at the time. Later, Miller & Lux's land holdings were distributed to smaller, private canal companies, some of which have since morphed into water and irrigation districts. Today they are Central California Irrigation District, Firebaugh Canal Water District, San Luis Canal Company, and Columbia Canal Company. Their continuing importance lies in the fact that they retain titles to the early riparian, appropriative, and prescriptive water rights Miller & Lux

assembled and owned long before 1914. Attorney Paul Minasian (2016, 14–16, Sec. 5) disclosed these rights to SWRCB, based largely on the Haines Decree of 1932.

18. This complex history is detailed by Miller (1993, Chs. 5–6).

19. "U.S. Purchases Friant Dam Site, Madera Rights for $300,000," *Fresno Bee*, June 5, 1939; "U.S. Buys Site of Friant Dam," *Sacramento Bee*, June 5, 1939. News articles from U.S. Bureau of Reclamation (1936–42).

20. Annual average deliveries to the Madera and Friant-Kern Canal water service contractors from delivery data for 1985–2010 available from the Bureau of Reclamation Mid-Pacific Region web site for Central Valley Project operations, accessed in 2011. Data analysis in author's collection.

21. Data analysis obtained from Central Valley Project's Operations Office web site, in author's collection. Accessible online at http://www.usbr.gov/mp/cvo/vungvari/water_allocations_historical.pdf, accessed May 20, 2016.

Chapter 9

Glass Half Full

DROUGHT REVEALS THE TENSIONS in governing a capitalist, hydraulic society such as California, where competition over scarce water supplies drives conflict. Deficits of Nature and needs of capitalists came into clear conflict in the early 1930s, just as most of the state's major urban aqueduct systems became operational. Already, at the onset of the Depression, California was in a drought that began in late 1928. It extended through the summer irrigation season of 1934 and remains one of the longest and worst droughts in the state's recorded history. Figures 9.1 through 9.3 show that every major watershed in the Central Valley experienced significant flow reductions from long-term averages.

Neither organizing new districts, nor regulating new water rights, nor adjudicating water rights brought more water supplies. But as California's population more than doubled to 3.4 million from 1900–1920, the quest for coordinated water resource development gained momentum. Cities swelled to account for over three-quarters of its population (Thompson 1955, 10). Agricultural productivity expanded through technological innovation and cultivation of newly irrigated lands, and the advent of refrigeration fueled the growth of domestic and Asian food-commodity markets. Yet during the 1920s, farmers fell on hard times: the end of World War I led to crop surpluses and falling commodity prices, and drought compounded those problems.

By the 1920s, irrigation- and water-district bond issues had stabilized since their rickety Bridgford Act days. An example of water's growing importance to California's financial structure is clear from a transcript of a special hearing before the Office of the Superintendent of Banks, March 29, 1931, in San Francisco, to address drought and its effects on the security of public irrigation bonds.

"We have in our state banks millions of dollars in irrigation bonds—millions of dollars in loans on agricultural property—orchards and farm land in general," declared Superintendent Edward Rainey as he opened the hearing. Present at the hearing besides Rainey were Colonel Walter Garrison, Director of Public Works for the state; Edward Hyatt, California's State Engineer; Harlowe Stafford, a state hydraulic engineer who previously served as San Joaquin Sacramento Delta water supervisor in the 1920s; hydraulic engineering consultants Walter Huber and John D. Galloway; L.B. Cheminant of the San Francisco City Engineer's office; and John Sharon of the San Francisco Water Department. Also present were a number of bank examiners, banking regulators, and Dan S. Canny, the Secretary of the California Bond Certification Commission (a precursor of the California Debt Allocation

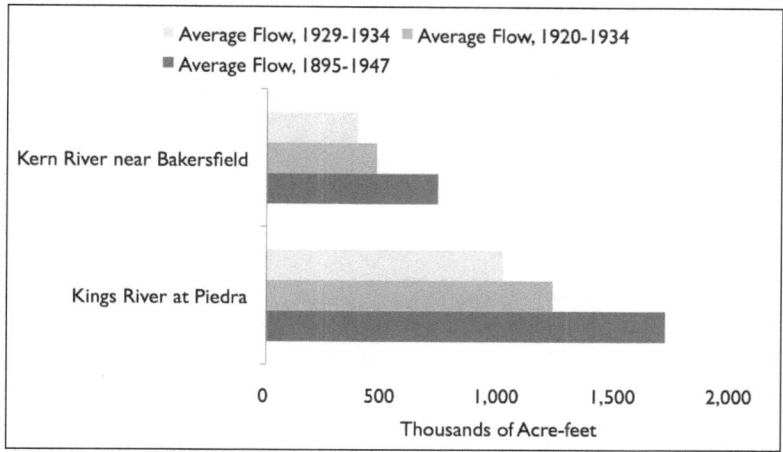

FIGURE 9.1. Drought effects on river runoff, Tulare Lake Basin. Source: State Water Resources Board 1951.

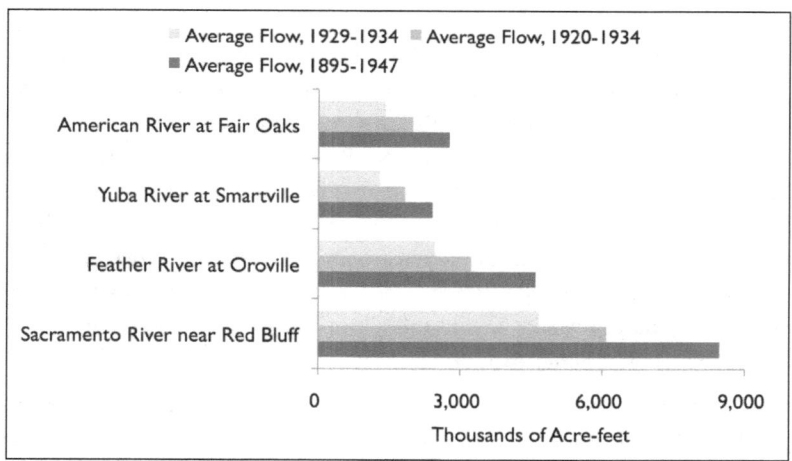

FIGURE 9.2. Drought effects on river runoff, Sacramento River Basin. Source: State Water Resources Board 1951.

Committee). All were there to discuss, Rainey continued, "the rainfall, upon which a lot of paper [outstanding bonds and farm loans] depends in California and the prosperity of the farmers and in talking about the situation we thought it might be a good thing to have a meeting and face the facts...." (Superintendent of Banks 1931).

Rainey asked Hyatt to summarize the situation. The State Engineer recounted dry years back to 1920, gloomily reporting that river runoff totals in the winter of 1931 would continue the dry trend.

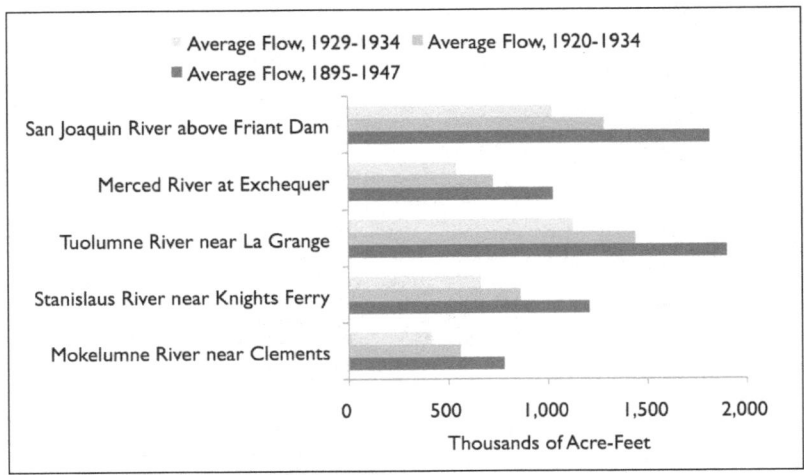

FIGURE 9.3. Drought effects on river runoff, San Joaquin River Basin. Source: State Water Resources Board 1951.

MR. HYATT: Right up to date, as of March 19th, we have an estimate of the probable run-off of the various streams estimated on a 40 year runoff [record], ... 35% [of the average of the 40-year records] on the Sacramento—the lowest is about 30% on the Kings and the highest 45% on the Tuolumne and Merced. The estimate of the low-flow discharge for late July and early August on the American is nothing—50 second feet. Estimated on the salinity intrusion [into the Delta] it is much better than 1926 and 1924 and the estimate will not be as bad as 1924, but apparently will be as bad as any except 1924 and in the Sacramento valley rice area a 20% increase over 1930. (Superintendent of Banks 1931, 2)

But 1931 turned out to be the worst year for salinity intrusion in the Delta before World War II. Going into the spring of 1931 after two dry years, farmers and their bankers were anxious: without water, how would growers generate income to pay their irrigation district assessments? Those assessments defrayed the districts' bonded debt, owed to bond holders throughout the country. Also, most growers had to use bank credit to plant and cultivate their crops. If they could not sustain their crops, how could they pay back their loans?[1]

In the 1920s, Sacramento Valley growers intensified rice cultivation. To address the dry-year problems, Hyatt described to bank regulators the voluntary response of many water diverters there.

MR. HYATT: In Sacramento they have had serious years already. In 1920, on account of the high price of rice they planted a tremendous acreage and that year the stream was practically used up and there was such alarm that a water conservation committee was formed and operated and prevented any serious damage to the rice industry. Again in 1924 it was apparently a bad year and they formed a local committee known as the Sacramento–San Joaquin Water Problems Conference and they functioned again that year. They actually distributed the water and prevented any serious loss. That old committee is still in existence and meet[s] once a year. It is a fine committee to work through. Headed by the power companies, etc. It raised friendly subscriptions in 1924.

MR. RAINEY: For what purpose?

MR. HYATT: To finance a program and actually distribute the water and prevent waste. There was an intensive campaign to prevent waste and keep the use to the minimum and also keep down to some extent the planting of rice. That committee could probably be called into existence again. Since 1924, Mr. Stafford has been on the river [as water supervisor], not so much with the idea of restricting diversions but to get an idea of the acreage rather and made some effort toward reducing waste. We now have an excellent record of the area in the valley and in the last few years they have been coming in to find out about, this time of the year, to find out about water conditions to govern plantings and at the present time we got many inquiries, wanting to know of the water conditions. Now, if it is as bad as it seems there ought to be some warning, but whether or not that should be a general warning is another question. We can put out a warning sub-rosa and perhaps reduce the acreage.

MR. RAINEY: From the point of view of this Department it should be sub-rosa.

MR. HYATT: A general warning has a bad effect. So far as the delta is concerned, we simply can not help it—salt is going up in there and no measures can be taken except to keep diversions to the minimum. . . . On the salinity, I don't know what could be done except to work in the Sacramento [Valley] to keep as much water coming down as possible. (Superintendent of Banks 1931, 3–4)

Like any prudent bank regulator, Edward Rainey's instinct was to avoid causing panic among farmers, lenders, districts, and bondholders, while shoring up operations of the districts whose assets provided security to their bonds. These enterprises involved incorporating local areas—essentially communities of farmers and growers—as special irrigation districts to issue bonds for irrigation works, levee construction and maintenance, swamp reclamation (what we today know as wetlands), water storage, and municipal utilities. As public districts, they were empowered to bond for all manner of hydraulic works.

State Engineer Hyatt was also sensitive to the needs of the irrigation and water districts whose bonds, as well as their croplands, were withering. Rainey pressed Hyatt at the hearing for the names of the Delta committee members to learn as much about it as he could and to urge Hyatt, his staff, and hydraulic consultants Walter Huber and John D. Galloway to get out in the field to ensure that the district boards and managers operated their water systems so as to keep making payments on their bonds. Hyatt reassured the bankers that he would shuttle about the valleys, "sub-rosa," to impress on the districts' boards the perils of delivering too much water to the farmers.

During the first quarter of the twentieth century, dozens of private electric utility companies and irrigation districts rushed to acquire dam and powerhouse sites throughout the Sierra Nevada and southern Cascade Range. At these sites, they constructed dynamos and diversion works for generating electricity. A powerhouse owner could reap fantastic profits selling power to California's growing cities and thirsty farms pumping groundwater. But when water supplies ran low, hydropower's profitability also suffered, and irrigation districts found it difficult to make bond payments. Such was the case in 1931.

Galloway described local political challenges facing the district boards. Districts had to meet their payment obligations to bondholders while depending on desperate farmers to pay their water bills, who in their turn clamored to receive water for crops *now*.

> MR. GALLOWAY: In the case of Merced [Irrigation District on the Merced River, draining Yosemite Valley], which is an outstanding example, the temptation will be to send all the water through the [electricity generating] powerhouse [maximizing revenues to the district at the expense of the farmers, but facilitating payments on district bonds]. If they have nerve enough to hold that water and let it accumulate they will get a great deal more energy out of the water there than in the low ebb; also it will hold the water back for the dry period this summer [so farmers can get through the peak irrigation season]. However, if they have that nerve with the people down there—that is quite a question. If a delegation of farmers make [sic] a loud demand to get some water, they will come pretty close to getting it without some backing up by a state authority. A survey of the whole situation might help; they might say it is none of your business....

By 1931, it had been so dry for three years that the farmers needed to irrigate just to germinate seeds. "If they have nerve enough to hold that water" is very likely an oblique reference by engineer Galloway to the Merced Irrigation District's several court-decreed water right settlements and negotiated agreements with riparian landowners and farmers. Since 1895, riparian landowners along the lower Merced River, west of Yosemite Valley, had won agreements from agricultural developers such as Charles Crocker (of Union Pacific Railroad fame), and later the Merced Irrigation District, that protected their paramount riparian rights.[2] (Crocker's Merced River diversion dam was later sold to the fledgling District.) One recent pact, the Cowell Agreement, was completed in 1926 prior to the District's construction and operation of Exchequer Dam, its signature structure. The Cowell riparians required the District to release their entitled flows from Exchequer Dam in order to continue irrigating their farms and ranches. Those flows had always to be met prior to the District's own contract obligations to its customers. "If they have the nerve enough to hold that water" is thus an allusion by Galloway to the dam owners' power to turn off the river's flow for their own purposes. In doing so, they could generate more electricity over the summer and have a better chance at making payments on their bond obligations. (After all, as Samuel Wiel observed in 1928, a lawsuit is a poor match for a dam.) Merced Irrigation District's official history confirms this interpretation of Galloway's remarks.

The district's new reservoir at the time, Lake McClure (behind Exchequer), held water amounting to about 3 percent of the lake's capacity at the start of 1931, or about 7,400 acre-feet. "The District continued to be harassed by the riparian owners on the Merced River under the Cowell Agreement. The [district] officials were hailed [sic] into court in a contempt proceeding," which the court continued when all parties agreed on appointment of a watermaster to assure proper handling of diversions. But in the meantime, the District saw its hydroelectric power generation nearly disappear. It transferred scheduled bond payments to its general fund "in order to keep the District in operation" even though some $480,000 was due on July 1, "and there was no money for the payment."[3]

"If a delegation of farmers . . . demand [sic] to get some water, they will come pretty close to getting it. . . ." Here Galloway likely refers to the fact that, legally speaking, Merced Irrigation District probably *couldn't* withhold that water from its riparian neighbors because the District had only acquired post–1914 appropriative rights, which were subordinate to riparian rights along the Merced.

Galloway continued his explanation to Mr. Rainey,

> The trouble is that the local boards don't have the backing of some State authority to stand behind them—the farmers will demand water and use all they can get on their land, and it is pretty hard to resist their claims. (Superintendent of Banks 1931, 8, 10)

So, no authority in the state could prevent the riparian water right holders from insisting on their lawful supplies during a drought. Even a 1928 constitutional amendment approved by voters to require that all water rights at least be reasonable and not wasteful did not appear to curb or eliminate the riparian's paramount right to receive water in dry years.

Merced Irrigation District spent most of the rest of 1931 negotiating with bankers and bondholders about its bonded debt obligations. In the end, the district won a ten-year extension (from forty to fifty years). The district was also able to change its bonds from "serial" (owing interest to bond holders every six months) to "sinking" status, which did not require payments except when the bonds came due. This change successfully shifted some financial risk from districts to bondholders.

But the problem extended beyond irrigation with surface water to groundwater pumping. Such pumping relied on the hydroelectricity that many districts generated from their own powerhouses.

MR. RAINEY: What is the situation of the water tables in the valleys, Mr. Hyatt?

MR. HYATT: More or less the same all over the state. [It is] most aggravated in Tulare—there is a steady depreciation of water and when it doesn't rise in a normal year or better, that means you have taken out more than comes in on the average, and that is the case in the greater part of the upper San Joaquin [Valley]. With the steady depreciation the last ten or twelve years it means they have to go on down another ten or fifteen feet this summer.

MR. RAINEY: What is the limit?

MR. HYATT: Two limits—some run out [of water] entirely and leave. Others get so deep the power charges are more than the land will produce and they have to quit. Others hang on. . . . Every [good] year helps [with recharge], but three or four to bring it back where it should be. In Tulare County [the water tables] will never come back.

MR. GALLOWAY: It will never come back south of Kings River. (Superintendent of Banks 1931, 17–18)

The explosive expansion of irrigation in the Tulare Lake basin was stimulated initially by artesian wells, which flowed naturally due to pressure on full aquifers (water-bearing geologic strata) from the overlying ground—like an oil well gushing. Later, irrigation continued artificially through development of hydroelectric generating capacity in the Sierra Nevada and the invention and widespread use of motorized pumps for extracting underground water. Growers in Tulare and Kern Counties exploited the cheap and abundant electricity by extracting groundwater with pumps to irrigate their field, row, orchard, and vineyard crops like there was no tomorrow. The pumping was so intense that land elevation subsided as much as 30 feet by the early 1930s. (Galloway proved to be right: groundwater elevations have never recovered in this region of California due to the intensive reliance on pumping; see chapter 5.)

The discussion in the hearing transcript veers into an exchange between bankers and water engineers regarding California's climate. It seems there was very little scientific understanding about long-term weather dynamics. Bank examiner Lowell asks the engineers, "Do you think we are now on a permanently lower level of rainfall?" Galloway answers, "I don't think so."

MR. HYATT: How about the old rainfall records—anything worse?

MR. STAFFORD: 1898–99 were about [the worst] but not as bad as 1924.

MR. GALLOWAY: 1883, the San Francisco records show was worse than 1924.

MR. HOLLY [a banking regulator]: I think the driest year was in 1864.

MR. GALLOWAY: In the past we only had two or three dry years, with good years.

MR. HYATT: We came across some old records which showed the Kern River at one time didn't run any water and the cattle all died. We have never seen anything like that. I believe that was about 1800, thereabouts. We don't think the climate has changed[,] it is just in a cycle. . . . We are going to get some good wet years and the delta is going under water again. We will have a different set of troubles then.

From the standpoint of today's more widespread grasp of climate dynamics, facilitated by computerized general circulation and weather-forecasting models, and remote satellite imagery, the analysis of climate illustrated in this March 1931 transcript displays a somewhat naïve faith. Hyatt vaguely refers to cycles, and the engineers try to reassure the Superintendent of Banks that the wet years will return, though without application of nearly as much analytic capacity as employed for the river flow shortfalls earlier in the hearing. On the other hand, it was their personal and professional experience that the wet years would eventually return, just as the dry had done.

The low Delta experienced the brunt of the drought's direct effects. By September 1931, six months after the San Francisco hearing, low river flows meant salty water reached clear to the small Sacramento County town of Isleton along the Sacramento and nearly to Tracy in southern San Joaquin County along the San Joaquin River.

* * *

With memory of the drought of 1928–34 still fresh, Sidney T. Harding, the Berkeley irrigation engineer began what became a lifelong interest: following climate research (Figure 9.4). As the state planned its huge water-resource system, he considered how to apply climate-related findings to engineering practice and forecasts of water supply. He wondered whether California's climate could really provide the water supply then being planned for the Central Valley Project, on which so

FIGURE 9.4. Sidney T. Harding, longtime professor of irrigation engineering at the University of California, Berkeley. Courtesy of Special Collections and University Archives, WRCA, UCR Library, University of California at Riverside.

many Californians pinned hope. Looking deeper into the past, he collected research into California's prehistoric climates from as many sources as he could find. This included river runoff, lake levels, and geological signals of weather variations in California and the enclosed lakes of the Great Basin.

Harding asked a Berkeley audience in March 1934, first, "What do we know of California's past rainfall before direct measurements were started?" Second, did the available records "furnish a basis on which future rainfall may be forecast?" At the time, California's precipitation records dated back to just 1849 in San Francisco, and only more recently for most other California weather stations (what he referred to in his talk as "direct records"). He analyzed crop yield records kept by Spanish missions from 1769 until their secularization by Mexico in the early nineteenth century. He researched tree-ring data ("indirect records"). They at least revealed a qualitative, relative picture about how much water was available in past climates to affect how and where trees grew, lake levels, and whether rivers flowed. The indirect records from fluctuating lakeshores and dead tree trunks available to Harding could only tell a story of more or less water and when it was last there. But he concluded, somewhat tepidly, that records of rainfall and lake levels were sufficient to allow "reasonably dependable estimates . . . of the probable critical or minimum amounts of rainfall that should be expected to occur in the future" (Harding 1934, 24).

Harding learned that when Pyramid Lake, the final stop for the Truckee River in northwestern Nevada, was found by Captain John C. Frémont's exploration party in 1844 it was at elevation 3,860 feet. The lake rose to about 3,885 feet by 1869, before it experienced a precipitous 20-foot decline between 1871 and 1889. Harding contended that an extended dry period accounted for the drop in surface level.

Eagle Lake near Mount Lassen in northern California stood at about 92 feet on a local gage (the Bly Gage, according to Harding) in 1875. It rose to 100 feet in 1900 and 108 feet by 1908, where it stayed through 1916. Tunnel diversions lowered it after 1924. And at Mono Lake, Harding believed that in 1857 the lake level stood at 6,390 feet above mean sea level, rising to about 6,437 by 1916 or so. Mono declined from there until 1933, when its level stood at 6,427. Diversions to Los Angeles began in the late 1930s (Harding 1935a, 87–90, Fig. 1; Harding 1935b, 572–74, Table 1).

These rising and falling lake levels, Harding argued to his Berkeley audience, demonstrated that California and Great Basin precipitation trends could vary substantially, as such changes indicated highly variable runoff. He concluded that all the lakes had low stages prior to 1860.[4] Then there was a general rise until about 1915 followed by decline. This also included Lake Tahoe and Great Salt Lake in Utah. Each lake's surface level in 1915 was higher than at any period since 1840, said Harding, implying that the water glass in this picture of past climates was at least half full.

Tree-ring records yielded additional insights, he said. Through them, he took his Berkeley listeners even farther back in time. Between 1750 and 1850, the lakes were continuously lower than at any time after 1850, suggesting a century of comparatively dry times. The high stages of 1915 were higher than any other period in the 250 to 300 years accessible through the tree-ring information. Thus, the general trend seemed promising for water development. Harding later commented,

> Within the last 30 to 70 years the Great Basin area has apparently experienced its most moist period of the last 300 years. . . . The last one hundred years have been continuously more moist than the preceding one hundred years. . . . The current period of deficient water supply since about 1917 has not resulted in as great an accumulated deficiency as has occurred in the past. (Harding 1935a, 90)

From today's vantage, we might now look at the long, dry periods Harding found with more concern (Ingram and Malamud-Roam 2013), but Harding took an optimistic, forward-looking view: the lakes might have been much lower a hundred years before (and had been so for a century or longer), but to him as the record arced closer to the mid-1930s the lakes seemed to get fuller.

> The record does not support the conclusion that the climate of this area is becoming progressively drier. Although the conclusion that the climate is becoming more moist is probably not justified either, there is more indication of a tendency toward increase in moisture over the last 300 years than there is toward a decrease. (Harding 1935a, 90)

The passage displays his rhetorical gift for diluting a conclusion with qualifications that left his preferred implication intact.

In 1935, Harding extended his research to the direct (measured) runoff records of six different rivers in various parts of California: the San Gabriel and Santa Ana of the south coast; Kern and Kings of the Tulare Lake basin; and the Tuolumne and Sacramento of the Delta's watershed. In these records, representing just thirty-nine years of direct stream runoff data between 1896 and 1934, Harding found wide variation in river flows up and down the state. He saw climatic conditions resulting in relatively long, continuous periods during which stream runoff might be "materially above or below the long-time mean." Southern California streams such as the San Gabriel, the Santa Ana, and the Kings were "subject to more severe and longer continued variations in runoff than streams in northern California." He noted that the San Joaquin Valley seemed to be subject to this tendency too. Southern California streams were prone to "periods of 10 or more consecutive years of average runoff below half of the long-time mean," and were also subject to similar periods in which the runoff might exceed one and a half times the mean.

Harding's quantified picture of California's highly variable climate showed that, around a "best-fit" statistical line, the data points of southern California stream flows did not gyrate wildly so much as exhibit lengthy periods of drought or abundance. The data points showed periods of stability interrupted by radical shifts in California's hydrologic and hydraulic fortunes. The graphs he drew for northern California streams were less dramatic: generally more abundant than dry but still highly variable, he told his readers.

> These variations may result in accumulated departures from the mean of as much as 7 to 10 times the mean annual runoff in Southern California streams, and 4 to 5 times the mean in the rest of the state. (Harding 1935b, 574)

Today, Southern California streams are viewed as "flashy," prone to long dry spells interrupted by tropical monsoons that can bring flash floods and mudslides. Harding's use of the term "departures" signals his awareness of meteorologists' and hydrologists' reliance on statistical "anomalies" to identify tendencies in climate and weather. This method of analysis was begun through pathbreaking research by Sir Gilbert Walker of the India Meteorology Department and extended worldwide by many others in early twentieth-century meteorology.[5]

Yet Harding's data and climate research carried a mixed message. He told his Berkeley audience that the Great Basin "discloses no cycle or system of variation in rainfall which can be used to forecast the rainfall for any particular single year or series of the future." He added, "While the available records are sufficient to indicate the probable general character of future rainfall, there is no present basis on which the occurrence of maximum or minimum years or sequence of years can be forecast."

California's climate future for water-supply planning purposes would look a lot like the past, Harding said. Even though the usable but impressionistic hydrologic past he referred to went back at most 350 to 400 years and included evidence of dry periods longer than any experienced by modern California, the "time and sequence of the occurrence of any particular fluctuations can not be forecast," he concluded. "If water projects are designed to meet demands during the observed dry periods, then when they occur," he argued, is "not a finally controlling factor in their feasibility."[6] California could count on dry years and wet years, and even groups of them, but there was no predicting *when*. Still, by planning for extended dry periods, water development could proceed (Harding 1934, 24).

From the vantage of early 1934, the state had seen a fourteen-year period in which most years had been dry. No one knew when significant rain and snow would return to California. Harding told his Berkeley audience with muted confidence that the direct record is not long enough yet to "contain the extreme conditions that may have occurred during longer periods." To design large-scale hydraulic systems, engineers needed to know what to assume about the climate in order to size and operate them properly. When multiyear droughts occur, said Harding, "Full development of the average run-off requires extensive storage to carry over from periods of excess to meet periods of deficiency."

Translating climate variability into a portfolio of snowmelt and river runoff scenarios was thus an engineering need of the first order to Harding. Long droughts in the indirect record posed the problem of sizing costly storage sufficient to cover dry year deficiencies. The longer the deficiencies, of course, the larger the storage facilities would have to be. He cautioned that "the extent and cost of such long period storage may exceed the value of the additional water supply made available. Fortunately," he continued, "many California areas have such storage capacity in their ground water basins where water is continuously available although the pumping lifts necessary to obtain it vary in the dry and wet periods" (Harding 1934, 1–2).

Yet even by 1934, groundwater overdraft was rampant and hard to reverse due to the rapid spread of pumpage and the many dry years of the 1920s and the early 1930s. Overdraft was already documented in the San Joaquin Valley. A later study by the United States Geological Survey in 1969 found that between 1905 and 1964 groundwater levels in the southeastern San Joaquin Valley (from Tulare to Wasco) declined 200 feet, and land surface levels had subsided up to 12 feet from their earlier elevations (Lofgren and Klausing 1969, B1).

Despite field evidence of lengthy droughts in California's prehistory, it would not do in the 1930s to assume, let alone recommend, that California's developing capitalist civilization would have to live within its means. To build reservoirs like Shasta and Friant was to raise hopes in people previously trounced by economic depression. In his Berkeley talk, and in subsequent 1935 articles for *Civil Engineering*, Sidney Harding took pains to conclude, despite just fifty years of direct precipitation records, "Past records furnish an adequate guide to the general character of the future rainfall" (Harding 1934, 23).

But in other *Civil Engineering* articles, Harding was more circumspect. In

February 1935, he acknowledged the paucity of data on which to base prospects for future runoff, adding that "caution should be used in planning water supply projects in this area based on this period." His September article clearly showed that the challenge for California would be how to get its population and economy through the dry periods to benefit from the wet ones. He summarized the problem in a highly variable weather region this way: "Either the development [of California] must be limited to the demand that can be met during periods of deficiency, or means must be found for retaining the runoff in periods of excess for use in years of deficiency."

Harding saw four options available to California society to address this problem. First, California could build lots of reservoirs. The trouble here was that "storage sites of sufficient capacity at practical costs are seldom available," the good sites growing scarcer as development proceeded. Moreover, evaporation during California's long, hot, dry season at many sites "would consume a large part of the supply stored."

Second, groundwater storage could be further developed. In his view, California had abundant "large masses of coarse alluvial fill" with fresh water aquifers in its numerous valleys. Shielded from the daily heat of the sun, these aquifers avoided evaporation losses and could be obtained for the cost of pumping—often with renewable hydroelectricity.

Third, the state could develop its streams only to a point. Accordingly, that was the point "in which present demand is met from direct flow, with limited storage, and much of the runoff is still unused. This practice meets present needs but does not represent the full practical use of the available supply" because it doesn't store runoff for those dry days to come again. Here, Harding was also alluding to Proposition 7, implying that letting runoff escape to the sea was a waste of water.

Finally, he recommended that on streams where full surface or underground storage was not available only the most reliable part of supplies from those streams should be used on "permanent development." The "irregular flow" should be applied, when available, only to grain or pasture—uses that could be interrupted with little social or economic cost. An example of this, Harding noted, was the irrigation of grasslands and swamps along the San Joaquin River and grain irrigation using the surplus water that reached Tulare Lake (from the Kings River). Both were areas where large agricultural interests such as Miller & Lux and the emerging cotton empires in Kings and Kern Counties controlled extensive landholdings and water rights (Arax and Wartzman 2004; Harding 1935b, 574; Igler 2001).

Harding saw each option as a specific approach for planning development and for mobilizing water-supply resources. They each occurred in different landscapes. Alone, none of them would be a panacea for the whole state. While the state's water law framework encouraged full beneficial use of scarce water resources, he wrote that his climate research findings demonstrated "that all the runoff of California streams cannot be used for irrigation development without the development of excessive carryover storage or a material variation in the area irrigated during different periods." Californians would have to be pragmatic, since they could not use all the water that might collect to storage. Thus, "Each stream is an individual problem in this regard" (Harding 1935b).

At that time, Harding found no discernible climatic cycles inscribed in the ancient shorelines and dead tree trunks of Great Basin lakeshores and Nevada playas. But he expressed hope that "eventually the different factors affecting rainfall may become more fully known." Because there had been significant droughts in the past, and because it was possible to determine approximate durations from the indirect record, Harding reasoned that future rainfall estimates could be based on "the expectation that past records reflect variations of the future," what climate scientists today call "stationarity." Subsequently, in 1937, Harding told an Oregon audience,

> Present records are adequate to warn us that we can only expect to have to face similar periods in the future and the plans for water supply should provide for their recurrence. The indirect records indicate that there have been drier periods within the last 250 years than any covered by our direct records. The length of below average periods is too long on many streams to permit the run-off to be fully equalized by carryover storage and some of the run-off of the above average periods cannot be made available for dependable use.

Harding wasn't about to urge restraint on state-led stimulation of water resource development in arid California. At the time, poverty, unemployment, and economic stagnation were rampant, and public investment in infrastructure, job creation, and new technologies all attracted widespread support as salve for Great Depression wounds. But he admitted ambivalence to his Oregon audience regarding society's ability to restrain its appetite for more water than could be affordably sustained.

> At present, recent years having been ones of generally below average water supply, most users will admit the wisdom of limiting our development to the areas we can maintain in similar future periods. Whether we will continue to recognize this situation during future periods of above average supply or whether we will then forget present experience and expand use beyond proper limits will be the real test of the soundness of our judgment. (Harding 1937, 15)

One wonders how a Central Valley audience would have received Harding's message. He nonetheless deserves credit for carefully framing the key water issue before California: given the incentives for state-supported capitalist development of water resources in California under way at the time, it remained to be seen whether the government and its client agencies in the water industry throughout the state would live within the means that Nature provided or not. That would be "the real test of the soundness of our judgment."

NOTES

1. Henderson (1999) provides an excellent discussion of the early geographical and financial characteristics and importance of agricultural credit in California's development.

2. There were numerous voluntary agreements and decrees along the Merced River before and as part of the formation and early operation of the Merced Irrigation District, including the Crocker–Huffman Decree (1895); Dale–Cook Judgment (1926); Cowell Agreement (1926); and Stevinson Decree (1930).

3. McSwain (1978, 107–08) himself was the appointed watermaster in this instance.

4. Geographer Scott Stine (1981) has since challenged Harding's determination of Mono Lake's 1857 elevation, but this does not change the historical context.

5. Walker pioneered use of correlation coefficients to identify atmospheric pressure correlations throughout the world and did not rely upon the simpler, statistical calculations of percentage difference from the mean of a stream's direct records.

6. Subsequently, Harding (1937, 14) presented a review of weather cycles based on sunspots to tree rings to the Oregon Reclamation Congress in 1937 and concluded that "it does not appear that the analysis of weather cycles has reached a point where it can be used for definite forecasting."

Chapter 10

Parable, Prophecy, Present

AS A YOUNG LAWYER, Samuel C. Wiel published an essay on "theories of water law" in the spring 1914 issue of *Harvard Law Review*. In it, he sought to let "possible theories of water law take form according to certain underlying ideas" and to consider the social systems that emerge from them. Consider his thought experiment a parable of sharing, where Wiel uses water rights law as his storytelling vehicle.

In his view, underlying all water law systems is the basic notion that "water running in streams and watercourses is not of itself the property of any person and cannot be" (Wiel 1914, 530). Wiel quoted the Roman jurist Justinian: "By natural law these things are common to all: the air, running water, the sea, and as a consequence the shores of the sea."[1] The law regulates the *use* of it, but water itself belongs to all, says Wiel. By regulating use, the law recognizes the rights of flow and use of water, but not the water itself as property. This status is accepted widely by courts and legislatures alike.

The prior appropriation system is founded on this concept of water as a common good, wrote Wiel, where "everyone . . . may take out freely from springs and streams what he wants, and that the first so to do shall have a prior right to continue to do so." Prior appropriation, as it was practiced in the states west of the Mississippi River, took on the requirement that use by the appropriator should be diligent or the right could be lost. "The system is eminently a pioneering system," wrote Wiel, because historically it originated in California "when the region was . . . all unowned, unclaimed and unguarded wilderness of vast extent."[2] Such a system worked under these conditions because the pioneer who appropriated water "left a surplus in the stream for others to appropriate; but to-day there are hundreds of appropriators on the most considerable sources of supply, and when another comes along on such streams he threatens the security of those who have gone before." As the region developed to the point where crowded conditions and exhausted supply take hold, Wiel observed, "appropriation itself comes to an end.

> Instead of carrying out the primitive idea that the water is *publici juris,* or the common property of all, it overthrows that idea by giving its use exclusively to those who have appropriated the water in the first place. Instead of being open to free use, the door is shut to all who have not already passed in. And indeed as between those already within the door, if a shortage now comes, even their numbers are cut down. The earliest appropriators are protected against the later, although . . . it may be the lion's share, and none may be left for those who come later. (Wiel 1914, 533)

To think this situation represents a case of "lifeboat ethics" would get ahead of Wiel's thought process. Holding to his prior-appropriation example, he introduces into his thought experiment on one hand the idea of "common right" and on the other the need to apportion deficiency of water supply during drought. Say it is a time well down the road (like today), when the community of appropriators from the stream "look over the forgotten records and get the gossip of the old-timers," and they determine that only some appropriators may take water, while others must endure privation of supply during the drought. Wiel observes, "Under the law of prior appropriation this has happened many times in Southern California. This is hardly fulfilling the idea of 'common right' with which the law begins." In recognition of the community's collective economic interest in sharing water, people—or at least some among them—might wonder whether, despite past reliance on priority, they should apportion the deficiency among all existing users. "Should this apportionment be made?" asks Wiel. "If it is, the principle of priority is seriously cut down."

Commitment to a common right to water in times of deficiency defines the other water rights system: the riparian doctrine. "Super-abundance of water allows each such owner to make the fullest use he pleases on his bordering land [adjacent to the river]; but when there is a deficiency the common law is a system of enforcing apportionment thereof," says Wiel. These owners share the water "ratably"—that is, each is allotted a *pro rata* share—"and no one of them gets a preference over the others in the eye of the law" (Wiel 1914, 534). Wiel sums up his two models of hydraulic social order.

> While the system of prior appropriation is a system of exclusive rights whereby the prior appropriator may exclude all others to the extent of his priority, the common-law system is one of correlative rights, as it is called, whereby the rights of landowners bordering upon the stream are interdependent and adjustable or relative to each other, so as to put them upon an equal footing in times of deficiency. (Wiel 1914, 534)

Wiel then asks his readers, which system is preferable? His answer distinguishes the "pioneering" stage of social and economic development from later stages when the pioneers have all passed on and the lands are filled with people. In the pioneering stage, prior appropriation is the superior system, he says, because "the pioneer gambles for high stakes, and unless those large stakes are secured to him after he succeeds, he will not gamble, and there would be no pioneering." Besides, the pioneer acknowledges that under a correlative system, "there is an inherent uncertainty among all as to how much will be theirs" when droughts come along. Here we find, once again, the illegibility of riparian rights, but that illegibility is useful for sharing the burdens in the commons.

But, says Wiel, where "streams [are] already developed by many users . . . we find a community of farmers to whom dates and order of settlement along the river are ancient history and largely forgotten." For Wiel, the classic complaint of any appropriator who says, "Take away my water and the land for which I braved hardships will revert to a desert" rings hollow. Regardless of the social order implied by legal doctrine, "Land reverts to desert upon shortage of water under every law; the only thing the law of prior appropriation does is to visit the loss wholly upon the subsequent appropriators, who now constitute most of the water users" (Wiel 1914, 535).

Prior appropriation is still held to be superior among western lawyers and engineers for enforcing priorities, writes Wiel. The seeming inequities of enforcing priorities, they argue, "[do] not come from injustice, but come from nature withholding its full supply that year, and nature is far more cruel than man; that the subsequent users, having taken rights dependent on nature for their existence, must blame nature and not man when the bounty is withheld."

Prior appropriation is based on a "technicality which is forgotten except in times of trouble," the technicality of priority dates. Wiel objects that in times of drought,

> [W]ater is a common necessity of the community which a given source of supply serves, and it is neither practical nor desirable to tell people to keep away from using water supplies unless they know for certain that a dry year will never come. People will and should use all the water there is in normal years, and industry cannot stand still, shrinking at some unforeseen calamity in the future. No blame can be justly attributed to the later users. (Wiel 1914, 535)

And yet such an impulse to share the common necessity of water during a drought flies in the face of deeply held commitments to vested property rights of prior appropriators. To them, sharing entails at least some confiscation of their property, writes Wiel, and could cause "an uprising." Here, Wiel points out that "the doctrine of apportioning deficiency of water" is hardly extreme, since it is at the core of riparian rights, "the most widely applied water law of any" in Europe and North America. He observes coyly,

> Since . . . apportionment in times of deficiency has been acquiesed [*sic*] in by a large part of the world, I suppose it could be peaceably done with us. (Wiel 1914, 536)

And Wiel notes that the California Supreme Court adopted apportionment of deficiency for groundwater, in *Katz v. Walkinshaw*, which we saw in chapter 5. Court decrees adjudicating the water rights of streams routinely apportion deficiencies, often with resort to a system of "rotation" among either riparian or appropriative right holders party to the decree. Under rotation, each party is assigned flow quantities for a set period of time so that no one is left out; and yet neither the decree nor the doctrine of prior appropriation collapses from use of rotation (Wiel 1914, 537). Wiel observes that "the doctrine of making existing appropriators' rights correlative, carrying apportionment in times of deficiency, is going on in conservative courts without causing disturbance, and rather, with approval" (Wiel 1914, pp. 537–38). When people focus on solving water problems, rather than adhering to ideological principles or rigid legal doctrine against all manner of evidence from reality, they see their way clear to apply what *works*.

Wiel's thought experiment at this point becomes static, so he relaxes assumptions to make it more dynamic, to see what happens next. He tinkers with the problem of how new users enter the respective systems of water law. Modern economists refer to this as the problem of "barriers to entry" with regard to how easy or difficult it is for new entrepreneurs or workers to enter a market in order to compete, or in water's case, to use the resource.

Wiel assumes a water resource and a community of farmers growing crops. The region experiences wet conditions for a period of years and attracts newcomers growing their own crops and diverting their own supplies of water. The water supply and the crops dwindle when the region enters a drought. The earliest appropriators can maintain their crops while the late arrivals lose their crops and are impoverished. Without a system of correlative rights to apportion the deficiency during the drought, "There would be a struggle for existence, the weaker would sell out, and in a few years" a reversion to the old equilibrium of farmers and their crops would be reestablished, possibly at a lower level of production.

Wiel is not satisfied with this example, based as it is on a wet/dry oscillation of climate. So he revises his climate assumptions in order that "the number of users would not be swollen by unusual conditions." Under such equilibrated conditions, absent any booms and busts in water supply, he offers that "apportionment of deficiency would work out as intended, oftener than it would defeat itself—among appropriators from streams, just as much among riparian owners, users of percolating water, and consumers from public-service canals." In those latter cases, the apportionment of deficiencies was the law in California then, as now. Wiel observes, "I assume, . . . that the correlative system is taken as preferable upon full-settled streams" (Wiel 1914, 539).

Prior appropriation, argues Wiel, undercuts the community, if applied under conditions of full development of a river. In today's media parlance, it precipitates "water wars." When rains fail, prior appropriation tells its adherents, blame Nature, not your senior neighbor. Yet, are we not ruled by laws, and are not laws made by human beings? In twenty-first-century California, the paradox of prior appropriation Wiel posed a century earlier is still with us: do drought or water rights under prior appropriation cause supply deficiencies to be exacted upon those coming later?

Wiel alludes to the Miller & Lux barony at the close of "Theories of Water Law":

> The riparian system has met with a flood of denunciation in the West. . . .
> Part of this loathing . . . is due to its distortion when applied in an unsettled region, especially where there are large holdings of bordering land in a few hands, as in the case of Mexican grants in California. Such abnormal situations twist the system and make it as exclusive for a few owners, even though not using the water, as prior appropriation ever could. But that is an opposition to the ownership of such large landholdings, rather than to the system as one of water law, and but a repetition of the denunciation of those land grants themselves. (Wiel 1914, 542–43)

The political rejection of riparianism among public officials, water attorneys, and the media was displaced from resentment, anger, and anxieties about economic and social opportunities imposed by *land monopoly* and, in particular, the specific monopoly of the San Joaquin River imposed by Miller & Lux. But in seeking to undercut riparian doctrine, some Californians would have stripped or abolished vested rights of many other Californians possessing riparian entitlements to the use and enjoyment of their adjacent stream. Apportionment of supply deficiency defined the collective obligations of each right holder; but each right holder did not necessarily or inherently represent or embody monopolistic practices, at least not at Miller & Lux's scale and span of control. Thus, there was no abolition of all riparian rights.

Still, the dead hands of Henry Miller wear one glove of riparian rights and one glove of appropriative rights. From within these gloves, like it or not, in wet years or dry, his hands still guide the flows diverted from streams and stored behind massive dams up and down the Central Valley of California.

* * *

The power of actual rather than theoretical water rights is exercised through position on the stream, possession of the water, and priority to store or divert. This power may be moderated, even controlled, through adjudication. In the early 1940s, with Shasta and Friant dams nearing completion, California Water Project Authority attorney Henry Holsinger surveyed the Central Valley Project, and worried. During his career with the state Department of Public Works, he had assisted with adjudications in the upper reaches of tributaries to the Sacramento River. Now fifty-three, Holsinger was experienced with both adjudication procedures in the Water Commission Act: the statutory proceeding, and the court referral proceeding. And as associate attorney with the Water Project Authority, he was intimately familiar with the water rights of the Central Valley Project, having studied them minutely for the Authority just a few years before (California Water Project Authority 1936–39).

The U.S. Bureau of Reclamation, which had taken over the project from the state of California in 1935, was preparing a number of Central Valley Project studies, analogous to today's environmental impact reports. They examined in detail specific ways in which the Central Valley Project—then the largest water resource storage and diversion project in the world—would affect California and the rest of the United States.

Holsinger, with the blessing of Water Project Authority director A.D. Edmonston, prepared a memorandum to Harlan Barrows, the University of Chicago geographer leading the Central Valley Project studies project, suggesting that a new study be added to those already under way. The new study, Holsinger proposed, would address the following problems:

> Problem No. 25. Is there necessity for a comprehensive adjudication of rights to the use of water on streams the natural regimen of which will be altered by operation of the project?
>
> Problem No. 26. If there is a need for such comprehensive adjudication, can the same be accomplished under existing law, and if not, what enabling legislation is necessary? (Holsinger 1942, 765)

With the Central Valley Project well into its construction phase, Holsinger doubtless knew that the Bureau and others would be skeptical of his argument.[3] It had to have created tensions between the U.S. Bureau of Reclamation and the California Water Project Authority when the Bureau assumed control: in the 1920s and 1930s, many of the staff members at the Authority had helped devise the studies and the designs that shaped the project, only to have the Great Depression sap the state's financing ability. Such tensions may somewhat explain Holsinger's uncommonly blunt language (for bureaucratic communication) in the proposal he submitted to Barrows in December 1942. He and the Water Project Authority may have felt that they had nothing to lose by trying. Near the beginning of the memorandum, Holsinger did not equivocate: "Never in the history of the State has there been an instance where a water conservation project was put in operation which involved such violent and extensive changes in the regimen of any stream" (Holsinger 1942, 765).

He plunged ahead, taking an emphatic, even sardonic tone at times.

> It would be pleasant to anticipate that all such difficulties and conflicts are now at an end and that this vast project, notwithstanding its radical alterations of stream regimen, will be peaceably accepted by those affected thereby without controversy, without objection and without resorting to litigation. However, attention to realities should convince any reasonable mind that any such anticipation is utopian and not reasonably possible of fulfillment. (Holsinger 1942, 766)

Section 8 of the 1902 National Reclamation Act states that in matters of water regulation, the Bureau of Reclamation is to be governed by the laws of the state. "The acquisition of water rights and their definition and enforcement are therefore governed" by California law, wrote Holsinger, "and this principle is applicable to the United States in relation to the Central Valley Project." Even though the feds had taken the project over, he opined that the state could still regulate it. He would be proved right, eventually.[4]

Holsinger acknowledged that the United States had acquired almost the entire flow of the San Joaquin River through its purchase of Miller & Lux grassland rights, exchange of its cropland rights, and receipt of state filings that enabled the Bureau to relocate the diversion points of those rights to the Friant Dam site, which the Bureau had also acquired. With this arrangement, he wrote, the United States achieved a strategic position at Friant, where the major storage point is upstream from all rights of owners who might enjoin it. He likened it to

> the water user "at the head of the ditch," an advantage by reason of position and possession. [When the] uppermost user . . . is in possession of the source of the supply by physical law necessarily the water will become available to the lower users only to the extent he who has control upstream allows it to flow past his point of diversion. . . . This position therefore casts a heavy burden upon the lower users. (Holsinger 1942, 768)

On the Sacramento River, Holsinger observed, the United States possessed fewer advantages. There were no monopolized water rights attached to lands that the Bureau could retire through negotiated compensation, "thereby enabling the use of a corresponding supply of water to be applied elsewhere" (Holsinger 1942, 768). Further, the Bureau did not control any prospects in the Sacramento Valley for an analogous exchange to relocate to storage. Nor was it looking to acquire any of the numerous senior water rights there. He concluded from eliminating these alternatives, "It is therefore the intention of the United States to recognize all existing rights to the use of water on Sacramento Valley lands between the Shasta Dam and the combined delta of the Sacramento and San Joaquin rivers" (Holsinger 1942, 768). These water right holders were a complex mix, including riparian and pre-1914 appropriative claimants, many of whom had also obtained senior post–1914 water rights from the Water Commission prior to 1927 (see Table 8.1).

On the San Joaquin River, the Bureau's advantage resided in its point of diversion being at the point of storage. After that water was diverted, the Bureau had exclusive control of the Friant-Kern Canal that would supply its customers without possibility of significant theft by any intervening users. But in the Sacramento Valley, Shasta Dam, as the point of storage, was 300 miles north of the point of diversion in the Delta. At that diversion, Shasta water would be lifted from the Delta to the Delta–Mendota Canal for delivery of the Bureau's substitute supply to the Exchange Contractors (as they were becoming known then). While water law in theory protects stored water from diversion by others, water released from storage looks just like other water as it flows in a channel. Between the point of storage and the point of diversion, Holsinger estimated there were some 300 water right holders, each of whom had his own ideas about his water rights (Holsinger 1942, 770).

The risk of having Shasta's stored water supplies poached after release toward its eventual Delta diversions, particularly in dry years, was "a practical certainty," Holsinger wrote. To combat this, the Bureau would have to surveil both banks of the 300-mile length of the river, and do so in the absence of adjudication. "The lawful drafts [diversions of water] alone, to say nothing of possible overdrafts, will be far in excess of the normal flow" (shown in Table 8.3). Thus, the function of the prior-appropriation doctrine alone in dry years on the Sacramento River would have dire implications for the Delta itself, the Delta diversions to Mendota, and, in turn, the Bureau's ability to uphold its end of the Exchange Contract. Such uncertainties placed the east side Friant-Kern farmers at risk, as Wiel had foreseen nearly thirty years before.

The "practical certainty" of supply poaching during drought was compounded by the fact that, unlike San Joaquin River water rights, rights in the Sacramento River basin had seen comparatively little litigation to adjudicate the main stem of the river. "In such a situation," wrote Holsinger prophetically,

> [I]t is evident that in view of radical changes in the natural regimen of stream flow, in order to foreclose endless conflict, misunderstanding and a multiplicity of litigation, it is necessary that preceding an attempt to actually make such changes in the natural stream flow, all rights, both vested and inchoate [those rights still being developed to full beneficial usage by the claimant], should be carefully and scientifically defined so that each and every right might be subject to as exact ascertainment as possible and that each might be justly enforced as against all others. If this is not accomplished the result will necessarily be uncertainty, doubt and conflict. (Holsinger 1942, 772)

Sacramento River basin water rights should be adjudicated, he said. To avoid doing so would leave grave uncertainties about all water titles in the Central Valley and would be a "strong derogation of the public interest and welfare." The practical result, he warned, would be poaching of Bureau-stored water: "It may be confidently predicted that those intervening users, finding an abnormal increment in the stream, will each for himself define and exercise their rights in their own favor with substantial elasticity." In the absence of a comprehensive definition and adjudication of Sacramento River water rights, the Bureau could expect that "interminable conflicts, disputes, and litigation will necessarily ensue" (Holsinger 1942, 773, 774).

Holsinger noted that the Bureau's rights to the Sacramento River at Shasta Dam dated only to 1927, so its ability to meet its side of the Exchange Contract would be limited by its junior rights.

> The moment it fails to discharge that commitment [of providing a substitute supply from Shasta to the Exchange Contractors at Mendota], it must cease the storage of water on the San Joaquin River [at Friant] commensurate with the rights of all other parties to the exchange. As a corollary thereto, the obligation to supply water from Friant will fall into default. (Holsinger 1942, 774)

Only through adjudication could an "effective ceiling" be placed on the senior water rights of the Sacramento River water users. This is doubly important because, as Holsinger correctly points out, "Before the United States can safely proceed with assurance of successful operation of the project, a comprehensive definition and enforcement must be secured with respect to all rights on both rivers which will be affected by operation of the project" (Holsinger 1942, 774–75).[5]

Obviously, he continued, the adjudication should have begun prior to construction, but it had not. At least do so before Central Valley Project operations begin, he implored the Bureau and his state superiors in late 1942. Holsinger was dubious of written agreements, usually executed between two or just a few parties. He argued that "the sole recourse is litigation" to quiet all water titles in the river basin. After describing the nuts and bolts of such adjudication, and addressing the federal government's likely (but, Holsinger believed, weak) claim of sovereign immunity from such litigation, he warned that adjudication was inevitable: "Eventually, either adequately or inadequately, either as a whole or piecemeal, the water rights here considered will of necessity pass through the courts."

Harlan Barrows recommended Holsinger's proposed study topics to Bureau Commissioner John C. Page. Page replied three months later to Holsinger's boss, state engineer Edward Hyatt,

> You and I have discussed this subject at various times over a period of years and I believe you are throughly [sic] familiar with my views which I feel are well supported by facts. In the light of all the circumstances, I find it unwise to recede from the position I have previously taken. In consequence I have advised Dr. Barrows that I cannot approve the inclusion of any problem relating to the "Adjudication of Water Rights" in the Central Valley Project studies.[6]

It is unclear to which "facts" Commissioner Page referred.

* * *

By the late 1940s, the Bureau of Reclamation anticipated that San Joaquin River flows between Friant and Mendota Pool would go dry: it intended to divert all its flow at Friant Dam into the Madera Canal to the Chowchilla Farms area on the northeast side of the river or south into the Friant-Kern Canal. State planning had anticipated that the Madera area would receive an average of 355,000 acre-feet of deliveries, while an average of about 1,365,000 acre-feet would flow annually through Friant-Kern Canal (California Department of Public Works 1930b, 99). Mendota Pool would receive water behind Mendota Dam from the Delta Mendota Canal's delivery of substitute supplies for the San Joaquin River Exchange Contractors. Several canals (most created originally by Robert Brereton or Henry Miller) ingested waters deposited in Mendota Pool, and flowed to the adjacent lands of the exchange contractors. Below Mendota Pool there would be some forty to fifty miles of dry riverbed, silent testimony to the Bureau's takeover of privately monopolized water rights. This operational vision would have consequences for San Joaquin Valley groundwater and its spring-run salmon runs.

In 1991, retired migratory fisheries biologist George Warner recalled the California Department of Fish and Game's attempts to salvage the Chinook spring run back in 1948, after Friant Dam stopped releasing water into the San Joaquin below the dam. The Chinook salmon runs along the San Joaquin River and its major tributaries rivaled those of the larger-flowing Sacramento River and its tributaries. "The impact of water development, however, drastically reduced San Joaquin runs long before major losses occurred on the Sacramento," he said (Warner 1991, 61). During the 1946 spring run past Mendota, state biologists estimated 56,000 salmon heading upstream to spawn, and 26,000 in 1947. There were numerous large, cold, gravel-filled pools still in place below Friant Dam in which many of the fish fashioned their redds (nests) and spawned. But beyond the dam, there was no longer any passage by which the fish could reach the coldest water and gravelly Sierra Nevada habitat where they historically spawned (Warner 1991, 63).

As the 1948 spring salmon run approached, state fish and game staff jury-rigged weirs, a holding pond, and a mast and boom to lift captured fish into smaller containers in which they would be transferred to tanker trucks borrowed from federal fish hatcheries. The biologists would make the trip from just above the river's confluence with the Merced River to Miller & Lux's old "Outside Canal," which ran full of irrigation water from the San Joaquin around the dry reach of the San Joaquin to Mendota Pool. From Mendota, Warner recalled, the fish could swim upstream to occupy deeper and cooler pools until they spawned (Warner 1991, 64).

This maneuver succeeded in hauling more than 1,900 salmon upriver until a huge snowmelt entered the Merced River in the spring of 1948, flooding Fish and Game's pond and operations on the San Joaquin adjacent to the confluence. The rest of the fish waiting there for transport were lost; the powerful homing instinct that returned them to their natal stream was their undoing that year.

But those fish that did make it upstream generally spawned successfully, Warner recalled. In early 1949, substantial numbers of downstream juvenile salmon, anywhere from 4 to 8 inches long, showed up at Mendota Pool and Dam preparing to migrate to sea. Below the dam, a dry channel awaited them all the way to the Merced River; the San Joaquin's "head, booster," had been cut off. Warner concluded of the 1948 salmon tragedy that the main beneficiaries were "the raccoons, herons and egrets" feasting on the young fish carcasses where the river ended (Warner 1991, 65).

In 1949, Fish and Game staff resolved to try to make the remaining spring-run San Joaquin salmon, soon arriving, use the Merced River instead: at least it was a hydrologically connected river. The Merced was the biologists' last hope to maintain population numbers for the whole river basin, even if the salmon's usual upstream habitat was now severed by lost flow and ultimately blocked by Friant. "Salmon arrived as expected," Warner recalled,

> but it was not home stream water. A few of the persistent San Joaquin fish were dipnetted, tagged, and released three miles up the Merced. These fish immediately turned downstream, almost beating the truck back to the weir! (Warner 1991, 66)

The fish preferred the warm and polluted San Joaquin River to the fresh, cool, and clear water of the Merced. After Friant diversions began in the San Joaquin River basin, there were still fall-run Chinook salmon and Central Valley steelhead trout using the other major tributaries: the Merced, the Tuolumne, and Stanislaus rivers. But the Bureau provided an object lesson for fish populations in what Samuel Wiel had meant in his admonition not to cut off the head or booster of a stream. Here at Friant was a "mountain installation" turning off a river, with devastating consequences to migratory fish helpless against the Bureau's monopoly power to control flow. Not only did the river dry up for over 40 miles, but spring-run Chinook salmon could no longer find their way, their water, upstream to spawn. They would soon be extinct on the San Joaquin. As of this writing, despite an active but as yet unfulfilled restoration program on that part of the river, they remain so.[7]

* * *

On September 25, 1947, riparian and groundwater users along the San Joaquin River below Friant Dam and above Mendota Pool sued the U.S. Bureau of Reclamation and a number of other Friant-related water users. The plaintiffs asserted that they, plus 125 other farm owners and another 1,000 ranchers owning a combined 600,000 acres of land, had vested water rights that were paramount to those of the Bureau of Reclamation at Friant. They complained in federal district court that they had not consented to have their water rights taken by the Bureau when it operated Friant Dam. Their water rights included riparian flows and rights of landowners nearby to pump groundwater that was replenished by natural flood flows of the San Joaquin River.

These riparian and overlying landowners won recognition in federal court of their rights to a reasonable portion of San Joaquin River flow below Friant to sustain their longstanding uses.[8] At that time, the court recognized the legitimate claim of plaintiffs in *Rank v. Krug* to about 200,000 acre-feet of riparian rights along the river in annual release by the Bureau from Friant. (More recently, the San Joaquin River Restoration Program reports that these riparian releases from Friant have dwindled to about 116,741 acre-feet annually; San Joaquin River Restoration Program 2011, 23.)

Before the federal district court, Bureau officials asserted that the agency was entitled to the entire flow of the San Joaquin River (just as Miller & Lux often claimed) on navigability and flood-control grounds (the latter of which Miller & Lux had not).[9] Federal District Justice Hall vociferously rejected the Bureau's argument that "any obstruction authorized by Congress which may impound the waters of [the upper San Joaquin River where it flows at Friant Dam] can be used [by the Bureau] to divert the entire flow . . . , regardless of the use to which such diversion is put, and regardless of any rights which Congress has said shall be recognized below such point of diversion under state law." If that argument held, he pointed out, the Bureau could "divert every stream in the west—from mountain freshet to flowing rivers . . . merely because of a flood that may occur in the incidence of once in 25 years." He rebuked the Bureau for overreaching.

> The extension of such doctrine would put every water right in California, if not the United States, in non-compensable jeopardy if somewhere some portion of the river system upon which that right depended, was navigable or caused floods. . . . The mere statement of the contention is sufficient to refute it. *The application of its extension explodes it as an instance of departmental zeal which is attempting to outrun the authority conferred by statute.*[10]

This time, a federal agency, the Bureau of Reclamation, not a privately held utility as twenty-five years earlier, preferred to ignore a constitutional protection afforded legitimate property owners. Nowhere in the process—from the purchase and exchange contracts to the Bureau's acquisition and construction of the Friant Dam site—had the Bureau offered to compensate riparian and overlying water rights holders between Friant and Mendota Pool. This was clearly an area where surface and subsurface flow were still connected.

Lead plaintiff Everett Rank and his 1,100 co-plaintiffs were not seeking to stop completion of Friant Dam. They merely sought recognition and enforcement of their water rights (or just compensation) in the San Joaquin and in the groundwater supplies they had long been using prior to Friant Dam. Those supplies depended upon the floods and freshets that Edward F. Treadwell and Samuel C. Wiel had debated about in the summer and fall of 1928. "Much of the testimony" in *Rank v. Krug*, reported civil engineer Charles H. Lee to a Stockton audience after the appeal was completed, "pertained to the source, course, and direction of subsurface waters" (Lee 1956, 3–4). This was done to help Justice Hall arrive at a "physical solution" that addressed the compensation issue. In the wake of Proposition 7's passage in 1928, physical solutions came into reasonable-use jurisprudence as a means of resolving conflicts but did not entail adjudication of the stream. During *Rank*, both parties submitted physical solution proposals to Justice Hall. He chose a plan from the plaintiffs, which he modified somewhat.

The plaintiffs proposed fourteen collapsible dams along the river below Friant (above Mendota Pool) to provide sufficient flow of 10 cubic feet per second over the lowest dam "after satisfying all intervening demands," said Lee (1956, 9). Collapsible dams can be of at least two basic designs. One type consists of a large air bladder spanning the entire channel width. When inflated, water fills the channel behind it, creating a pond. Deflating the bladder flattens it to the riverbed, allowing high flows to pass. Fixed dams, another type, are designed to pivot into position along a radial axis spanning the river channel. Raising one creates a pond. As with deflating the bladder design, lowering the radial dam to the riverbed allows for passage of high flows.

The plaintiffs' plan would have cost about $1.2 million in the 1950s, with an estimated annual cost of about $4,000 (Lee 1956). To provide the needed flows, the Bureau would have to release 200,000 acre-feet per year, about 11 percent of average annual flows of the San Joaquin River. "The amount demanded," Lee observed to his Stockton audience, "is but a small fraction of the flow of the river. . . . The plans of the defendant officials [of the Bureau] and of the State, the Court found, would neither provide enough water to operate river pumps nor make provision for sustaining or replenishing the underground supply for some 300,000 acres of land" (Lee 1956, 10). The Bureau and state officials "refused to concede any merit at all to plaintiffs' plan of physical solution," he added.

Their attitude, Lee said, probably reflected a poor grasp of the hydrogeology of the San Joaquin River's alluvial fan and "cone" (Lee 1956, 11–12). This cone distributed water from surface channels through a "complex structure" of boulders, cobbles, gravels, sand, silt, and clay. It was arrayed along subsurface stream channels radiating from the river's canyon mouth at the lowest face of the Sierra Nevada, with the cobbles upslope and the finer sediments downslope near the valley floor. All of it was distributed according to gravity's ability—through the "head" or "booster"— to make a river do the work of pushing sediment from higher to lower positions throughout its length.

Much *Rank* testimony dealt with the San Joaquin River cone, said Lee: first proving its existence, next proving that it is fed by seepage from the flow of the San Joaquin River, "and that this seepage is an appreciable element in the supply of wells extracting water from the cone." In addition, he continued, there was "great controversy" about the "influence of high river stages during the period of melting snows

[April through June, generally] upon the seepage losses" from the San Joaquin River into the cone. The Bureau defendants argued that as long as there was any water in the river "maximum seepage occurred," but Justice Hall did not accept this. Instead, he accepted expert testimony that "was in general agreement—namely, that the greater flow of the river and the higher the level of the water in the stream, the greater the seepage" to groundwater.

Lee thought that expert testimony in *Rank v. Krug* also cast doubt on the efficacy of spreading the Friant-Kern Canal's contributions across southern San Joaquin Valley lands to percolate to the aquifers below. This was originally an important strategy for the Valley in the state water plan of the 1930s. According to Lee, evidence presented at trial showed that 59 percent of the soils within seventeen contracting districts totaling some 666,000 acres of land were "non-absorbent, and that in many districts 100 percent of the soils are non-absorbent" probably due to impermeable clay layers common in Valley sediments (Lee 1956, 14). These conditions posed difficult and costly drainage problems.

The alluvial fans—giant cones of boulders, cobbles, gravels, sands, and silts that had spilled out of the mountains over California's eons—were the storage structures that the state needed to figure out how to put water into, for it was these structures that had enabled the San Joaquin Valley to grow and develop, said Lee. He predicted,

> The failure to make full use of the absorptive capacity of all natural stream channels in the valley will eventually deprive many existing landowners of their well supplies and will insure permanent waste of valuable surplus waters. (Lee 1956, 15)

The small size of Millerton Lake behind Friant Dam limited the Bureau's ability to use surface storage to carry over supplies in wetter years for groundwater storage later. But more importantly, Lee was convinced that the way into those cones for surface seepage to underground storage was through the existing river channels. "*Rank v. Krug*," he said, "by providing a physical solution, points the way toward greater utilization of our natural resources" and protection of vested land and water rights (Lee 1956, 15). He also believed that the court decision in 1956 held two warnings: first, there needed to be larger reservoirs, not small ones like Friant, for more carryover storage from one year to the next. Second, he urged that California use existing river channels such as the San Joaquin's to recharge the alluvial cones of the eastern San Joaquin Valley. This would also recharge deeper aquifers. It was the only way, Lee said, "that a successful joint use of surface and underground storage can be attained."

Since 1956, California has built and operated several large new reservoirs, including Trinity, Folsom, New Melones, and San Luis in the Central Valley Project, as well as Oroville in the newer State Water Project.

As Samuel C. Wiel had predicted in his 1928 essays in the *California Law*

Review, the *Rank v. Krug* lawsuit forced some water to be released from a dam to protect the water rights of "lower level" water right holders. It wasn't easy, and the yield of those releases, as noted, has dwindled with the passage of time along the San Joaquin River between Friant and Mendota Pool. But even with Charles Lee's subsequent "warnings," the San Joaquin River below Gravelly Ford would see no further flow or seepage from the river channel to replenish the aquifers of the San Joaquin Valley floor. Like a link cut from Samuel Wiel's sausage example, from the point on the river where the "physical solution" of *Rank v. Krug* dribbled into a sandy stream bed, the river was dry until the Merced reached the San Joaquin's channel nearly 50 miles beyond.

The *Rank* physical solution illustrated precisely Wiel's attempts to introduce hydraulic truths into water law and politics: a river cannot deliver water to claimants and make it to the sea when its head or booster is cut off, when its stream no longer flows. (In the San Joaquin River's case, it could not even reach the next major tributary.) If humans take too much of a river's flow, then beds go dry as water seeps its way down in the grip of gravity seeking its lowest point. The less water we put into our rivers, Charles Lee warned in 1956, the deeper the San Joaquin Valley's groundwater elevations will fall. By implication, it takes water in river channels in alluvial valleys to make and have water underground.

Nearly a half-century would pass before flows released from Friant Dam would connect Gravelly Ford with the Merced River, a river that had a head, a booster—energized by simple, eternal, omnipresent, costless gravity—able to reach the Delta. A 1988 lawsuit precipitated a fragile effort to reestablish that connection—a story for another day.[11] A lawsuit remains, indeed, a poor match for a dam, and a river once severed, ever so difficult to restore.

* * *

Henry Holsinger's prophecy of adjudication for the Sacramento River basin has yet to occur. In the 1950s, responding to just such a threat amid protests at the initiation of Central Valley Project operations, the Bureau and the California Department of Water Resources embarked on a "cooperative study" process for "trial distributions" of water throughout the Sacramento River and its lower Delta. The stated purpose was to see how the system could be operated, given known water rights disclosed by water right holders at the time (California Water Project Authority 1955; USDOI and DWR 1957). Based on results from the 1950s studies, intensive negotiations with Sacramento River senior appropriators ensued, and the State Water Rights Board convened hearings. Subsequently, the Bureau executed hundreds of "settlement contracts" for water service to all the senior rights holders up and down the Sacramento River (Martin 1968). Every year they are served first before the junior water contractors of the Central Valley Project. The settlement contracts appear to have staved off the threat of adjudication of Sacramento River surface water, at least for the time being. Settlement contract terms were for forty years. In 2004, they were renegotiated for another forty.

In 2014, California staggered from a near-rainless 2013 and reports of well failures spread throughout the San Joaquin Valley and coastal basins of the golden state. State legislators enacted and Governor Jerry Brown signed into law the Sustainable Groundwater Management Act (SGMA, pronounced "sigma"). The new law attempts to place groundwater pumping and use on a more sustainable footing, to create that "large permanent usefulness" of which Sidney Harding wrote in the late 1920s.

While SGMA aspired to a rationally planned transition from overdrafted groundwater basins to basins adhering to sustained yields among a community of pumpers, it became clear that especially in the twenty-one identified basins rational planning would give way to conflict and litigation (Figure 10.1). Additional legislation was enacted in 2015 to streamline adjudication procedures and link them to sustainability goals (Sabalow 2015).[12]

The State of California anticipates that climate change will mean more frequent droughts and greater risk of "extreme weather events," which in California can mean flooding. Both will likely result in less water available for storage. Moreover, rising average temperatures will mean less snowpack in the Sierra coupled with less runoff from rainstorms and snowmelt.

Averages, however, are informed by extremes in the overall climate pattern. The occasional blizzard can still create bountiful snowpack. But with rising average temperatures, even winters in California will be warmer, and winter heat waves can cause rapid snowmelt. If not properly monitored and planned for, such rapid snowmelt can result in downstream flooding. The state's numerous multiple-use reservoirs (for water supply, recreation, temperature management for migratory fish spawning downstream, and flood control) must leave more space empty to allow for this possibility. Public safety and welfare demand that more space be allotted to flood-control protection, but this reduces the storage of runoff for use at other times.

Meanwhile, the cities and farms of the Central Valley Project's source areas (the Sacramento Valley and the Delta) continue to expand. State law prioritizes that these areas receive sufficient supply to enjoy that development. But with all the other pressures on the supply sources for the Central Valley Project and the State Water Project, there is less water available for export from the Delta.

In late 2015, an elected Kings County supervisor, Doug Verboon, showed a *Fresno Bee* reporter a neighbor's well recently bored a short distance from his own walnut orchard. "Now you can see the concern you have with your neighbors when it comes to property rights," Verboon told the reporter, as if channeling ancient state supreme court justices Jackson Temple and Lucien Shaw. "Because whose water is he taking now?" Verboon added, "It's almost turned into a competition: who can have the deepest well in the aquifer near your farm. We need to have some kind of

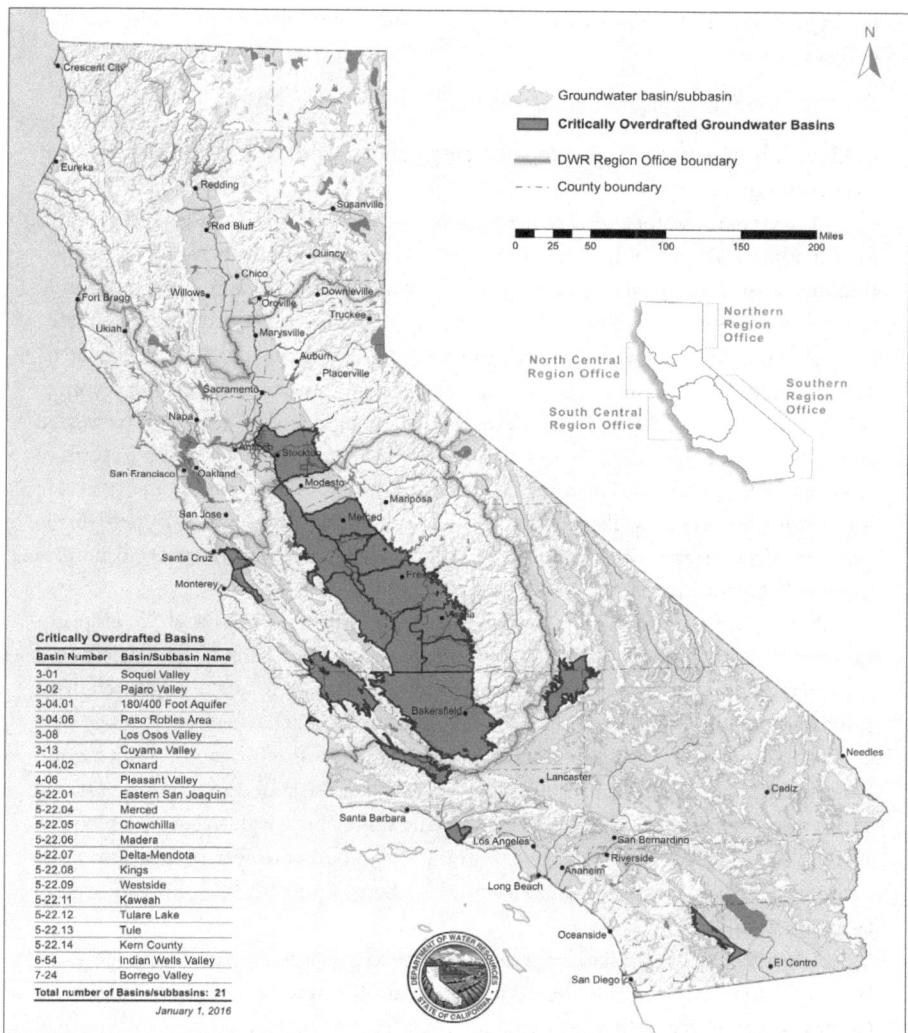

FIGURE 10.1. Critically overdrafted groundwater basins, January 2016. Courtesy of California Department of Water Resources.

ordinance to protect us from trying to kill each other off. We don't want to be fighting over water to survive" (Sabalow 2015).

One former, award-winning farmer from Kings County got out of farming and into agricultural real estate because he lost his imported surface-water supplies. To the same *Fresno Bee* reporter, he described the impacts of groundwater loss, echoing the San Joaquin Valley Water Committee of 1929 and the California Water Plan of 1957: shuttered schools, broke local governments, and vast brown fields of dust (Sabalow 2015).

* * *

California is now the fully developed reality that Wiel posited in broad terms over a century ago.

Today, senior water rights remain a veiled power behind the allocation of water in wet years. When the Bureau's Central Valley Project had no water of its own to allocate in the dry spring of 2014, senior water rights became overt economic and legal powers. On January 17, after nearly thirteen consecutive months without rain following two dry years, the State Water Resources Control Board's Division of Water Rights issued a notice curtailing the rights of the most junior appropriators since 1948 (State Water Resources Control Board 2014a). Rights issued to the Bureau of Reclamation and the California Department of Water Resources after 1951 were curtailed. The notice stated ominously, "Some riparian and pre-1914 water right holders may also receive a notice to stop diverting water if their diversions are downstream of reservoirs releasing stored water and there is no natural flow available for diversion."

A few months later came a board notice extending the curtailment to all post-1914 water rights holders (State Water Resources Control Board 2014b). The board considered going farther up the pecking order of seniority to curtail rights claimed prior to 1914 but backed away. Rather than hold to the Exchange Contract's 25 percent reduction cap on Mendota deliveries from Shasta, the Bureau of Reclamation announced that it could "only allocate 40 percent of the stated maximum contract entitlement of 840,000 [acre-feet] at this initial stage of the water year which equals 336,000 acre-feet rather than the maximum of 650,000 acre-feet critical year entitlement," in all a 60 percent reduction, rather than 25 percent (U.S. Bureau of Reclamation 2014, 2).

Attorney Paul Minasian, representing the San Joaquin River Exchange Contractors Authority, reminded board and Bureau officials of his clients' seniority in Central Valley water rights.[13] The exchange contractors had an option no one else in the hearing room had: they could call on Friant Dam near Fresno for up to three-quarters of their usual supply instead of Shasta, 400-plus miles north. On May 27, a federal judge in Fresno refused to stop water releases down the San Joaquin River from Friant Dam, so they could be diverted to Friant's water contractors, stating that about 200,000 acre-feet was expected to be released to the Exchange Contractors by late August. According to the *Fresno Bee*, "In rejecting the bid for a temporary restraining order, the court said the water allocation is a result of the way Congress wrote laws, not government regulators prioritizing fish and wildlife above farmers and the economy," a reference to federal Endangered Species Act protections for Delta fish (Grossi 2014).

In July 2015, the Bureau of Reclamation again announced it would release water into the San Joaquin River from Friant Dam for delivery to the Exchange Contractors. "As a result of the continuing drought," it said, "there is not enough water supply from the Sacramento–San Joaquin River Delta alone to fulfill Reclamation's contractual obligations to the exchange contractors. As was the case last year, these contractual obligations will be satisfied from both Delta and San Joaquin River sources." From the Bureau's announced flow schedule, the supplies to come from Friant would be somewhere between 81,000 and 103,000 acre-feet, delivered by August 15, 2015.

Friant Water Authority hired a new general manager in early 2016, a young engineer from the Bureau of Reclamation named Jason Phillips. Eric Borba, a Porterville area farmer and the Authority's chairman, told the *Bee* that the Authority had high hopes for Phillips. "Friant is facing a third year of a zero allocation. We need a leader who will thrive in the highly dynamic environment of California water. . . . We all want the same thing—we need water" (Griswold 2016).

* * *

So this was the big story in 2014 and 2015: an update to Samuel Wiel's 1914 parable of a pioneer society's willingness to share water in a modern economy. The Exchange Contractors asserted the power of the concentrated, monopolized water rights to the San Joaquin River, which they held and from which the Bureau borrowed. The law of priority operated. And the ghostly gloves on Henry Miller's dead hands operated through the actions of the Exchange Contractors, the Bureau, the federal court, and the State Water Board during drought. Those hands still exact deference from anyone holding younger priority dates to the pioneer mode of property in water: first in time, first in right.

During drought, under the law of California water, prior appropriation's victims along the Friant-Kern Canal are still told, by a federal judge one year and the Bureau the next, that they will receive little or no water from the canals extending from Friant Dam. They are to believe that the blame for such cruelty falls solely on Nature, which the law of prior appropriation follows. Sharing a sustained water supply in a modern capitalist economy is put off to another day.

NOTES

1. This quote from Justinian has since become a founding tenet of the public trust doctrine in California law, which has only been applied to water resources since the 1970s.

2. Of course, as we showed in chapter 2, California may have appeared "unowned, unclaimed, and unguarded," but it was in no way unoccupied when the miners showed up to stake the mining and water claims that were the historical roots of prior appropriation doctrine. California Indians were forced to abandon Sierra and foothill homelands that had provided sustenance and sacred places to them since time immemorial. The Gold Rush forced creation of an "open access" condition where the U.S. government failed to enforce its rights as

major landowner in the mining districts, and miners imposed their own system of rules and laws in the absence of other authoritative governance.

3. The first piece of the Central Valley Project was the Contra Costa Canal, begun in October 1937, soon followed by Shasta Dam in 1938 and Friant Dam in 1939 (United States Bureau of Reclamation 1994a–c, 1996).

4. Rank v. Krug, 90 F.Supp. 773 (1950), held in 1950 that the Bureau, according to Section 8 of the National Reclamation Act of 1902, was subject to California water rights law. See also United States v. State of California, 694 F.2d 1171 (1982), for a similar outcome.

5. In Holsinger's manuscript version (1942), p. 16, this passage reads, "Before the United States can enter into a contract [to sell water it has stored for later use], it must know definitely what it has to grant." It appears that the final version in the Central Valley Project Documents, Part One, is even more explicit as to Holsinger and Edmonston's meaning than the manuscript version.

6. Letter from John C. Page, Commissioner, Bureau of Reclamation, to Edward Hyatt, Executive Officer, Water Project Authority, dated March 10, 1943 (United States Congress 1956, 784). Holsinger was not copied on Page's letter, but it is also attached to the "Necessity" manuscript of his memorandum at the Water Resources Collections and Archives at the University of California at Riverside, Call No. G4316 G2-2.

7. There are plans, through the San Joaquin River Restoration Program, to restore spring-run Chinook to the upper San Joaquin River, but their efforts are delayed due to periodic lack of water and downstream seepage issues, the kinds of river losses Samuel Wiel wrote of in the 1920s and 1930s. And the program is under recurring political attack by some conservative local members of Congress. Source fish for reintroduction would come from a tributary to the Sacramento, it is hoped.

8. Rank v. Krug, 90 F.Supp. 773 (1950). In addition to the water rights complaint lodged against the Bureau and its Madera and Friant canal customers, there was a complaint from Northern California Fisheries, Inc. (Case No. 832-ND), that the Bureau's operation of Friant Dam had to be restrained to preserve the river's salmon runs. Justice Hall rejected this cause of action because neither the adjacent landowners nor the fisheries group possessed legal standing.

9. Friant Dam was never planned to have a significant flood-control role on the San Joaquin; it stores less than a third the total face amount of the Miller & Lux historical water rights, while the average unimpaired (approximately natural flow of the river) is about 6 million acre-feet per year. The dam's purpose was diversion for irrigation and groundwater recharge. See Lee (1956, 13–14).

10. Rank v. Krug, 90 F.Supp. at 794, emphasis added. The defendants' theory that *any* structure authorized by Congress constituted license to divert the entire flow of that stream reflects the culture of the Bureau in the 1950s and 1960s, chronicled in Reisner, 1986, especially chapters 3–8.

11. NRDC v. Patterson, 333 F.Supp.2d 906 (2004).

12. Assembly Bill 1390 and Senate Bill 226 were signed into law by Governor Jerry Brown on October 9, 2015, amending the California Code of Civil Procedure to streamline adjudication processes.

13. "If the SWRCB questions whether Protestant San Joaquin River Exchange Contractors Water Authority, who are entitled under the Second Amended Exchange Contract to receive water from the Central Valley Project or in certain circumstances from their water rights on the San Joaquin River, are legal users of water, the decision in the *Bay Delta Consolidated Cases* (2006) 136 Cal.App.4th 674 conclusively establishes their standing." Minasian and Harman (2014, 15).

Appendix A

Summaries of Key Miller & Lux–related San Joaquin River California Supreme Court Cases

There were thirteen cases in which Miller & Lux was either a direct party in interest to the case or provided crucial legal, expert, and evidentiary support. These cases span two decades (1899–1919) and contribute legal precedents or accumulated case law in such areas as reasonable use of water among riparians; determination of a riparian right; assertion of a prescriptive right; whether a riparian's use of water had to be reasonable with respect to an appropriator (it did not, anticipating the 1926 *Herminghaus* decision); and what constitutes a private water utility for purposes of regulation.

CASE NAME	CITATION	OPINION AUTHOR	DESCRIPTION
Miller & Lux and San Joaquin & Kings River Canal & Irrigation Co. v. Enterprise Canal & Land Company and Jefferson G. James.	142 Cal. 208 (1904)	McFarland	James and Enterprise Canal & Land Co. built a canal to appropriate San Joaquin River water upstream of Mendota Dam, where San Joaquin & Kings River Canal & Irrigation Co. diverted water for its Outside Canal. San Joaquin's appropriative rights were senior to James' appropriation, but James defended his right by claiming Mendota Dam was an unlawful obstruction to navigation along the river. The Court rejected James's defense as unconnected to the problem in the case and ruled James's diversion illegal.

CASE NAME	CITATION	OPINION AUTHOR	DESCRIPTION
Miller & Lux v. Enterprise Canal & Land Co. and Jefferson G. James	145 Cal. 652 (1905)	McFarland	This case derives from 142 Cal. 208 above. James, using his Enterprise Canal Co., dug a ditch from a diversion point upstream of Miller & Lux's Mendota diversion and routed the ditch to his lands located along Fresno Slough. James claimed he was a riparian owner too because he owned land along Fresno Slough, as part of the San Joaquin River. High flows in the San Joaquin River at times back up into Fresno Slough from the San Joaquin. Court disagreed, citing Fresno Slough's origins as a Kings River distributary when Tulare Lake levels are high. Miller & Lux succeeded as well with arguing that James could not go upstream along the San Joaquin to divert water to his lands many miles from the mouth of the slough. Court decreed that James had no riparian rights to the San Joaquin River anyway and could not divert from the San Joaquin because evidence showed Fresno Slough is not part of the San Joaquin system.
Miller & Lux v. Madera Canal & Irrigation Company	155 Cal. 59 (1909)	Sloss	A Fresno River case, tributary to the San Joaquin River. Riparian proprietor (Miller & Lux) was entitled to the ordinary and usual flow of the stream. That is, even flood flows from the Fresno River are part of the usual and ordinary flows of the San Joaquin River, if such flows are themselves typical for the stream. Reasonableness of riparian use was only a matter between different riparians, not as against appropriators, presaging the 1926 *Herminghaus* case.

CASE NAME	CITATION	OPINION AUTHOR	DESCRIPTION
Elizabeth Turner and Merced Security Savings Bank v. James Canal Company	155 Cal. 82 (1909)	Shaw	Third case dealing with James's view of Fresno Slough hydrology and riparian status. (Miller & Lux was a tenant using Turner-owned land.) Court finds riparian rights depend on land situated next to water providing opportunity to divert and use water, their natural advantages and benefits resulting therefrom, and presumption that landowner acquired the land with riparian use in mind. James was awarded reasonable use of flows for diversion from Fresno Slough at times when the San Joaquin River and Fresno Slough are hydrologically connected.
San Joaquin & Kings River Canal & Irrigation Co. v. Fresno Flume & Irrigation Co.; and Miller & Lux v. Fresno Flume & Irrigation Co.	158 Cal. 626 (1910)	Henshaw	Fresno Flume's dam on Stevenson Creek (high in the Sierra) was found by the Court to actually improve flows in the San Joaquin River: before its installation, flows were merely absorbed by mountain meadow lands. Miller & Lux and its canal company were not injured by Fresno Flume's dam and flume works.
J. J. Stevinson v. San Joaquin & Kings River Canal & Irrigation Co.	162 Cal. 141 (1912)	"The Court"	Downstream of Miller & Lux's diversion, Stevinson wanted to divert water to develop an irrigation colony. The Court found that his delay (*laches*) in protesting Miller & Lux's new Outside Canal diversion was not actionable. Miller & Lux was found to have promised no added diversions from the San Joaquin River to Stevinson, who was unaware of the new diversion until it happened.

CASE NAME	CITATION	OPINION AUTHOR	DESCRIPTION
San Joaquin & Kings River Canal & Irrigation Co. v. J. J. Stevinson	164 Cal. 221 (1912)	Shaw	Miller & Lux and its canal company sought to divert 500 cfs* for public use. To do this, Miller & Lux sought to condemn J. J. Stevinson's interest in this water. Stevinson argued in defense that (1) Miller & Lux's proposed use for the water was not "public"; (2) Miller & Lux is a Nevada corporation, hence "foreign," and therefore ineligible to exercise eminent domain powers; (3) some of the water would be lost to seepage in conveyance; and (4) a portion of the diversion would be for Miller & Lux's private use. The Court disagreed, enabling the condemnation to go forward.
California Pastoral & Agricultural Co. v. Madera Canal & Irrigation Co.	167 Cal. 78 (1914)	Angellotti	Madera Canal & Irrigation appropriated 100 cfs legally, but tried to get another 250 cfs by prescription against Miller & Lux's riparian right to the Fresno River (held by its subsidiary landowner, California Pastoral & Agricultural Co., see Fig. 4.1). The extra water was deemed not reasonably necessary in evidence to Madera's overall appropriation. Court reiterates that an appropriative right consists in what amount of water is reasonably necessary for some beneficial use. Water used above and beyond what is reasonably necessary by the appropriator is considered waste.
Elizabeth Turner and Las Animas & San Joaquin Land Co. v. East Side Canal & Irrigation Co.	168 Cal. 103 (1914)	Shaw	Turner and her land company (from whom Miller & Lux leased land for cattle grazing) sought to overturn a Merced County Superior Court decision providing 280 cfs to East Side (Stevinson's corporation). The Court reversed this award, overturning East Side's claim to adverse prescription as the basis for its right to divert.

CASE NAME	CITATION	OPINION AUTHOR	DESCRIPTION
Miller & Lux v. Enterprise Canal & Land Co. and Jefferson G. James	169 Cal. 415 (1915)	Shaw	New trial granted from 145 Cal. 652 (above). Court found that it is not necessary for a riparian to show harm to an upstream appropriator for the flow to be restored. Court affirmed Miller & Lux's prescriptive right acquired by its alteration of Aliso, Brown, and Lone Willow sloughs to its east-side lands. Court sustained James's contention that Fresno Slough diversions are riparian when the slough is connected hydrologically to San Joaquin River. However, James was limited to what would be reasonable use of water to his riparian lands on the slough.
Elizabeth Turner and Las Animas & San Joaquin Land Co. v. East Side Canal & Irrigation Co.	169 Cal. 652 (1915)	Shaw	East Side Canal & Irrigation threatened to divert 500 cfs when Turner et al. were diverting just 75 cfs, both as riparians. Merced County Superior Court found that East Side was entitled only to 281 cfs. East Side's excess diversions were found to be wasteful and unreasonable, and did not justify the 500 cfs diversion.
Miller & Lux v. J. G. James Company	179 Cal. 689 (1919)	Wilbur	James Company lands were originally part of a larger tract of riparian lands that were subsequently conveyed with stipulations that preserved the conveyed parcels' share of riparian use. Against Miller & Lux's appeal, the Supreme Court upheld James's ability to deliver water to these parcels under a riparian right to a parcel not connected. (Miller & Lux won the next case by losing this case because the subsequent owner of James's riparian subdivision did not seek compensation for private taking of water for public use, nor to stop timely Miller & Lux's adverse use.)

CASE NAME	CITATION	OPINION AUTHOR	DESCRIPTION
Miller & Lux v. Jefferson G. James and J. G. James Company	180 Cal. 38 (1919)	Wilbur	The Court affirmed Miller & Lux's two main water rights to San Joaquin River flows: 760 cfs (priority date of 1871) and 600 cfs (1899, affirmed through prescription in 1904) against James's claim that the latter right was an appropriation for public use by the San Joaquin & Kings River Canal & Irrigation Co., and therefore he was owed compensation. However, the Court found that James "slept" on his rights (*laches*) to sue for compensation from Miller & Lux's claim of water for public use and an adverse use that ripened into a prescriptive right.

*cfs = cubic feet per second

Appendix B

Text of Proposition 7 from 1928 California Constitution

ARTICLE 10 WATER

SEC. 2. It is hereby declared that because of the conditions prevailing in this State the general welfare requires that the water resources of the State be put to beneficial use to the fullest extent of which they are capable, and that the waste or unreasonable use or unreasonable method of use of water be prevented, and that the conservation of such waters is to be exercised with a view to the reasonable and beneficial use thereof in the interest of the people and for the public welfare. The right to water or to the use or flow of water in or from any natural stream or water course in this State is and shall be limited to such water as shall be reasonably required for the beneficial use to be served, and such right does not and shall not extend to the waste or unreasonable use or unreasonable method of use or unreasonable method of diversion of water. Riparian rights in a stream or water course attach to, but to no more than so much of the flow thereof as may be required or used consistently with this section, for the purposes for which such lands are, or may be made adaptable, in view of such reasonable and beneficial uses; provided, however, that nothing herein contained shall be construed as depriving any riparian owner of the reasonable use of water of the stream to which the owner's land is riparian under reasonable methods of diversion and use, or as depriving any appropriator of water to which the appropriator is lawfully entitled.

This section shall be self-executing, and the Legislature may also enact laws in the furtherance of the policy in this section contained.

(Passed by the voters of California, November 6, 1928, by a vote of 913,125 YES [77.2%] to 270,163 NO [22.8%].)

Appendix C

Authorities

1850 Cal. Stats. Ch. 95.
1927 Cal. Stats. Ch. 286 (Feigenbaum Act).
Antioch v. Williams, 188 Cal. 451 (1922).
Bassett v. Salisbury Manufacturing Co., 43 N.H. 569 (1863).
Bay Delta Consolidated Cases, 136 Cal. App.4th 674 (2006).
Bear River Co. v. York Mining Co., 8 Cal. 332 (1857).
Brown v. Board of Education, 347 U.S. 483 (1954).
California Const. Art. X, §2.
Chicago, Milwaukee & St. Paul Railroad v. Minnesota, 134 US 48 (1890).
Conger v. Weaver, 6 Cal. 556 (1856).
Creighton v. Evans, 53 Cal. 55 (1878).
Davis v. Gale, 32 Cal. 26 (1867).
Eddy v. Simpson, 3 Cal. 249 (1853).
Evans v. Ross, 67 Cal. 19 (1885).
Fall River Valley Irrigation District v. Mount Shasta Power Company, 202 Cal. 56 (1927).
Heilbron v. Last Chance Water Ditch, 75 Cal. 117 (1888).
Herminghaus v. Southern California Edison, 200 Cal. 81 (1926).
Katz v. Walkinshaw, 141 Cal. 116 (1903).
Kidd v. Laird, 15 Cal. 161 (1860).
Lux v. Haggin, 4 Pac. 919 (1884).
Lux v. Haggin, 69 Cal. 255 (1886).
Irwin v. Phillips, 5 Cal. 140 (1855).
Miller & Lux v. Enterprise Canal, 142 Cal. 208 (1904).
Miller & Lux v. Enterprise Canal, 145 Cal. 652 (1905).
Miller & Lux v. Enterprise Canal, 169 Cal. 415 (1915).
Miller & Lux v. Madera Canal, 155 Cal. 59 (1909).
Moore v. Smaw, 17 Cal. 199 (1861).
Munn v. Illinois, 94 U.S. 113 (1877).
National Audubon v. Superior Court, 33 Cal. 3d. 419 (1983).
Pope v. Kinman, 54 Cal. 3 (1879).
Rank v. Krug, 90 F.Supp. 773 (1950).
San Joaquin & Kings River Canal v. Stevinson, 164 Cal. 221 (1912).
Santa Clara County v. Southern Pacific, 118 U.S. 394 (1886).
Slaughterhouse Cases, 83 U.S. 36 (1873).
Stevinson v. San Joaquin & Kings River Canal, 162 Cal. 141 (1912).
Toskin v. Winzell, 27 Nev. 88 (1903), 73 Pac. 593.
Turner v. East Side Canal, 168 Cal. 103 (1914).
Turner v. East Side Canal, 169 Cal. 652 (1915).
U.S. Congress, Act of 1866, approved July 26, 1866, Rev. Stats. Sec. 2339, 14 Stats. 253, c. 263.
U.S. Const. 1865. amend. XIII, §1, proposed 1 February 1865, ratified 18 December 1865.
U.S. Const. 1868. amend. XIV, §1, proposed 16 June 1866, ratified 28 July 1868.
Union Water v. Crary, 25 Cal. 504 (1864).
Walker v. Lillingston, 137 Cal. 401 (1902).

References

Adams, F. 1905. "The Distribution and Use of Water in Modesto and Turlock Irrigation Districts, California." In U.S. Department of Agriculture, Office of Experiment Stations, *Bulletin No. 158, Annual Report of Irrigation and Drainage Investigations*, 93–139. Washington, D.C.: Government Printing Office.

Alevizon, B., and Vorster, P. 1998. *From the Sierra to the Sea: The Ecological History of the San Francisco Bay-Delta Watershed*. Bay Institute of San Francisco.

Appleby, J. 2010. *The Relentless Revolution: A History of Capitalism*. New York, NY: W. W. Norton.

Arax, M., and Wartzman, R. 2004. *The King of California: J. G. Boswell and the Making of a Secret American Empire*. New York, NY: PublicAffairs.

Attwater, W. R., and Markle, J. 1988. "Overview of California Water Law," *Pacific Law Journal* 19(4):957–1030.

Barkan, J. 2010. Liberal Government and the Corporate Person. "*Journal of Cultural Economy*" 3(1):53–68. doi:10.1080/17530351003617578.

Barley, S. R. 2007. Corporations, Democracy, and the Public Good. "*Journal of Management Inquiry*" 16(3):201–215. doi: 10.1177/1056492607305890.

Barnes, D. H. 1987. *The Greening of Paradise Valley: Where the Land Owns the Water and the Power: The First 100 Years of the Modesto Irrigation District*. Modesto, CA: Modesto Irrigation District.

Basye, G. 2011. *Battling the River: A History of Reclamation District 108*, 2nd ed. Sacramento, CA: California State Library Foundation.

Benchmark Maps. 1998. California Road & Recreation Atlas.

Black's Law Dictionary. 2010. Abridged 9th edition.

Blomquist, W. 1992. *Dividing the Waters: Governing Groundwater in Southern California*. San Francisco, CA: ICS Press.

Brechin, G. 1999. *Imperial San Francisco: Urban Power, Earthly Ruin*. Berkeley, CA: University of California Press.

Brewer, W. 1966. *Up and Down California in 1860–1864: The Journal of William H. Brewer*, 3rd ed. Berkeley, CA: University of California Press.

Bromley, D. 1991. *Environment and Economy: Property Rights and Public Policy*. Cambridge, MA: Blackwell.

Browning, P. 1991. *Place Names of the Sierra Nevada: From Abbot to Zumwalt*. Berkeley, CA: Wilderness Press.

CalFED [CalFED Bay–Delta Program]. 2000. *Phase II Report, Technical Appendix to the CalFED Bay–Delta Program*. Final Programmatic Environmental Impact Statement/Report. July.

California Department of Finance. 2000. *California Statistical Abstract*. December.

California Department of Finance. 2013. *Historical Census Populations of Counties and Incorporated Cities in California, 1850–2010*. California State Data Center. March. Accessed 27 December 2015, http://www.dof.ca.gov/research/demographic/state_census_data_center/historical_census_1850-2010/view.php.

California Department of Public Works. 1923. *Water Resources of California. A Report to the Legislature of 1923.* Public Works Bulletin No. 4. Sacramento.
———. 1926. Part III, Biennial Report. November 1.
———. 1927a. *Ground Water Resources of the Southern San Joaquin Valley,* by S. T. Harding, consulting irrigation engineer. Public Works Bulletin No. 11. Sacramento.
———. 1927b. *Summary Report on the Water Resources of California and a Coordinated Plan for their Development. A Report to the Legislature of 1927.* Public Works Bulletin No. 12. Sacramento.
———. 1930a. *Report of the Sacramento–San Joaquin Water Supervisor for the Period 1924–1928.* Public Works Bulletin No. 23. Sacramento.
———. 1930b. *Report to the Legislature of 1931 on State Water Plan.* Public Works Bulletin No. 25. Sacramento.
———. 1931a. *Variation and Control of Salinity in Sacramento–San Joaquin Delta and Upper San Francisco Bay. Report on State Water Plan Prepared Pursuant to Chapter 832, Statutes of 1929.* Public Works Bulletin No. 27. Sacramento. http://www.water.ca.gov/waterdatalibrary/docs/historic/Bulletins/Bulletin_27/Bulletin_27__1931.pdf.
———. 1931b. *San Joaquin River Basin, Report on State Water Plan Prepared Pursuant to Chapter 832, Statutes of 1929.* Public Works Bulletin No. 29. Sacramento.
———. 1940a. *Administrative Determination of Water Rights by the Division of Water Resources.* Sacramento.
———. 1940b. *Butte Creek Adjudication: Abstract of Claims.* December. Sacramento.
———. 1942. *Butte Creek Adjudication: Order of Determination,* Butte County Superior Court Decree No. 18,917. Entered on April 14. Sacramento.
———. 1952. *Feasibility of Acquiring the Central Valley Project.* March. Sacramento.
California Joint Legislative Water Problems Committee. 1929. *Report of the Joint Committee of the Senate and the Assembly Dealing with the Water Problems of the State,* January 18. Sacramento.
California Water Project Authority. 1936a. *Central Valley Project: Reports on Acquisition of and Plan of Exchange for Waters of the San Joaquin River, Advance Copy.* Report No. 1: *Present Use of Water From San Joaquin River on Irrigated Crop Lands by Diversions between Lone Willow Slough and Merced River.* August. Sacramento.
———. 1936b. *Central Valley Project: Reports on Acquisition of and Plan of Exchange for Waters of the San Joaquin River, Advance Copy.* Report No. 2: *Plan of Exchange of Water Supplies by and through San Joaquin Pumping System of the Central Valley Project, Physical Works and Source of Substitutional Supply.* August. Sacramento.
———. 1936c. *Central Valley Project: Reports on Acquisition of and Plan of Exchange for Waters of the San Joaquin River, Advance Copy.* Report No. 3: *Definition of Rights to the Waters of the San Joaquin River Proposed for Diversion to Upper San Joaquin Valley.* August. Sacramento. Available at Water Resources Collections and Archives, University of California at Riverside, call no. G438 F6 no. 3; or at University of California Northern Regional Library Facility, Richmond, California. Accessible from University of California Northern Regional Library Facility, Richmond, California, Microfilm 78383.
———. 1937a. *Central Valley Project: Reports on Acquisition of and Plan of Exchange for Waters of the San Joaquin River, Advance Copy.* Report No. 4: *Valuation of Rights to the Waters of the San Joaquin River Proposed to be Acquired for Diversion to the Upper San Joaquin Valley.* March. Sacramento.
———. 1937b. *Central Valley Project: Reports on Acquisition of and Plan of Exchange for Waters of the San Joaquin River.* Report No. 4: *Valuation of Rights to the Waters of the San*

Joaquin River Proposed to be Acquired for Diversion to the Upper San Joaquin Valley. March. Sacramento.

———. 1937c. *Central Valley Project: Reports on Acquisition of and Plan of Exchange for Waters of the San Joaquin River, Advance Copy.* Report No. 5: *Opinion of Counsel Relative to the Validity of Rights to the Use of the Waters of the San Joaquin River Proposed to be Acquired for Diversion to the Upper San Joaquin Valley.* March. Sacramento.

———. 1937d. *Central Valley Project: Reports on Acquisition of and Plan of Exchange for Waters of the San Joaquin River, Advance Copy.* Report No. 5a: *Validity of Certain Water Rights Proposed for Purchase from Miller & Lux Incorporated and Subsidiary Companies.* April. Sacramento.

———. 1937e. *Central Valley Project: Reports on Acquisition of and Plan of Exchange for Waters of the San Joaquin River, Advance Copy.* Report No. 6: *Chowchilla Farms, Inc.* November. Sacramento.

———. 1937f. *Central Valley Project: Reports on Acquisition of and Plan of Exchange for Waters of the San Joaquin River, Advance Copy.* Report No. 7: *Lands East of San Joaquin River Between Chowchilla Farms and Stevinson Colony Subject to Uncontrolled Overflow.* December. Sacramento.

———. 1938. *Central Valley Project: Reports on Acquisition of and Plan of Exchange for Waters of the San Joaquin River, Advance Copy.* Report No. 8: *Properties of Edison Securities Company.* December. Sacramento.

———. 1939a. *Central Valley Project: Reports on Acquisition of and Plan of Exchange for Waters of the San Joaquin River, Advance Copy.* Report No. 9: *Properties of East Side Canal and Irrigation Company, J. J. Stevinson Corporation, Stevinson Water District, and Affiliated Interests.* April. Sacramento.

———. 1939b. *Central Valley Project: Reports on Acquisition of and Plan of Exchange for Waters of the San Joaquin River, Advance Copy.* Report No. 12: *Lands Adjacent to San Joaquin River Between Friant and Gravelly Ford Canal.* June. Sacramento.

———. 1939c. *Central Valley Project: Reports on Acquisition of and Plan of Exchange for Waters of the San Joaquin River, Advance Copy.* Report No. 5d: *Report of Progress on the Matter of the Formulation of an Opinion Concerning the Validity and Ownership of Water Rights of East Side Canal and Irrigation Company, James J. Stevinson, a corporation, and Stevinson Water District.* August. Sacramento.

———. 1955. *Sacramento River and Sacramento-San Joaquin Delta Trial Water Distribution 1954, Report of Analysis.* April. Sacramento.

Carroll, J. 2008. "You take the iron; I'll take the top hat," *San Francisco Chronicle*. January 31.

Chandler, A. E. 1913. "The 'Water Bill' Proposed by the Conservation Commission of California," *California Law Review* 1:148–168.

Chapman, J. S. 1903. *Points and Authorities, for Houghton & Houghton*. Filed March 1 in the case of *Katz v. Walkinshaw*, California Supreme Court. Accessible from California State Archives, Sacramento.

Commonwealth Club of California. 1911. "Marketing Irrigation Bonds," *Transactions* 6(8): December.

Cowell Agreement. 1926. Merced County Court Case No. 6131, January 27.

Crocker-Huffman Decree. 1895. Merced County Court Document No. 1097, February 11.

Dale-Cook Judgment. 1926. Merced County Court Document No. 5996, March 2.

Davis, C. F. 1984. *Where Water is King: The Story of the Glenn-Colusa Irrigation District.* Willows, CA: Glenn-Colusa Irrigation District.

Davis, M. 2001. *Late Victorian Holocausts.* New York, NY: Verso.

DSC [Delta Stewardship Council]. 2013. *The Delta Plan.* May. http://deltacouncil.ca.gov/delta-plan-0.

Didion, J. 2003. *Where I Was From.* New York, NY: Knopf.

Downey, S. 1947. *They Would Rule the Valley.* Self-published. San Francisco.

DWR [California Department of Water Resources]. 1957. *The California Water Plan.* Bulletin 3, May. Sacramento.

———. 1976a. *Special Report on Dry Year Impacts in California.* February 1. Sacramento. http://water.ca.gov/waterconditions/docs/8_special_report-1976.pdf.

———. 1976b. *The California Drought—1976.* May. Sacramento. http://www.water.ca.gov/waterconditions/docs/11_drought-1976.pdf.

———. 1977. *The California State Water Project,* Appendix E: "Water Operations in the Sacramento–San Joaquin Delta During 1976." Bulletin 132–77. Sacramento.

———. 1978. *The California State Water Project,* Appendix E: "Water Operations in the Sacramento–San Joaquin Delta During 1977." Bulletin 132–78. Sacramento.

———. 2003. Bulletin 118: California's Groundwater, Update 2003. October. Sacramento. http://www.water.ca.gov/groundwater/bulletin118/report2003.cfm

Encyclopedia Britannica Online, s.v. "Treaty of Guadalupe Hidalgo," accessed December 27, 2015, http://www.britannica.com/event/Treaty-of-Guadalupe-Hidalgo.

Etcheverry, B. A., Herrmann, F. C., and Walker, C. 1936. *Miller & Lux Water Rights Appraisal,* December 12. Accessible at University of California at Riverside, Special Collections, Water Resources Collections and Archives, Call No. BLOTE 101.

Fresno County Superior Court. 1932. Judge Haines' Opinion [regarding] Miller & Lux v. Madera Irrigation District; San Luis Canal Company v. Madera Irrigation District; and San Joaquin & Kings River Canal & Irrigation Company, Inc. v. Madera Irrigation District, Nos. 25729, 25730, and 25731. Accessed at University of California, Berkeley, Northern Regional Library Facility, Richmond, California, Call No. L190 M502.

Garone, P. 2011. *The Fall and Rise of the Wetlands of California's Great Central Valley.* Berkeley, CA. University of California Press.

George, H. 1902. *Our Land and Land Policy: Speeches, Lectures, and Miscellaneous Writings.* New York, NY: Doubleday and McClure.

Gerencser, S. 2005. "The Corporate Person and Democratic Politics," *Political Research Quarterly* 58(4):625–635.

Goodall, M. R., Sullivan, J. D., and De Young, T. 1978. *California Water: A New Political Economy.* New York, NY: Allanheld, Osmun/Universe Books.

Goodwyn, L. 1976. *Democratic Promise: The Populist Moment in America.* New York, NY: Oxford University Press.

———. 1978. *The Populist Moment: A Short History of the Agrarian Revolt in America.* New York, NY: Oxford University Press.

Grantham, T., and Viers, J. 2014. "100 years of California's water rights system: patterns, trends and uncertainty," *Environmental Research Letters* 9. http://dx.doi.org/10.1088/1748-9326/9/8/084012.

Griswold, L. 2016. "Friant Water Authority names new chief executive," *Fresno Bee,* January 11.

Grossi, M. 2014. "Federal court rejects bid to stop flow from Friant Dam," *Fresno Bee,* May 27.

Gudde, E. G. 1998. *California Place Names: The Origin and Etymology of Current Geographical Names,* 4th ed. Berkeley, CA: University of California Press.

Handlin, O., and Handlin, M. F. 1945. "Origins of American Business Corporation," *Journal of Economic History* 5(1):1–23.

Harding, S. T. 1934. "Climatic Variations and California's Water Supply," Engineering Faculty Lecture, March 2. Accessible at the University of California, Riverside, Special Collections, Water Resources Collections and Archives, Sidney T. Harding Papers, Call No. Harding 134-9.

———. 1935a. "Changes in Lake Levels in the Great Basin Area: Three Hundred Years of Record Studied to Determine Trend in Available Water Supply," *Civil Engineering*, February.

———. 1935b. "Variations in Runoff of California Streams: Shifting Lake Levels Give Quantitative Indications Extending Back Three Centuries," *Civil Engineering*, September.

———. 1936. *Water Rights for Irrigation: Principles and Procedure for Engineers.* Palo Alto, CA: Stanford University Press.

———. 1937. "Weather Cycles." Presentation to the Oregon Reclamation Congress, Portland, Oregon, October 21. Accessible at University of California, Riverside, Special Collections, Water Resources Collections and Archives, Sidney T. Harding Papers, 1912–1969, Item No. 134-13.

———. 1960. *Water in California.* Palo Alto, CA: N-P Publications.

Hart, J. 1996. *Storm Over Mono: The Mono Lake Battle and the California Water Future.* Berkeley, CA: University of California Press.

Haskell, C. C. 1900. *Appellants' Reply Brief on Rehearing.* In the case of *Katz v. Walkinshaw.* April 6. Accessible at California State Archives, Sacramento, CA.

Henderson, G. L. 1999. *California and the Fictions of Capital.* New York, NY: Oxford University Press.

Hine, R. 1953. *California's Utopian Colonies.* San Marino, CA: Huntington Library.

Hollowell, J., and Hollowell, C. 2010. *Take Me to the River: Fishing, Swimming, and Dreaming on the San Joaquin.* Berkeley, CA: Heyday.

Holsinger, H. 1936. "Comments Pertaining to Some Fundamental Theories of California Water Law," address before Sacramento Section American Society of Civil Engineers, February 4. Accessible at University of California, Riverside, Special Collections, Water Resources Collections and Archives, Call No. G408 F6-1.

———. 1942. "Necessity for Comprehensive Adjudication of Water Rights on the Sacramento and San Joaquin Rivers in Aid of the Central Valley Project," Memorandum of the California Water Project Authority, December 10. In: United States Congress (1956). Manuscript accessible at University of California at Riverside, Special Collections, Water Resources Collections and Archives, Call No. G4316 G2-2.

Hon. Elisha McKinstry Eulogy. 1906. 141 Cal. 745.

Hon. John Evan Richards Eulogy. 1933. 215 Cal. 777.

Hope, B., and Sheehan, M. 1983. "The Political Economy of Centralized Water Supply in California," *Social Science Journal* 20(2):29–39.

———. 1985. "Miller and Lux: A Study in Monopoly Power," *Social Science Journal* 22(1):36.

Horwitz, M. J. 1973. "The Transformation in the Conception of Property in American Law, 1780–1860," *University of Chicago Law Review* 40:248–290.

———. 1977. *The Transformation of American Law, 1780–1860.* New York, NY: Cambridge University Press.

Hundley, N. 2009 [1975]. *Water in the West: The Colorado River Compact and the Politics of Water in the American West.* Berkeley, CA: University of California Press.

———. 2001. *The Great Thirst: Californians and Their Water,* rev. ed. Berkeley, CA: University of California Press.

Hutchins, W. 1923. *Irrigation District Operation and Finance.* Washington, D.C.: U.S. Department of Agriculture, Department Bulletin No. 1177, September 22.

———. 1956. *The California Law of Water Rights*, Sacramento, CA: State of California.
Hyatt, E. 1925. "Control of Appropriations of Water in California," *Journal of the American Water Works Association* 13(2):134.
———. 1927. Newspaper clippings concerning the *Herminghaus* decision and its aftermath. Available in collection of State Engineer Edward Hyatt, University of California, Riverside, Special Collections, Water Resources Collections, Folder Hyatt 5.
———. 1934. "The Central Valley Project of California: An Approved Method of Combating Aridity and Salt-Water Encroachment and of Improving Navigation." *Civil Engineering* 4(9):465, 483–86.
———. 1935a. "Salinity Problem of Sacramento–San Joaquin Delta and Upper San Francisco Bay Regions and Remedial Measures for Its Solution Including a Salt Water Barrier." Presentation to Waterways Division, American Society of Civil Engineers, Los Angeles, July 4. Available at University of California, Riverside, Special Collections, Water Resources Collections and Archives.
———. 1935b. "Combating a saline invasion in California: plans are prepared for protection of Sacramento–San Joaquin Delta Region." *Civil Engineering* 5(9):567, 581–82.
Igler, D. 2001. *Industrial Cowboys: Miller and Lux and the Transformation of the Far West, 1850–1920.* Berkeley, CA: University of California Press.
Ingram, B. L., and Malamud-Roam, F. 2013. *The West Without Water: What Past Floods, Droughts, and Other Climatic Clues Tell Us About Tomorrow.* Berkeley, CA: University of California Press.
Institutes of Justinian. 535. Book II, Title I. Accessed March 4, 2016 (in the Latin), http://faculty.cua.edu/pennington/Law508/Roman%20Law/JustinianInstitutes.htm.
Isenberg, A. C. 2005. *Mining California: An Ecological History.* New York, NY: Hill & Wang.
Jackson, D. C. 1995. *Building the Ultimate Dam: John S. Eastwood and the Control of Water in the West.* Lawrence, KS: University Press of Kansas.
Jackson, W. T., and Paterson, A. M. 1977. *The Sacramento–San Joaquin Delta: The Evolution and Implementation of Water Policy: An Historical Perspective.* Contribution No. 163, June: California Water Resources Center, University of California, Davis.
Jacobsma, R. 2010. "San Joaquin River Settlement Water Supply Impacts and Water Management Goal." Presentation to the State Water Resources Control Board, November 15, 2010. http://www.waterboards.ca.gov/waterrights/water_issues/programs/bay_delta/docs/prsntns111510/friant.pdf.
Jelinek, L. 1982. *Harvest Empire: A History of California Agriculture,* 2nd ed. San Francisco, CA: Boyd & Fraser.
Johnston, C. T. n.d. American Society of Civil Engineers, Paper 1256, cited in Wiel (1928a).
Jordan, F. C. 1928. *Statement of Vote at General Election held on November 6,* Proposition 7. California Secretary of State. Sacramento.
Katz v. Walkinshaw Transcript on Appeal. 1900. Filed with the California Supreme Court, July 6. California State Archives, Sacramento.
Kelley, R. 1989. *Battling the Inland Sea: American Political Culture, Public Policy, and the Sacramento Valley.* Berkeley, CA: University of California Press.
Kindleberger, C. P. 1989. *Manias, Panics, and Crashes: A History of Financial Crises,* rev. ed. New York, NY: Basic Books.
Kitch, E. W., and Bowler, C. A. 1978. "The Facts of Munn v. Illinois," *Supreme Court Review, Vol. 1978,* 313–43.
Lee, C. H. 1956. "Important Court Decisions Affecting California Water Development." Presentation to Central Valley Council, California State Chamber of Commerce, Stockton,

California, March 2. Accessible at the University of California at Riverside, Special Collection, Water Resources Collections and Archives,. L190 R3, no. 4.

Liebman, E. 1983. *California Farmland: A History of Large Agricultural Landholdings*. Totowa, NJ: Rowman & Allanheld.

Lincoln, A. 1864. *Letter to Col. William F. Elkin, November 21*. In Archer H. Shaw, ed., 1950, *The Lincoln Encyclopedia*. New York, NY: Macmillan. http://www.ratical.org/corporations/Lincoln.html.

Lindley, C. 1914. A Treatise on the *American Law Relating to Mines and Mineral Lands within the Public Land States and Territories and Governing the Acquisition and Enjoyment of Mining Rights in Lands of the Public Domain*, 3rd ed. San Francisco. Reprint 1988, Littleton, CO: F. B. Rothman.

Lister, R. C. 1993. *Bank Behavior, Regulation, and Economic Development: California, 1860–1910*. New York, NY: Garland Publishing.

Littleworth, A. L., and Garner, E. L. 2007. *California Water II*, 2nd ed. Point Arena, CA: Solano Press Books.

Lofgren, B. E., and Klausing, R. L. 1969. *Land Subsidence Due to Ground-Water Withdrawal, Tulare–Wasco Area, California*. U.S. Geological Survey Professional Paper 437-B, in cooperation with the California Department of Water Resources, p. B1.

Lustig, R. J. 1982. *Liberalism: The Origins of Modern American Political Theory, 1890–1920*. Berkeley, CA: University of California Press.

Malone, T. E. 1966. "The California Irrigation Crisis of 1886: Origins of the Wright Act." PhD diss., Stanford University, Palo Alto, CA.

Martin, B. 1968. *The Sacramento Valley Contract Negotiations, 1945–1964*. Accessible at University of California, Riverside, Special Collections, Water Resources Collections and Archives, Call No. G433 J8-1.

McCurdy, C. W. 1976. "Stephen J. Field and Public Land Law Development in California, 1850–1866: A Case Study of Judicial Resource Allocation in Nineteenth Century America," *Law & Society* 10:235–266.

McSwain, K. R. 1978. *History of the Merced Irrigation District, 1919–1977*. Merced, CA: Merced Irrigation District.

McWilliams, C. 1976 [1949]. *California: The Great Exception*. Santa Barbara, CA: Peregrine-Smith.

Mead, E., ed. 1901. *Irrigation Investigations in California*. U.S. Department of Agriculture, Office of Experiment Stations, January 24. Washington, D.C.: Government Printing Office.

Mendenhall, W. C. 1908. Preliminary report on the ground waters of the San Joaquin Valley, California. U.S. Geological Survey Water-Supply Paper 222. Washington, D.C.: Government Printing Office.

Mendenhall, W. C., Dole, R. B., and Stabler, H. 1916. *Ground Water in the San Joaquin Valley, California*. United States Geological Survey Water-Supply Paper 398. Washington, D.C.: Government Printing Office.

Miller, H., and Haggin, J. B. 1888. *Contract and agreement between Henry Miller and James B. Haggin*. Accessible at University of California, Berkeley, Bancroft Library. Call No. F862.25 M47.

Miller, M. C. 1989. "Water Rights and the Bankruptcy of Judicial Action: The Case of Herminghaus v. Southern California Edison," *Pacific Historical Review* 58(1):83–107.

———. 1993. *Flooding the Courtroom: Law and Water in the Far West*. Lincoln, NE: University of Nebraska Press.

Minasian, P. R. 2016. San Joaquin River Exchange Contractors Water Authority's Protest and Notice of Intent to Appear—California WaterFix Petition for Change Hearing. January 4. Accessed March 2, 2016, http://www.waterboards.ca.gov/waterrights/water_issues/programs/bay_delta/california_waterfix/noi_protests/docs/sjrec_protest.pdf.

Minasian, P. R., and Harman, P. C. 2014. Protest, Objection, and in the Alternative, Petition for Reconsideration of Temporary Urgency Change Order to the State Water Resources Control Board, February 28. http://www.waterboards.ca.gov/waterrights/water_issues/programs/drought/docs/tucp/comments/sjrecwa_minasiano30314.pdf.

Mulholland, C. 2000. *William Mulholland and the Rise of Los Angeles*. Berkeley, CA: University of California Press.

On the public record. 2015. "Either you own the legacy of your farming ancestors or you don't," June 11. Blog entry, http://onthepublicrecord.org/2015/06/11/either-you-own-the-legacy-of-your-farming-ancestors-or-you-dont/.

Online Archive of California. 2014. *Inventory of the Sidney T. Harding Papers*. Accessed December 27, 2015, http://oac.cdlib.org/findaid/ark:/13030/tf7d5nb33k.

Orsi, R. 2005. *Sunset Limited: The Southern Pacific Railroad and the Development of the American West, 1850–1930*. Berkeley, CA: University of California Press.

Paterson, A. M. 1978. "Rivers and Tides: The Story of Water Policy and Management in California's Sacramento–San Joaquin Delta, 1920–1977." PhD diss., University of California, Davis.

———. 1987. *Land, Water, and Power: A History of the Turlock Irrigation District*. Glendale, CA: Arthur H. Clark.

Pisani, D. 1980. "Water Law Reform in California, 1900–1913," *Agricultural History* 54:295–317.

———. 1984. *From the Family Farm to Agribusiness: The Irrigation Crusade in California and the West, 1850–1931*. Berkeley, CA: University of California Press.

———. 1992. *Reclaiming a Divided West*. Albuquerque, NM: University of New Mexico Press.

———. 1996. "Enterprise and Equity: A Critique of Western Water Law in the Nineteenth Century." In *Water, Land, and Law in the West*, edited by D. Pisani, pp. 7–23. Lawrence, KS: University Press of Kansas.

Pitzer, G. 2015. "Allocating Water in a Time of Scarcity: Is It Time to Reform Water Rights?" *Western Water*. August:4–13.

Preston, W. L. 1981. *Vanishing Landscapes: Land and Life in the Tulare Lake Basin*. Berkeley, CA: University of California Press.

Reisner, M. 1986. *Cadillac Desert: The American West and Its Disappearing Water*. New York, NY: Viking.

Richards, L. L. 2007. *The California Gold Rush and the Coming of the Civil War*. New York, NY: Knopf.

Righter, R. W. 2005. *The Battle Over Hetch Hetchy: America's Most Controversial Dam and the Birth of Modern Environmentalism*. New York, NY: Oxford University Press.

Robertson, R. D. 1917. *Irrigation of Rice in California*. University of California, College of Agriculture, Agricultural Experiment Station Bulletin No. 279, May. Berkeley.

Rohrbaugh, M. 1968. *The Land Office Business: The Settlement and Administration of American Public Lands*. New York, NY: Oxford University Press.

Sabalow, R. 2015. "Tensions, threats as California's new groundwater law takes shape," *Fresno Bee*, November 21.

Sacramento Chamber of Commerce and Division of Water Rights, California Department of Public Works. 1924. *Proceedings of the Sacramento River Problems Conference*, January 25–26.

San Joaquin County Superior Court. 1929. In the Matter of the Determination of the Rights, Based Upon Prior Appropriation of the Various Claimants of the Waters of the Stanislaus River and its Tributaries in California, No. 16873, Dept. No. 1, November 14. Accessed December 27, 2015, http://www.swrcb.ca.gov/waterrights/board_decisions/adopted_orders/judgments/docs/stanislausriver_jd.pdf.

San Joaquin River Restoration Program. 2011. *Draft Program Environmental Impact Statement/Environmental Impact Report, Executive Summary.* April. Accessed December 28, 2015, http://www.usbr.gov/mp/nepa/documentShow.cfm?Doc_ID=7556.

San Joaquin Valley Water Committee. 1929. *The San Joaquin Valley in the State-Wide Water Problem of California.* Before the Federal-State Water Resources Commission and Joint Legislative Committee on State Water Resources, State of California. Accessible at the University of California, Berkeley, Bancroft Library. Call No. F868 S173 S3. Also, accessed May 23, 2016, https://archive.org/stream/sanjoaquinvalley1927unse/sanjoaquinvalley1927unse_djvu.txt.

Schulz, C. W., and Weber, G. S. 1988. "Changing Judicial Attitudes Towards Property Rights in California Water: From Vested Rights to Utilitarian Reallocations," *Pacific Law Journal* 19(4):1031–1110.

Sharp, J. 1926. "Storage of Water in California by Riparians and Appropriators," *California Law Review* 14(3):198–213.

Shaw, L. 1922. "The Development of the Law of Waters in the West," *California Law Review* 10(6).

Short, F. 1902. *Application for Re-Hearing, Amicus curiae.* Filed November 28 in the case of *Katz v. Walkinshaw,* with the California Supreme Court. California State Archives, Sacramento.

Sklar, M. J. 1988. *The Corporate Restructuring of American Capitalism, 1890–1916: The Market, the Law, and Politics.* New York, NY: Cambridge University Press.

Slater, S. 1999. "Water Rights, Water Wrongs: Learning from the Past, Looking to the Future." Author's notes from conference sponsored by the San Francisco Estuary Institute, Oakland, California, November 2.

Soulé, F. 1901. "Irrigation from the San Joaquin River," in *Irrigation Investigations in California,* edited by E. Mead. U.S. Department of Agriculture, Office of Experiment Stations, January 24. Washington, D.C.: Government Printing Office.

Starr, K. 2005. *California: A History.* New York, NY: Modern Library.

State of California. 1913. Report of the Conservation Commission of the State of California. January 1. Sacramento: State Printing Office.

State Water Commission of California. 1917. *Report.* January 1. Sacramento: State Printing Office.

———. 1921. *Third Biennial Report, 1919–1920.* Sacramento: State Printing Office.

State Water Problems Conference. 1916. *Report.* November 25. Sacramento: State Printing Office.

State Water Resources Board. 1951. *Water Resources of California.* Sacramento.

State Water Resources Control Board. 2014a. "*Notice of Surface Water Shortage and Potential for Curtailment of Water Right Diversions.*" January 17. http://www.swrcb.ca.gov/waterrights/water_issues/programs/drought/docs/notice_of_curtailment.pdf.

———. 2014b. "Notice of Unavailability of Water and Immediate Curtailment for Those Diverting Water in the Sacramento and San Joaquin River Watersheds with a Post–1914 Appropriative Right." May 27. http://www.swrcb.ca.gov/waterrights/water_issues/programs/drought/docs/sac_curtailment052714.pdf.

———. 2015a. "Order for Additional Information in the Matter of Diversion of Water from Sacramento and San Joaquin Watershed and Delta." Order WR 2015-0002-DWR, Division of Water Rights. http://www.waterboards.ca.gov/waterrights/water_issues/programs/drought/docs/2015sacsjinfoorder.pdf.

———. 2015b. *Fact Sheet: August 2015 Statewide Conservation Data*. Updated October 1. Accessed December 27, 2015, http://www.waterboards.ca.gov/waterrights/water_issues/programs/drought/docs/fs100115_conservation.pdf.

Stegner, W. 1962. *Beyond the Hundredth Meridian: John Wesley Powell and the Second Opening of the West*. Boston: Houghton Mifflin.

Steinberg, T. 1991. *Nature Incorporated: Industrialization and the Waters of New England*. Amherst, MA: University of Massachusetts Press.

Stevinson Decree. 1930. Merced County Court Case No. 6179. February 11.

Stine, S. 1981. *A Reinterpretation of the 1857 Surface Elevation of Mono Lake*. Report No. 52, April. California Water Resources Center, University of California, Davis.

Stoll, S. 1998. *The Fruits of Natural Advantage: Making the Industrial Countryside in California*. Berkeley, CA: University of California Press.

Stroshane, T. 2012. "Water Availability Analysis for Trinity, Sacramento, and San Joaquin River Basins Tributary to the Bay–Delta Estuary." Testimony submitted by the California Water Impact Network on behalf of California Sportfishing Protection Alliance and AquAlliance, October 26, Workshop #3: "Analytic Tools for Evaluating Water Supply, Hydrodynamic, and Hydropower Effects of the Bay–Delta Plan." http://www.waterboards.ca.gov/waterrights/water_issues/programs/bay_delta/docs/comments111312/tim_stroshane.pdf.

Superintendent of Banks. 1931. *Special Hearing Re: Water Conditions in California, held in the Office of the Superintendent of Banks*, San Francisco, March 20, 2 p.m. Accessible at the University of California at Riverside, Special Collections, Water Resources Collections and Archives, Call No. HARDING Box 29, Item 159.

Thompson, W. S. 1955. *Growth and Change in California's Population*. Los Angeles, CA: The Haynes Foundation.

Treadwell, E. F. 1928. "Modernizing the Water Law," *California Law Review* 17(1):1–18.

———. 1931 [2005]. *The Cattle King: The Biography of Henry Miller, Founder of the Miller & Lux Cattle Empire*. Lafayette, CA: Great West Books.

United States Bureau of Labor Statistics. 2014. *CPI-U for all urban consumers, Table 24*. http://www.bls.gov/cpi/cpid1411.pdf.

United States Bureau of Reclamation. 1936–1942. *Central Valley Project News Clippings Archive*. University of California at Berkeley, Bancroft Library, Call No. 92/24c.

———. 1994a. *Sacramento River Division, Central Valley Project*, prepared by Eric A. Stene. http://www.usbr.gov/projects//ImageServer?imgName=Doc_1303395363655.pdf.

———. 1994b. *Delta Division, Central Valley Project*, prepared by Eric A. Stene. http://www.usbr.gov/projects//ImageServer?imgName=Doc_1303394251242.pdf.

———. 1994c. *Friant Division, Central Valley Project*, prepared by Robert Autobee. http://www.usbr.gov/projects//ImageServer?imgName=Doc_1303394667366.pdf.

———. 1996. *Shasta Division, Central Valley Project*, prepared by Eric A. Stene. http://www.usbr.gov/projects//ImageServer?imgName=Doc_1303395822724.pdf.

———. 2013. *Water Transfer Program for the San Joaquin River Exchange Contractors Water Authority, 2014–2038. Final Environmental Impact Statement/Environmental Impact Report*. State Clearinghouse No. 2011061057, January. http://www.usbr.gov/mp/nepa/nepa_projdetails.cfm?Project_ID=9086.

———. 2014. "2014 Notice of Water Supply Conditions and Availability—Critical Year Water Supply—Second Amended Contract for Exchange of Waters." Contract No. I1r-1144—Central Valley Project, California, Water Year 2014. Letter of Michael P. Jackson, Area Manager, to Steve Chedester, San Joaquin River Exchange Contractors Water Authority, February 15. http://mavensnotebook.com/wp-content/uploads/2014/02/Settlement_SJRECWA_Allocation_2-15-2014.pdf.

United States Congress. 1956. *Central Valley Project Documents, Authorizing Documents*. 84th Congress, 2nd Session. House Document No. 416. Washington, D.C.: U.S. Government Printing Office

———. 1957. *Central Valley Project Documents, Part 2: Operating Documents*. 85th Congress, 1st Session. House Document No. 246. Washington, D.C.: U.S. Government Printing Office

USDOI [United States Department of the Interior]. Bureau of Reclamation. 1939a. "Central Valley Project, California, Contract for Purchase of Miller & Lux Water Rights," July 27. Contract Symbol Ilr-1145.

———. 1939b. "Contract for Exchange of Waters," August 26. Contract Symbol Ilr-1144.

———. 1956. "Amended Contract for Exchange of Waters," March 17. Contract Symbol Ilr-1144 Amendatory, including Exhibit A: Map of the service areas of Central California Irrigation District, Columbia Canal Company, San Luis Canal Company, Firebaugh Canal Company, State Game Refuge.

———. 1962. *East Side Division, Central Valley Project, California: A Report on the Feasibility of Water Supply Development*. Sacramento: The Bureau.

———. 1968. "Second Amended Contract for Exchange of Waters," February 14, 1968. Contract Symbol Ilr-1144 Second Amendatory, including: Exhibit A: Map of the service areas of Central California Irrigation District, Columbia Canal Company, San Luis Canal Company, Firebaugh Canal Company, State Game Refuge.

USDOI and DWR [United States Department of the Interior, Bureau of Reclamation, and California Department of Water Resources, Division of Resources Planning]. 1957. *Report on 1956 Cooperative Study Program, Vol. 1*, March.

Vincent, Jr., W. G. 1925. "The Interconnected Transmission System of California." *Journal of Electricity* 54:563–75.

Walker, R. A. 2004. *The Conquest of Bread: 150 Years of Agribusiness in California*. New York, NY: New Press.

Warner, G. 1991. "Remember the San Joaquin." In *California Salmon and Steelhead: The Struggle to Restore an Imperiled Resource*, edited by Alan Lufkin. Berkeley, CA: University of California Press.

Water and Forest. 1902. Vol. 2(3):8, October.

Waters, B. 1902. *Petition for Rehearing*. Filed November 26, in *Katz v. Walkinshaw*, L.A. No. 967.

West, C. H. 1924. "Sacramento Valley West Side Area: Reclamation District #2047, Glenn–Colusa Irrigation District, Jacinto Irrigation District, Princeton–Codora–Glenn Irrigation District, Provident Irrigation District, Compton–Delevan Irrigation District, Maxwell Irrigation District, Williams Irrigation District, Zumwalt Project, Roberts Ditch Company, Cheney Slough Project." Federal Land Bank of Berkeley and the Division of Rural Institutions of the University of California, Cooperative Investigations, December 1. Accessible at University of California, Riverside, Special Collections, Water Resources Collections and Archives, Call No. G4084 E4 c.2.

Wiel, S. C. 1909. "The Water Law of the Public Domain." *American Law Review* 43:481–515.

———. 1913. "A Short Code of Underground Water." *California Law Review* 2(1):25–33.

———. 1914. "Theories of Water Law." *Harvard Law Review* 27(6):530–44.

———. 1923. "One Aspect of the Colorado River Interstate Agreement." *California Law Review* 11(3):145–55.

———. 1928a. "The Pending Water Amendment to the California Constitution and Possible Legislation." *California Law Review* 16(3):169–207.

———. 1928b. "The Pending Water Amendment to the California Constitution, and Possible Legislation." *California Law Review* 16(4):257–80.

———. 1928c. "Legal Report Proposing a Plan of Water Legislation Reconciling Public Development and Private Rights." Presentation to the Joint Committee of the California Senate and Assembly Upon Water Resources, November 1, 81 pages.

———. 1929a. "The Recent Attorneys' Conference on Water Legislation." *California Law Review* 17(3):197–213.

———. 1929b. "Need of Unified Law for Surface and Underground Water." *Southern California Law Review* 2(2):358–69.

———. 1949. *Lincoln's Crisis in the West*. Self-published.

Wiel, S. C., Shaw, L., Young, Governor C. C., Chapman, W., and Wright, H. M. 1927. *Rights to the Use of Water in California*. February 23.

Williams, J. C. 1997. *Energy and the Making of Modern California*. Akron, OH: University of Akron Press.

Williamson, A. K., Prudic, D. E., and Swain, L. A. 1989. *Ground-Water Flow in the Central Valley, California*. U.S. Geological Survey Professional Paper 1401-D. Washington, D.C.: Government Printing Office.

Wood, G. 1991. *The Radicalism of the American Revolution*. New York, NY: Knopf.

Worster, D. 1985. *Rivers of Empire: Water, Aridity, and the Growth of the American West*. New York, NY: Pantheon.

Young, E. 1960. "The Adoption of the Common Law in California," *American Journal of Legal History* 4(4):355–363.

Zonlight, M. A. C. 1979. *Land, Water, and Settlement in Kern County, California, 1850–1890*. New York, NY: Arno Press (1949 MA thesis, Dept. of Economics, University of California, Berkeley).

Index

Page numbers in *italics* indicate illustrations.
The letter "t" after a page number indicates table data.

absolute ownership rule *(cujus est solum),* 91–92, 133, 143, 144, 145
acre-foot (defined), 22, 25n5, 114, 119n12
Act of July 26, 1866, 37–38, 40, 61
Adams, Frank, 104, 106, 109, 132–33
adjudication process, 112, 115, 116, 117, 145, 152, 187, 188, 190, 191, 197
administrative law, 41
adverse use, 84, 120
agribusinesses, irrigated, water shortages to, 22
agricultural economy, monopolistic domination of, 7
agricultural irrigation water-supply system, 4
agricultural monopolists, water usage practices of, 3
agricultural productivity, expansion of, 168
agricultural use, wetland reservoir conversion to, 10
Allison, Almira, 85, 86
Alta California, 27
alternating current transmission, 80
American dream, 48
American freedoms, traditional, shrinking of, 39
American individualism, 41, 42
American River, 15
Antioch, 20
appropriation: diligent use of, 38, 45n23; end to, 183; formalizing process of, 38; riparian rights *versus,* 143–44, *160t–162t*; system, critique of, 109–11; as U.S. government grant, 36
appropriative doctrine: common law doctrine differing from, 62; defined, 20; historic development of, 29; law recognizing, 37–38
appropriative right, 35
appropriative water rights: acquisition of, 145; of canal company, 70; cases, 29, 59; definition and overview of, 4; existence dependent on, 148; overview of, 14–15; pre- and post-1914, 113; process of seeking, 109; protection of, 138; on public domain, 40; retaining, 20; riparian rights *versus,* 143–44
appropriative water rights doctrine, 41
appropriative water rights holders, 30
appropriators, riparian priorities over, 40
artesian (spontaneously flowing) wells, 78–80, *79, 80,* 84–90
artificial cascades, 15–16, 23–24
"astroturf" movement, 63
atmospheric pressure ridge (near west coast), 13, *14*
Attwater, William, 29, 37

Bailey, Paul, 93–94, 95, 96, 114, 115, 122, 155
Bakersfield, 16
Barlow, C. A., 121
Bates, Edward, 37
Bay–Delta estuary, 21, 25n4
Bensley, Robert, 66
boards, 42–43
bonds (defined), 106, 118n4
borer mollusk, 20
Bottoms, P. H., 124
Boulder Canyon Project Act, 1928, 133
Brereton, Robert, 66, 67, 68, 192
Brewer, William, 47, 86
Bridgford Act, 1897, 105, 168
Brock, Alfred T., 106
Bromley, Daniel, 73, 75n10
Brown, Jerry, 3, 10n1, 17, 198
Brown v. Board of Education (1954), 40, 46n30
Burnett, Peter, 33, 45n17

INDEX

California: development, financing, *50, 51,* 76; economic development, 38, 57; before Gold Rush, 27; land and rivers owned by, 31; population increase, 12, 168; statehood, 28, 29, 54

California Aqueduct, 11

California Civil Code: amendments of 1872, 61; appropriation and prior appropriation covered in, 109; appropriation covered in, 110, 127; riparian diverter rights covered in, 109; Section 1422, 62, 63; Sections 1410 through 1422, 38; water rights under, 104

California Conservation Commission, 77–78, 91, 102, 113, 125, 141n19

California Constitution, 28, 29–30, 123

California Constitution, Proposition 7. *See* Proposition 7

California doctrine, 143

California Geological Survey, 47, 86, 179

California Indians, 27, 183, 201n2

California Pastoral & Agricultural Company, 69, *70, 206t*

California Pastoral & Agricultural Co. v. Madera Canal & Irrigation Co. (1914), *206t*

California society, 47

California Supreme Court: appropriate rights cases, 29; composition of, 122, 140n8; groundwater overdraft cases brought before, 83, 87, 89, 90, 185; riparian rights upheld by, 38; surface water doctrine, 143–44; water rights cases brought before, 70–71, 72–73

California Water and Forest Association, 102, 107–8, 112, 113

California Water Commission: cases handled by, 116–17; establishment of, 42–43; riparian rights and, 145, 153; river salt concentrations, high found by, 20; water availability, impossibility of knowing, 114

California Water Commission Act, 1913, 127, 140

California Water Plan, 23

California Water Project Authority, 162

Calloway, O. P., 47–48, 67, 103

Calloway Canal: construction of, 50; financing of, 51; illustrations, *49;* landed empire along, 52; planning, 47–48; water diverted into, 57

Calloway Weir: diversions at, 57, 60; headgates, 51, 62–63, 139; illustrations, *49;* planning, 47–48

Campbell, John L., 85

canal control, securing, 8

canals, cases involving, *203t–204t*

capital, raising, 39

capitalism, games paralleling, 26

capitalist development, 58

Carey Act, 106

Carquinez Strait, 20

Carr, William (Billy), 51, 52, 54, 59

carriage water, role in salinity control, 21

case law, 10

cattle industry, 73

centralized government, distrust of, 76

Central Valley, 9, 10, 18–19, *154t*

Central Valley, eastern, 15

Central Valley Project: artificial cascades, 23; controversial nature of, 29; dam and canal technology, 9; demand for, 23; design of, 4, 6; developing and planning to operate, 5; entities dependent on, 17; environmental impact of, 8; foundations of, 6, 73; funding for, 102; history, sources on, 6; operation of, 4; origin of, 4–5; overdraft, impact on, 144, 165n1; overview of, 4; partnerships, 163; planning, 3; purchase and exchange contracts, 16; regulatory authority over, 146; San Joaquin River dried up by, 74; state rights applications (state filings), 149; State Water Project coordination with, 17; supply and demand under, 198; survey of, 187–91; water reserves through, 22; water rights and, 15, 21, 149; water shortage impact on, 200

Central Valley Project Act, 143

Central Valley Project reservoirs, 13

Chapman, J. S., 90

Chapman, W. S., 67, 68

Chinatown (movie), 27, 44n2

Chowchila Canal, 72

citizen, definition and rights of, 40

citizen, government distance from, 43

citrus orchards, 78

Civil War, 28, 36, 37, 42, 90–91

claim jumping, 31, 32, 33

Clean Water Act, 21

climate change, 3, 6, 10n1, 198
coastal communities, drought impact on, 14
commissions, individual redress through, 42–43
commodity agriculture, 76
common law, 33, 35, 60, 62, 91
Common Law of England. *See* English common law
common law riparian doctrine, 58
commons, 93
Commonwealth Club of San Francisco, 106
compensation: addressing issue of, 150, 152; arranging, 151; for private property taken, 148–49; water rights and, 9, 122, 123, 124, 125, 127
competition, control or elimination of, 83
Comstock Lode silver rush, 52
conflict of interest, 5–6
Conger v. Weaver (1856), 35, 36
continuous stream flow, role in salinity control, 21, 25n4
contractual arrangements, 3
contractual law, 41
Corning Canal, 4
corporate chartering, laws governing, 39
"corporate liberalism" (term), 42
corporate personhood, 40, 111
corporations: legal status of, 42; personhood rights applied to, 40; reach of, 42; rise of, 38–39, 43
correlative rights, 30, 143
court decisions, 33, 45n17
Creighton v. Evans (1878), 38

damage, 151, 152
dams: building era, 146; legal issues, 138, 139–40, 146, 196–97
Delta: description of, 18; salinity objectives in, 21–22; salt problem in, 18, 20, 170, 175; watershed and service area, 19
Delta fish, 200
Delta-Mendota Canal, 4, 15, 16, 189–90
Department of Water Resources (DWR), 11, 17, 21–23, 197
Depression, 168
desert, 47
Desert Land Act, 50, 52, 54, 60
design (defined), 27
Didion, Joan, 76

Dred Scott decision (1857), 39
drought: climate change contributing to, 198; economic depression combined with, 101, 168; rice cultivation during, 18–20; river runoff, effects on, *169, 170*; water allocation during, 5; water rights in, 5, 16, 74, 146; water supplies in, 164
drought, 1860s, 47
drought, 1868-1873, 66
drought, 1877-1879, 8, 57
drought, 1928-1934, 11–12, 13, 21, 175, 179
drought, 1976-1977, 8, 11–14, 17–18
drought, current, 3, 201
drought, extended, 10
drought, future, 3, 10n1
drought, historic, 5
due diligence, 20, 31, 32, 149
due process, 33, 40, 43
Dutton, William J., 107
"duty of water," 129

East Side Canal, 72
economic depression, 1870s, 67, 101
economic depression, 1930s, 163, 168
economic development, 8
"economic multiplier" (defined), 103
economic opportunity, competition for, 43
Eddy v. Simpson (1853), 29
efficiency, property right based on, 58–59
efficient water use, 58, 111, 138
electricity distribution systems, 80
electricity transmission, 80, 82
electricity transmission networks, 105, 118n3
Elizabeth Turner and Las Animas & San Joaquin Land Co. v. East Side Canal & Irrigation Co. (1914), *207t*
Elizabeth Turner and Las Animas & San Joaquin Land Co. v. East Side Canal & Irrigation Co. (1915), *207t*
Elizabeth Turner and Merced Security Savings Bank v. James Canal Company (1909), *205t*
Ellery, Nathaniel, 107
eminent domain: appropriator compared to state applying power of, 61–62; compensation in cases of, 149, 151, 152; private property, obtaining for public purposes, 127; proceedings, 159; right to exercise, *206t*
engineered structures. *See* canals, dams

England, drought in, 13
English common law: appropriation doctrine differing from, 62; California adoption of, 29–30; groundwater treatment in, 83; priority of use roots in, 31; riparian doctrine in, 57, 61, 63
Enterprise Canal & Land Company, 69
equal economic opportunity, 26
equal protection of the law, 40, 43
Etcheverry Bernard, 82
exchange contract, 15, 17
"exchange contractors," 15, 73–74, 164, 189–90, 201
exchanged rights, 73–74
extraction, restraint of, 83
"extreme weather events," 198

"face amount" (concept), 146, 165n2
Fall River Valley Irrigation District v. Mount Shasta Power Company (1927), 122, 140n8
farm economy recession, 21
farmers, bankruptcy of, 106
farms, providing water to, 47–48
Feather River, 11, 15
federal land, possessory claims on, 33
Feigenbaum Act, 1927, 5, 146, 149, 150, *150t*
"fertility" of the lands, 30, 55
Field, Stephen J., 33, 138, 139
Fifth Amendment, 61
financial and ecological means, living within, 6
Finkle, F. C., 87–88
"first in time, first in right" (adage), 14, 20, 149
fish reintroduction, 193, 202n7
fish transport, 192, 193
flood control, 121–22
flooding, 198
Florence Lake, 124
Fourteenth Amendment, 40
franchise, 35
Free Parking (Monopoly® game), 26
free speech as corporate right. *See* corporations.
Fresno County cadastral maps, 69, *70, 71*
Friant Dam, 24, 189, 194, 201
Friant-Kern Canal, 4, 15–16, 24–25, 189
Friant-Kern Canal cascade, 16
Friedlander, Isaac, 66, 67, 68

Galloway, John D., 168, 172, 173, 174, 175
Gate, The, *34*
George, Henry, 39, 40–41
gold, 37, 45n21
Gold Rush, 8, 15, 37, 183, 201–2n2
Gold Rush miners. *See* miners
government, citizen distance from, 43
government as monopolist, 43
Grant, Ulysses S., 37, 45n21
grasses, water-loving, production of, 55–56
"greatest good for the greatest number," 60, 61–62
Green, Sherwood, 121
groundwater: addressing, 158; commons, regulating, 96–97; conditions, 7; efficacy, questionable of, 101; irrigation development, 105, 118n3; landmark case, 9, 185; law, 83–84; levels, drop in, 23, 82, 84, 144, 199–200; management during drought, 8; as natural subsidy, 76–77; pumping, 9, 80, 82, 84; reliance on, 22, 24; storage, 180; as supply source, 13; types of, 83; usage, 9, 22–23
groundwater overdraft: basins, *199*; causes of, 82–83; Central Valley Project impact on, 144, 165n1; controversy over, 5; drought, 1976-1977 impact on, 24; explaining, 8; groundwater reliance resulting in, 23
Guadalupe Hidalgo, Treaty of, 27

Haggin, James Ben Ali: background and economic activities, 51; Calloway canal project taken over by, 51, 103, 139; land acquisition by, 52; land and water development schemes of, 8; land irrigation by, 56; in lawsuit, 43; in *Miller v. Haggin* case aftermath, 63; as monopolist, 76; prerogatives and privileges enjoyed by, 41; subdivisions, interest in, 52; water diverted for, 57
Haines, Charles G., 162
Harding, Sidney T.: background, 82; climate research conducted by, 175–82; engineered structures interpreted in political-legal terms by, 10; groundwater law, writings on, 84; groundwater level decline documented by, 82, 94–95; illustrations, *176*; on "large permanent usefulness," 198; water handling, opinion on, 7

Haskell, C. C., 87, 90, 94
Hayes, Rutherford B., 52
Henderson, George L., 48
Herminghaus, Amelia, 120–21, 123–24
Herminghaus v. Southern California Edison Company (1926): aftermath of, 143; analysis of, 9, 131; arguments and decision reached, 123–30; compensation issue stemming from, 150, 152; groundwater use and, 78; impact of, 145; legal precedents for, 72; public reaction to, 10, 120–23, 135; riparian water rights upheld in, 9; views based on, 148
Hildreth ranch, 53
Holsinger, Henry, 7, 10, 187–91, 197
Homestake Mining Company, 52
Horwitz, Morton, 58, 91, 92
household water consumption past and present, 22, 25n5
Huber, Walter, 168, 172
Huntington, Collis P., 52, 121
Hyatt, Edward, 116, 168, 169, 170–71, 172, 174, 175
Hyde, E. A., 54
hydraulic barrier, 21, 22, 25n4
hydraulic issues, 111
hydraulic mining operation requirements, 33
hydroelectric energy, 9
hydroelectricity, 82
hydroelectric power plants, 80
hydrological data, 11, 25n1
hydrologically connected (defined), 69
hydropower transmission grid, 80

Igler, David, 57
immigrants to California, 28, 48
India Meteorology Department, 178
individual rights, 39
industrial factory system, 58
industrialization era, 38
"insecurity of other [non-riparian] rights to water," 120
irrigated agriculture: crop acreage, expanding, 24; during drought, 172; expansion of, 77, 78, 80, 81, 82, 129–30, 144; land area, increase in, 64
irrigation: conventions focusing on, 112–13; education on, 134; extent of, 108; federal government involvement in, 112; geography and climate impact on, 101; socioeconomic benefits of, 103–4; surface-water supplies for, 103
irrigation development, 103
irrigation districts: authorizing, 42; challenges, 104–7; in disarray, 109; forming of, 3, 104; funding, 3, 106, 107; organizing, 9; purpose of, 102; spread of, 145
irrigation systems, utilizing, 20
Irwin v. Phillips (1855), 29, 35

James, Jefferson G., 69
James, Walter, 50
J. J. Stevinson v. San Joaquin & Kings River Canal & Irrigation Co. (1912), 205t
Johnson, Hiram, 113
Johnston, Clarence, 83
judicial activism, 33, 92
junior water rights, 15, 197
Justinian (Emperor of Rome), 7, 183

Katz, Marcus, 84
Katz family, 85, 87
Katz v. Walkinshaw (1903), 9, 83, 84–90, 94, 113, 120, 123, 143, 185
Kern County, 8
Kern County Land and Water Company (later Kern County Land Company), 51, 52, 63, 64n2
Kern River, 47, 53
Kern River Island & Canal Company, 48
Kidd v. Laird (1860), 29

lake levels, rising and falling, 176–77
land, U.S. government ownership of, 31–32, 35
land-development schemes, 8
land for settlement, 103
land monopolists, holdings of, 40–41, 41t
land monopoly, 5, 40; struggles with, 5
land ownership, 48, 50
land patent (defined), 32
land rights, 25, 30
landscape, descriptions of, 47
landscaping, drought-tolerant, 24
land value, water role in, 145
"large permanent usefulness" (euphemism), 9, 198

Lee, Charles, 194–96, 197
Legal Advisory Committee, 154–55
liberalism, 42
limited liability corporations, 39
Lincoln, Abraham, 36–37, 42
Lindley, Curtis H., 32, 45n14
local irrigation and reclamation districts, 104–5
losses *versus* waste, 135
Lustig, R. Jeffrey, 39, 41
Lux, Charles, 6, 53
Lux v. Haggin (1886): aftermath of, 63–64, 101, 102, 103; arguments and decision reached, 59–63, 126; Herminghuas case arguments similar to, 125, 127; overview of, 8, 39, 43; reasonable use doctrine adopted after, 59; stage set for, 57
Lynch, James, 106

Madera Canal, 4, 24
Madera Canal and Irrigation Company, 72
"manifest destiny," 38
market failure, 101, 144–45
Markle, James, 29, 37
Maxwell, George, 105, 117–18n2
McCurdy, Charles, 33
McDonald, William, 85
McKinstry, Elisha W., 60, 61–63, 101
Mead, Elwood, 110, 112, 153
Mendenhall, W. C., 78, 79
Mendota (name origin), 68, 75n2
Mendota area, 8–9
Mendota Pool: diversion at, 101; lands adjacent to, 123–24; lands downstream of, 70; San Joaquin River diversion at, 69; San Joaquin Valley hydrologic activity, role in, 68; water transported to, 16, 192; waterways linked with, 15
Merced Irrigation District, 172, 173–74
Merced River, 193
Mexican land grants, 54
Mexican law, 60
Mexico, war with, 27
military, government property defense role of, 31, 44–45n13
Miller, Henry: biography, 53, 67, 126, 151; canal companies, dealings with, 66–67; death, 54; illustrations, 74; land acquisition by, 52–55, 55, 56–57, 68; land holdings, 69, 70, 71; legacy of, 159, 187; *Miller v. Haggin* case settlement accepted by, 63; *Miller v. Haggin* decision, reaction to, 63, 65n16; as monopolist, 76; prescription, water rights through, 84; San Joaquin River shaping, role in, 6
Miller, M. Catherine, 41–42, 54, 67, 73, 124
Miller & Lux: canal companies, dealings with, 66, 67–68; canals built by, 71; canals owned by, 72; case law, 8–9; cases involved in, 69, 203t–208t; compensating, 159; competitor canal building, 72; corporate descendants, 15, 73–74, 163; decline, 73; economic and political power, 73; economic weapons used by, 56; flood flows, criticism of, 125, 141n19; grassland and cropland rights, 189; Herminghaus case influenced by, 124; *Katz v. Walkinshaw* case, involvement in, 90; land acquired by, 54; land certificates of purchase, 59, 62; law importance recognized by, 42; legal and economic legacy of, 5; legal doctrine shaped by, 4, 111; legal status and holdings, 40; as monopoly, 7, 43, 56, 73, 74, 77, 101, 103, 143, 186–87; net assets, 54; partnerships, 163; prerogatives and privileges enjoyed by, 41; as public utility, 72; riparian water rights, 53–54, 72; San Joaquin River use by, 3; Southern California Edison (SCE), dealings with, 72, 124–25; vertical integration, 56; water properties assembled by, 4; water reduced for, 57; water reform, role in, 113; water rights, 145, 162–63, 194, 202n9; water rights cases and, 70–71, 72–73; water rights law and, 5, 69
Miller & Lux and San Joaquin & Kings River Canal & Irrigation Co. v. Enterprise Canal & Land Company and Jefferson James (1904), *203t*
Miller & Lux v. Enterprise Canal & Land Company and Jefferson James (1905), *204t*
Miller & Lux v. Enterprise Canal & Land Company and Jefferson James (1915), *207t*
Miller & Lux v. Fresno Flame & Irrigation Co. (1910), *205t*
Miller & Lux v. Jefferson G. James and J. G. James Company (1919), *208t*

Miller & Lux v. J. G. James Company (1919), *208t*
Miller & Lux v. Madera Canal & Irrigation Company (1909), 125–26, *204t*
mill owners, hydraulic heads created by, 58
Minasian, Paul, 200
mineral land, 33
miners: appropriative rights of, 29; eviction, threatened of, 36–37; as federal grantees, 37; lawmaking role of, 31, 32–33; possessory rights of, 33; prior appropriation by, 35; self-governance by, 32, 45n16; as trespassers, 27, 32, 35
"miners inch" (defined), 109
mining claims, 31, 33, 38, 45n23
mining districts, *34*, 38
minorities, discrimination against, 28, 40, 46n30
Modesto Irrigation District, 104, 105
monopolies: agricultural economy dominated by, 7; concern over rise of, 40–41; controversy over, 38–39; *Lux v. Haggin* not addressing, 62; preventing, 102; regulation of, 139–40; resisting during drought, 5; riparian rights an, 73; technology as counterstrategy against, 9; water, impact on, 40–41
monopolistic combination, alternatives to, 83
monopolists, 8, 30, 43, 103
monopolization, structure of, 40
monopolized water politics, 27
monopoly: struggles over, 5
Monopoly® (board game), 26–27
monopoly capital, concentrated, 111
monopoly power, 9, 27
Moore v. Smaw (1861), 32, 35, 36
Mount Shasta Power Company, 122

National Reclamation Act, 1902, 112, 189
natural ecosystems, restoring, 6
natural law, 7
natural use theory, 58, 59, 74
natural water flow, physical substitutes for, 135–36
nature, descriptions of, 47
navigable waters, protecting, 152
New Almaden quicksilver mine, 36–37
"non-injury rule," 84

Northern California Fisheries, 194, 202n8
Northwest Ordinance, 1787, 28, 31

Office of Irrigation Investigations, 104, 108
option (defined), 53, 64n4
Ordinance, 1807, 36–37
over-appropriation, ratio of, 102–3
overdraft. *See* groundwater overdraft

Pacific Gas and Electric Company, 131
Page, John C., 191
Panic of 1857, 53
Panic of 1893, 106
pastoral water uses, 58
patent, 35, 36
patentee's rights, 35
patenting (defined), 32
Peck, James F., 125, 126
percolating water, 83, 88, 144
person(hood) (defined), 39–40
petroleum deposits, 83
Phillips, Jason, 201
physical barriers, salinity control with, 21, 22, 25n4
Pisani, Donald, 105, 113
Plessy v. Ferguson (1896), 40, 46n30
police power *versus* vested property rights, 33
political influence, 43
pollution case decisions, 33, 45n17
Pope v. Kinman (1879), 38
Populist agrarian movement, 106
power of location, design and priority, 27
power production, 78
precipitation, mean annual, *12*
prescription doctrine, 38, 46n23
prescriptive rights, 72, 84, 120
presumption doctrine, 35, 36
prior appropriation: analysis of, 183, 184–86; common law practice as origin of, 58; during drought, 201; establishing, 35; historic development, 30–31, 183, 201n2; impact of, 37; overview of, 28–29; public domain, water acquisition through, 61; *versus* riparian rights, 57–59, 187; riparian rights paramount to, 35–36
prior appropriation doctrine, 29, 32, 36
priority: due diligence, separation from, 149; in law, 29; overview of, 58; reasonable use

doctrine as challenge to, 59; in water law, 27, 28
"private property regime" (defined), 73, 75n10
private speculators, government land sold to, 28
private *versus* public property rights, 29
production-to-profit business model, 56
Progressive-era movements, 109
property: acquiring and controlling, 26; laws defining, 42; organizing, profit increase resulting from, 26; rights, 58; unconstitutional taking of, 33; value, 26–27, 111
Proposition 7: analysis of, 138–39; authorship of, 139, 142n38; case law stemming from, 158; groundwater use prior to, 78; impact of, 152; passage of, 3, 134, 140, 143, 157; "reasonable use" standard and, 145; text of, 209
proprietary individualism, pitfalls of, 82–83
public domain, 31, 35–36, 37, 40, 61
public lands, 31, 35
public lottery, 26
public municipal corporations, 9
public trust doctrine, 7, 183, 201n1
public use, 122
public wealth, 76
pump technology, 80, 82

Railroad Commission, 42
Rainey, Edward, 168, 169, 171, 174
rainfall, low, 48
rainfall, variations in, 11
Ralston, William C., 53, 66, 67
Rank, Everett, 194
Rank v. Krug, 194–96, 197
reasonable use standard: adoption of doctrine, 59; analysis of, 138; cases focusing on (landmark case), 9; cases upholding, 123; groundwater competition and, 92; ideas on, 7; law and legislation, 137; overview of, 58–59; price of, 139; riparians accountable for, 144; water law, incorporation into, 145
Reber, Charles, 85
recession, post-World War I, 21
regulatory commissions, 42
reservoirs, 11, 13
resource development, 101
return flows, 135, 136, 137, 138
reuse of water, 137, 138–39, 144

rice cultivation, 10, 18–20
rice growers, suit against, 20
Richards, John E., 126, 127–28, 129–30, 150
Richards, Leonard L., 32
Rights to the Use of Water in California (pamphlet) (Wiel), 130–31, 131
Riley, Bennett, 28
riparian claims, prior water rights protection against, 38, 45–46n23
riparian diverters, rights of, 109, 113
riparian doctrine: analysis of, 184; battles against, 60–61; criticism of, 120, 121; historic roots of, 57–58; as preeminent water-law doctrine, 60, 61, 69; recasting, 74
riparian lands, maps of, 112
riparian property rights, 73
riparian rights: abolition of, 30, 45n12; application of, 30; *versus* appropriation, 143–44, 160t–162t; grandfathering of, 103; land monopoly, association with, 40; law and legislation, 209; limits to, 127–29; miners' appropriative rights compared to, 29; monopoly combined with, 187; overview of, 14; *versus* prior appropriation, 28, 35–36, 57–59; protecting and upholding, 38, 63–64, 134; quantifying, 152–53; relief from doctrine of, 146, 148; transfer of, 35; upholding of, 9; as vested property rights, 38, 57
riparians, 30, 58, 120–21, 150, 151
riparian storage, 127–28
Riparian Suits Association, 57
risk, 58–59
river (defined), 132, 133, 136, 142n33
river flows, median, *154t*
river flows, preserving, 7–8
River Problems Committee, 13
River Problems Conference, 1924, 21
river runoff, drought effects on, *169, 170*
rivers: industrialization of eastern, 31; ownership of, 31; restoration, challenges of, 197
Riverside Park site, 47
Riverside Water Company, 85, 90, 91
Robie, Ronald, 17–18, 22
rod (defined), 47, 64n1
Roman-era quotes, 7, 183
runoff, 114, 115, *169, 170*

Index

Sacramento River: appropriators along, 146; water from, 16; water rights on, 15, 189, 191, 197–98
Sacramento River Basin, 10, *147t–148t*, *169*, 190
Sacramento Valley, 15, 20, 189
salinity control, 19, 21–22
salinity problem, 18, 20–21
salmon, 192, 193
salt water borers, 20
San Bernardino, artesian wells in, 84–93
San Francisco, rainfall in, 57
San Francisco Bay, 18
San Francisco County, *50*, *51*
San Francisco earthquake, 1906, 133
San Joaquin and Kings River Canal, 66, 70, 75n1
San Joaquin and Kings River Canal and Irrigation Company, 66, 67, 71, 72
San Joaquin and Kings River Canal and Irrigation Company v. Fresno Flame & Irrigation Co. (1910), *205t*
San Joaquin and Kings River Canal and Irrigation Company v. J. J. Stevinson (1912), *206t*
San Joaquin Power and Light Company, 72
San Joaquin River: Central Valley Project impact on, 8; Class I water deficiency in, 24; control of, 73; diverting of, 16, 69, 71–72, 189; drying up of, 74, 192; flow and descent of, 68–69; land along, 69, *70*, *71*; monopoly control over, 3, 6, 8; over-appropriation ratio at, 102–3; pumping system, *156*; ranches along, 53; restoration program, 193, 202n7; rights to, 15, 73, 145, 190, 194; riparian and pre-1914 appropriative water rights on, *160t–162t*; water released into, 201
San Joaquin River Basin, 78, 97, 100n30, *170*
San Joaquin River Exchange Contractors, 8, 17, 24, 73–74, 200
San Joaquin River snowmelt, 15–16
San Joaquin Valley: artesian wells in, 78, *79*; California Aqueduct role in water supply for, 11; drainage of, 68; during drought, 1976-1977, 14; groundwater levels, declining in, 82, 94–99, *98*, 144; growth and development, 196; irrigated agriculture in, 77, 80, 81; monopoly challenged in, 9; rivers, 77; underground water throughout, 18; water rights, 8, 15, 16; water supply, 94–99
Schulz, Clifford, 29, 36, 37
"securities made uncertain," 120
senior water rights, 15, 16, 197, 200
"separate but equal" doctrine, 40, 46n30
settlement, encouraging, 8
settlers, 27, 28
Shasta Dam, 15, 16, 21, 190
Shasta Lake, 16
Shasta Reservoir, 17
Shaver Lake, 124
Shaw, Lucien, 88–89, 90, 91
Sherman Anti-Trust Law, 56
Sierra, western, 15
Sierra Nevada, 18–19
Sierra rivers, 15
Silicon Valley, 3
slavery, 27, 28, 32–33, 39–40
small proprietorships, 41
snowpack during drought, 1976-1977, 12, 13–14
society, duties imposed on, 6
Soulé, Frank, 108, 109–11
Southern California Edison (SCE): commentaries on, 131; expansion sought by, 124; Miller & Lux dealings with, 72, 124–25; suit against, 120–30
Southern Pacific Railroad: canal construction-related transport facilitated by, 66, 75n1; establishment in San Joaquin Valley, 66; land along, 52; lands acquired from, 48; as monopoly, 101; "robber barons" of, 76, 121
Spanish land grants, 54
"species of property," 33
Stafford, Harlowe, 168, 171, 175
Stanislaus River, 116
Starr, Kevin, 28
state rights applications (state filings), 149, *150t*
State Water Plan, 145, 146
State Water Problems Conference, 1916, 120, 146
State Water Project: artificial cascades, 23; controversial nature of, 29; demand for, 23; entities dependent on, 17; funding for, 102; reservoirs, storage levels of, 13; voter approval of, 17; water reserves through, 22; water rights bases for, 149; water rights reallocated to, 21

State Water Resources Control Board: groundwater, handling of, 83; regulatory authority of, 21; responsibility and authority of, 5, 113; statewide savings rate reported by, 3, 10n1
state water system, 8
Stevinson, J. J., 72
Stevinson irrigation colony, 157, 166n12
stream-flow records, 114
streams, nature of, 136–37
subsidies, 76
subterranean channels, water flowing in defined, 83
suburban development, 12
surface water, 102, 144
surface water doctrine, 143–44
surface water management, 8
surface-water rights, 8, 14–15, 143
surface water rights claims, 9
surface water shortages, 8
sustainability, 9
Sustainable Groundwater Management Act, 2014, 83, 99n3, 198
Sutter's Mill, 27, 36

Tehama-Colusa canal, 4
Temple, Jackson, 88–89, 90, 92, 113
Tevis, Lloyd, 51–52, 66
Thirteenth Amendment, 39, 40
"through Delta conveyance" (principle), 21, 25n4
Timbuctoo, Yuba County, 34
torredos, 20
Treadwell, Edward: debates, 194; as H. Miller's biographer, 53, 67, 126; on Legal Advisory Committee, 150, 151–52; as Miller & Lux attorney, 124; Miller & Lux production-to-profit business model described by, 56; as Southern California Edison (SCE) representative, 125, 129; water handling, opinion on, 7; water rights and compensation issues addressed by, 9
tree-ring records, 177
Tulare County, 82
Tulare Lake Basin, 77, 78, 169
Turlock Irrigation District, 104, 105
Turner, Elizabeth, 71
Tyler, Rachel, 85, 86

underclass, placating, 26, 43–44n1
underground water, 144
undeveloped lands, conversion into farms, 47
"uneconomic use," 120
urban Californians, water conservation measures by, 24
urban development, 12, 82
U.S. Bureau of Reclamation: CVP operated by, 4, 188; governing of, 189; irrigation supplies provided by, 73, 74; partnerships, 163–64; precursor to, 112; rights claimed by, 5; San Joaquin River drying anticipated by, 192; water delivery, role in, 201; water rights sales to, 15; water service contracts executed by, 17
U.S. Constitution, 16, 29–30, 31, 39–40, 61, 127
U.S. Department of Agriculture, Office of Irrigation Investigations, 104, 108
U.S. Department of the Interior, 32
U.S. Dept. of Agriculture, 102
"use it or lose it" (adage), 14–15, 20, 32, 149
U.S. General Land Office (GLO), 31–32, 54, 61
U.S. government, land owned by, 27–28, 31, 33, 35
U.S. government, water owned by, 35
Usher, John, 37
U.S. Reclamation Service, 112
U.S. Supreme Court, 56
usufruct, 28, 29, 30, 133

Verboon, Frank, 198–99
vested property rights: appropriative rights as, 29; police power *versus*, 33; protecting, 39, 61, 111; riparian rights as, 38, 57, 74; risk reduced in, 58; risks to, 122
vested water rights, 103
vigilante justice, 32, 45n16
Vincent, W. G., Jr., 80, 82
vineyards, 78

Walker, Gilbert, 178
Walkinshaw, Margaret D., 85, 86, 87, 90, 92
Walnut Irrigation District, 106
Warner, George, 192, 193
Wasco, 82
waste, causes of, 135–36
water, government ownership of, 29, 35, 44n5
water agencies, 18

water as object of contention, 42
Water Commission Act, 1914, 103, 113, 115–16, 117, 129, 144, 145, 146
water commons, flowing, 7
water companies, 33, 85
water conservation: calls for, 12; goals, surpassing, 3, 10n1; ongoing importance of, 3, 10n1; urban measures, 24
water consumption, 78
water demand *versus* supply, 144–45
water-development schemes, 8
water distribution, 4, 101, 117
water diversion, notice of intent, 38, 109
water diversion, right of, 29, 44n5
water entitlements, perceived, 6
water facillities, 6
water handling, 7
water history sources, 6
water industry, 17
water law, 3, 5, 29, 111
water litigation, 109
water management, 21
water measure units, standard, 110
water monopoly, 5
water movement, 6
water over-appropriation, addressing, 9
water overflow, 125, 141n19
water ownership, 48, 50
water politics, 27
water reserves, 22
water resource development, 9, 10
water resources, regulation of, 134
Water Resources Center Archives, 7
water rights: adjudicating (*see* adjudication process); analysis of, 187; claims, 5–6, 108–9, 109–11; common, 184–85; defined, 14; dominant type of, 4; and drought, 5; emerging framework of, 40; expansion of, 9; government regulation of, 102–3; grandfathering of, 103; hierarchy, changes in, 113, 119n11; institution of, 14; irrigation district success, role in, 107; litigation and conflict, 8; "mightily mixed," 107; monopolization of, 25; monopoly over, 5; pre- and post-1914, 113, 144, 146, *147t–148t*, 164; prior, investigating, 113; private, government involvement with, 101; quantifying, 146, 165n2; rationalizing and regulating, 102;
regulating acquisition and protection of, 42; stability of, 4; state acquisition of, 146; system of, 8; transfer of, 35
water rights cases, 8
water rights doctrine, 113
water rights holders, protection for, 38, 45–46n23
Water Rights in the Western States (Wiel), 130
water rights law, 3, 5, 27
water rights reform, 112–14
water rights system, 3, 8, 10, 107
Waters, Byron, 86–87
water service, land with, 103
water service contracts, 16–17
watersheds, 27
water shortages, 8, 15, 143
water source, identifying, 87
water storage, 11, 12–13, 77–78, 121–22
water supplies: expansion sought for, 5; insufficient, allocating, 14; monopoly control, limiting, 9; municipalization of, 109; poaching, 190
water systems, 16
water usage productivity, competition over, 58
water use: claims, 143; for economic purpose, 4; regulating, 9; risks taken in, 18
water use efficiency, 3, 7
water utilities, 109
water year, characterizing and comparing, 11, 25n1
weather dynamics, long-term, 174–75
Weber, Gregory, 29, 36, 37
Wells Fargo, 52, 66
western states, riparian rights abolished in certain, 30, 45n12
wetland reservoirs, 10
Whitney, Josiah, 47
Wiel, Samuel C.: background, 130; on compensation issues, 9; dam issues analyzed by, 146, 196–97; debates, 194; defeat of, 7; engineered structures interpreted in political-legal terms by, 10; head, booster and flow question raised by, 105; *Herminghaus* amicus brief prepared by, 127, 141n26; *Herminghaus* case analyzed by, 9, 131, 135; law records historical content cited by, 6; on Legal Advisory Committee, 150, 151, 152–54, 155; on Lincoln, A. and

New Almaden mine controversy, 37; pioneers described as trespassers by, 35, 36; on prior appropriation, 30–31; on riparian water rights, 131–32, 134, 148, 152–53; river flow preservation advocated by, 7–8; Sacramento River basin adjudicating, commentary on, 10; state plan analyzed by, 9; on streams, 193; surface water regulation advocated by, 144; water handling, opinion on, 7; on water law systems, 183–87; on water rights, 9; on water sharing, 201; writings, 130–40, 146

wild irrigation, 70, 72, 151
Wilkinshaw, Margaret D., 85–86
Williams, James C., 80
women, property rights for, 28
Woolley, J. E., 122
Wright Act, 1887, 29, 42, 62, 103, 104, 105, 106

yeoman farmer, 48
Young, C. C., 122–23, 130, 131–32, 133–34, 136, 144, 146